Highlight
Marks 177-1
213-217 JL
6113

VOICES OF LATINO CULTURE
READINGS FROM SPAIN,
LATIN AMERICA,
AND THE UNITED STATES

ED. DANIEL S. WHITAKER

CALIFORNIA STATE UNIVERSITY, SAN BERNARDINO

D1616542

 KENDALL/HUNT PUBLISHING COMPANY
4050 Westmark Drive   Dubuque, Iowa 52002

Copyright © 1996 by Kendall/Hunt Publishing Company

Library of Congress Catalog Card Number: 96-77604

ISBN 0-7872-2591-6

All rights reserved. No part of this publication may be reproduced,
stored in a retrieval system, or transmitted in any form or by any
means, electronic, mechanical, photocopying, recording, or otherwise,
without the prior written permission of the copyright owner.

Printed in the United States of America

10 9 8 7 6 5 4

OUR CULTURE

There is so much about our culture
to be proud of—
from the things we value most,
like our language,
persevering spirit
and strong sense of family,
to the simpler pleasures,
like our music, foods and traditions
which have been handed down to us.

Our culture is timeless,
yet ever-changing, ever new
because we keep it alive
in each of us. . . .

Let our lives be a proud expression
of its beauty, strength, and hope.

Today, and each day of your life
feel proud of who you are
and celebrate all that makes you
someone so special.

En nuestra cultura,
tenemos tantas cosas
por las cuales
sentirnos orgullosos—

desde las cosas que valoramos mucho,
como nuestro idioma,
espíritu de perseverancia,
y nuestro sentido de unión familiar,
hasta las cosas más sencillas,
como nuestra música,
comidas,
y tradiciones que compartimos
y que han sido pasadas
de generación a generación.

Nuestra cultura
es antigua
y a la vez moderna,
porque vive
en cada uno de nosotros

Hagamos que nuestras vidas
sean un orgulloso reflejo
de su belleza, valor, y esperanza.

Hoy, y cada día de tu vida,
siente orgullo de ser quien eres
y celebra todas las cosas
que te hacen alguien tan especial.

© AGC, Inc.

Contents

PREFACE   vii

INTRODUCTION
1. EARL SHORRIS, "THE NAME OF THE PEOPLE"   3

PART I—READINGS FROM SPAIN
1. SENECA, "ON SELF-CONTROL" AND "ON TAKING ONE'S OWN LIFE"   9
2. "MARY," FROM THE KORAN   17
3. MAIMONIDES, "THE EPISTLE ON MARTYRDOM"   23
4. POEM OF THE CID, ANONYMOUS   27
5. LAZARILLO DE TORMES, ANONYMOUS   33
6. SANTA TERESA DE JESÚS, SELECTIONS FROM HER VERSES AND AUTOBIOGRAPHY   41
7. TIRSO DE MOLINA, THE SEDUCER OF SEVILLE   49
8. MIGUEL DE CERVANTES, DON QUIXOTE DE LA MANCHA   59

PART II—READINGS FROM LATIN AMERICA
1. POPOL VUH   67
2. GARCILASO DE LA VEGA, EL INCA, ROYAL COMMENTARIES OF THE INCAS   79
3. CHRISTOPHER COLUMBUS, LETTER DESCRIBING THE NEW WORLD   87
4. AZTEC POETRY   93
5. ITALO CALVINO, "MONTEZUMA"   107
6. BERNAL DÍAZ DEL CASTILLO, THE CONQUEST OF NEW SPAIN   115
7. BARTOLOMÉ DE LAS CASAS, A BRIEF RELATION OF THE DESTRUCTION OF THE INDIES   121
8. CARLOS FUENTES, "THE BIRTH OF THE HISPANO-INDIAN CIVILIZATIONS OF THE NEW WORLD"   125
9. SOR JUANA INÉS DE LA CRUZ, "VERSES AGAINST THE INJUSTICE OF MEN'S COMMENTS ABOUT WOMEN"   129
10. GERTRUDIS GÓMEZ DE AVELLANEDA, SAB   133
11. NICOLÁS GUILLÉN, "BALLAD OF THE TWO GRANDFATHERS" AND "TWO KIDS"   139

12. Frida Kahlo, "Moses"   145
13. Octavio Paz, "Mexico and the United States" and "Mexican Masks"   149
14. Cecilia Rodríguez and Marjorie Miller, "Muy Macho"   167

Part III—Readings from the United States
   1. Earl Shorris, "Someone from Mexico"   175
   2. Alberto Alvaro Ríos, "The Iguana Killer"   187
   3. Juan Delgado, The Green Web   195
   4. César Chávez, "A Step to Freedom"   203
   5. Earl Shorris, "Someone from Puerto Rico"   207
   6. Ed Vega, "The Angel Juan Moncho"   221
   7. Nicholasa Mohr, "A Time With a Future (Carmela)"   231
   8. Earl Shorris, "Someone from Cuba"   241
   9. Margarita Mondrus Engle, "Niña" and "Singing to Cuba"   253
  10. Julia Alvarez, "Snow"   261
  11. Judith Ortiz Cofer, "The Latin Deli: An Ars Poetica"   265

PREFACE

Latinos will soon be one of the largest communities in the United States; Carlos Fuentes predicts that within fifty years almost half the population of the United States will be Spanish-speaking. In fact, Latinos are the fastest growing minority in America. Los Angeles is already the second largest city of Spanish-speakers in the world, only surpassed by Mexico City. Overall, there are more than 25 million Latinos in the United States at the present time.

Moreover, the connection of Latinos with the United States is not a new phenomenon. Despite the recent focus on late twentieth-century immigration from Mexico, Central America, and other Spanish-speaking countries, other Latinos now living in this country can identify ancestors who were inhabitants in the current borders of the United States as early as the sixteenth-century. This longstanding relationship of many Latinos with the United States may be especially noted in California, New Mexico, Arizona, Texas, as well as Florida.

To trace the origin and contemporary role of Latinos, one must examine various and diverse cultures, both past and present. A working definition of "Latino" reflects these multiple roots: an important community in the United States whose cultural identity has been influenced by Spain as well as the indigenous peoples of North America, South America, and Africa. Any investigation of Latino civilization, then, will imply an analysis of the contributions and meshing of the cultures of all these regions. The Latino community is a multicultural, multiethnic group of individuals with both common roots and individual traits comprised of Mexican-Americans, Puerto Ricans, Cuban Americans, and Dominicans, as well as those with ties to the countries of Central America, South America and Spain.

Voices of Latino Culture: Readings from Spain, Latin America, and the United States is a selection of writings of the some of the most important Latino ancestors in the long development of this culture to its present form in the United States in the Twentieth Century. This text would be an ideal companion to Carlos Fuentes' epic history of Latino culture, *The Buried Mirror: Reflections on Spain and the New World*, or other similar text. While *The Buried Mirror* discusses the unfolding events that formed one of the world's greatest civilizations, *Voices of Latino Culture* focuses on individual women and men who helped create what we now call Latino.

After an exploration of the word "Latino" by Earl Shorris, we begin our survey of some the people who have influenced Latino culture from the Iberian Peninsula. From Roman Spain comes the stoic philosophy of Seneca; Islamic Spain is represented by a selection of the Koran; and the Medieval Jewish philosopher Maimonides outlines for us some very modern ideas about martyrdom. Next from the Spanish Middle Ages is a selection from the great Spanish epic poem about the life of El Cid. Speaking from Spain's "Golden Age" of the sixteenth- and seventeenth-centuries are the voices of Lazarillo de Tormes, Teresa de Jesús, Tirso de Molina (the "Don Juan" myth), and Cervantes.

Yet, the roots of the Latino community do not solely lie in Spain. When Christopher Columbus came ashore in 1492, he brought European culture to the "New" World, but that world was already inhabited by several great civilizations. These cultures--later joined by those of western Africa--rapidly influenced and changed the world of Queen Isabella and King Ferdinand. Epitomizing the richness of the indigenous cultures of North and South America are the creation stories of the Maya in the *Popol Vuh* and of the Inca in the *Royal Commentaries* by Garcilaso de la Vega, El Inca, the first two readings of this portion of *The Voices of Latino Culture*. Selections of anonymous Aztec poetry are followed by a imaginary interview with the great Aztec Emperor Montezuma himself (by Italo Calvino).

Other figures of the Spanish conquest that communicate with us are Columbus, Bernal Díaz, and Bartolomé de las Casas; Carlos Fuentes then summarizes the significance of the year 1492. The Mexican nun Sor Juana Inés de la Cruz from the Latin America colonial period writes of men's shortcomings in one of her most famous poems. The African presence in Cuba is described by Gertrudis Gómez de Avellaneda in her nineteenth-century novel *Sab*. Analyzing the present-day situation of blacks in Cuba, the poet Nicolás Guillén describes both his white and black grandfathers. Twentieth-century Mexican painter Frida Kahlo discusses the inspiration and technique of one of her paintings. Rounding out modern Latin America is Octavio Paz's seminal description of the "Mexican Mask" as well as a comparison between the United States and Mexico. Finally, a Latina and a gringa examine the role of machismo in Latino culture.

Moving to the United States, our readings begin with Earl Shorris, who in three probing and poetic essays examines the relationship of Mexican-Americans, Puerto Ricans, and Cuban-Americans with Anglo America. Writing as a Mexican-American, Alberto Ríos describes a boy who learns how life is different north and south of the border; and Juan Delgado allots us visions of Latino life in the U. S. from diverse perspectives. César Chávez relates how he first decided to establish the Farm Workers Association. Ed Vega and Nicholasa Mohr describe life in the United States as experienced by Puerto-Ricans who have left their island home. Cuban writer Margarita Mondrus Engle describes how a young Los Angeles girl and her family search for their roots in Cuba, and then notes the reflections of a grown woman who returns to Old Havana during the time of Castro. Words from Julia Alvarez, born in the Dominican Republic, tell of her adjustment to life in New York City. Finishing the selection of Latino voices in the United States is the poet Judith Ortiz Cofer who perceives the individual characteristics of each Latino group but who also stresses the strong ties that bind this group together.

A selection of significant writers of a specific civilization is always problematic, especially a text attempting to review a culture influenced by four continents. Moreover, the Spanish texts here are presented in English; and no matter how skillful the translator, much can be lost in the translation. Those with an intermediate or advanced level in Spanish are encouraged to seek and read these selections in their original form. Nevertheless, we hope the reader of this book will not only pause to consider the roots and contemporary role of Latino culture but also continue to read and listen to the voices that have formed this influential American community.

INTRODUCTION

1. EARL SHORRIS, "THE NAME OF THE PEOPLE"

How is it possible to give a name to a culture that has roots on four continents and whose history spans thousands of years? That is the challenge taken up by Earl Shorris in "The Name of the People" (the introduction to his *Latinos: A Biography of the People*, 1992). Shorris has excellent credentials to speculate on the naming of a culture—in this case Latino—since he is from El Paso, Texas. There he was exposed to the meshing of Anglo, Latino, and Native American trends that provide the content for some of his books (*Under the Fifth Sun*, a novel about Pancho Villa; and *The Boots of the Virgin*, a comic novel set on the U.S.-Mexican border). Later on in Voices of Latino Culture, we will return to Shorris as he explores the relationship of Mexican-Americans, Puerto Ricans, and Cuban Americans with Anglo America.

In "The Name of the People," Shorris reminds us of the difficulty of finding a name that will be broad enough to include the diverse elements of a culture yet specific enough to distinguish that culture from others. In the end, Shorris concludes, no one may be entirely pleased with any specific label.

THE NAME OF THE PEOPLE

One summer afternoon in Los Angeles I asked Margarita Avila, "If you were writing this book, what would you want it to say?"

"Just tell them who we are and that we are not all alike," she said, distilling into a single sentence what I had heard from people in Florida, Texas, New York, and other parts of California. Before I could begin, there was a word to be chosen, a name to be given to the noun represented by "we."

It was hot that afternoon and there was no breeze. Margarita Avila and Sylvia Shorris had been chatting easily in their Mexican-accented Spanish, discussing their sons in a style no Anglo-Saxon mother could understand. They spoke in the shadow of the evil eye, never daring to exhibit pride, characterizing Harvard and Yale as distant places, cold stone, strangers into whose care they had given their sons. They indicated great successes by speaking of little troubles, for the rule of the evil eye is that immodesty will be punished; it is the enforcer of humility. Both women knew the etiquette of the evil eye; each one listened carefully to what the other did not say.

Later, over lunch, I asked Mrs. Avila, whose interest in language leads her to keep four dictionaries in her house, what she had meant by the pronoun "we." She smiled, the grandmother of adolescents, still girlish, pretty in her white summer suit. "Mejicanos," she said.

"Yes, but there is a larger group," I insisted, hoping to learn what word she would prefer.

"We are Mejicanos," she said again, laughing now, looking over at her husband and then at Sylvia for confirmation. Everyone laughed. She had left the problem to me. No matter which other, more inclusive noun I chose, it would blur the distinct character of Mejicanos, and she was unwilling to do that. As the Avilas explain in the oral history of their family, which serves as part of the Epilogue to this book, culture, the nuances of language history are important to them.

Mrs. Avila knew all the other, less specific nouns and preferred not to use them. I think the variety of them must have pleased her, however, for she once

said to me that the difference between English well-spoken and Spanish well-spoken is in the propensity in Spanish for what H. W. Fowler, the arbiter of English usage, called "elegant variation."

"Hispanic?" I asked.

"Mejicano." She said.

"Mejicano. He said.

And Sylvia nodded too.

"Hispano, Latino, Latin, Spanish, Spanish-speaking."

"Mejicano," she said. And even I laughed then.

Gently, but very firmly, with laughter, but without permitting argument, she had made her point. No other word was acceptable, not because there were no other nouns or adjectives available, but because any less specific more encompassing word was damaging. To conflate cultures is to destroy them; to take away the name of a group, as of an individual, is to make pale the existence of the group.

Unfortunately, I do not have the luxury of taking Margarita Avila's advice. To carry out the mission of this book requires that the people have a name. But what?

"Tell them that we are not all alike" is good advice, but once that is done, what name should be given to the set of people who share—with many exceptions—a common language, some customs, and some ancestors? Any set that can be defined can be named. There must be one name, a single word that is not objectionable.

Leobardo Estrada, the demographer at UCLA, told me that in 1980 the U.S. Census was on the verge of choosing *Latino* as the correct word when someone said that it sounded too much like *Ladino*, the ancient Castillian now spoken only by descendants of the Spanish Jews who went into exile in the fifteenth century. *Latino* was replaced by *Hispanic* in the census. The battle was joined immediately on all sides. Political, racial, linguistic, and historical arguments were advanced; some were serious, a few were petulant, and at least one was offered as a joke.

Geographically, *Hispanic* is preferred in the Southeast and much of Texas. New Yorkers use

From LATINOS: A Biography of the People by Earl Shorris. Copyright © 1992 by Earl Shorris. Reprinted by permission of W. W. Norton & Company, Inc.

both *Hispanic* and *Latino*. Chicago, where no nationality has attained a majority, prefers *Latino*. In California, the word *Hispanic* has been barred from the Los Angeles *Times*, in keeping with the strong feelings of people in that community. Some people in New Mexico prefer *Hispano*.

Politically, *Hispanic* belongs to the right and some of the center, while *Latino* belongs to the left and the center. Politically active Mexican-American women in Los Angeles are fond of asking, "Why HISpanic? Why not HERpanic?"

Historically, the choice went from Spanish or Spanish-speaking to Latin American, Latino, and Hispanic.

Economically, Rodolfo Acuña, the historian, is correct when he says that Hispanic belongs to the middle class, which seems most pleased by the term. Anglos and people who oppose bilingual education and bilingualism prefer Hispanic, which makes sense, since Hispanic is an English word meaning "pertaining to ancient Spain."

I have chosen to use *Latino/Latina* for linguistic rather than political, geographic or economic reasons. Latino has gender, which is Spanish, as opposed to Hispanic, which follows English rules. Although the linguistic connection to culture in the group name may eventually be killed, I choose not to be among the assassins.

PART I—READINGS FROM SPAIN

1. SENECA, "ON SELF-CONTROL" AND "ON TAKING ONE'S OWN LIFE"

Lucius Annaeus Seneca, who died around A.D. 65, is perhaps best remembered for being the tutor of the young Nero. Later, as emperor, Nero ordered Seneca to kill himself (he was accused of participating in a conspiracy against his old pupil). As a citizen of Roman Spain (a province in the Roman Empire called *Hispania*), Seneca was the chief representative of his time of the Stoic philosophy. As a stoic, Seneca advocated the suppression of emotion, a love for all human beings, an acknowledgement of the vanity of the world, and an overall world view not too dissimilar from that of a contemporary—Jesus Christ. As a distant Latino *abuelo*, Seneca epitomizes the stoic virtues that eventually will be absorbed by Christianity in the Iberian Peninsula and later transported to the New World by the Spanish.

In this selection we find two letters to Lucilius, a young friend of the aging philosopher (there are 124 of these letters extant). In the first epistle ("On Self Control"), the Latin writer stresses the importance of restraining all emotions; in the second letter ("On Taking One's Own Life") Seneca addresses the very modern topic of one's right to choose the moment of death. Seneca's voice seems contemporary to us partly because his culture—one of diversity, cynicism, corruption, marked by the division of the rich and the poor—is so like our own today.

CXVI. ON SELF-CONTROL

The question has often been raised whether it is better to have moderate emotions, or none at all. Philosophers of our school reject the emotions; the Peripatetics keep them in check. I, however, do not understand how any half-way disease can be either wholesome or helpful. Do not fear; I am not robbing you of any privileges which you are unwilling to lose! I shall be kindly and indulgent towards the objects for which you strive—those which you hold to be necessary to our existence, or useful, or pleasant; I shall simply strip away the vice. For after I have issued my prohibition against the desires, I shall still allow you to wish that you may do the same things fearlessly and with greater accuracy of judgment, and to feel even the pleasures more than before; and how can these pleasures help coming more readily to your call, if you are their lord rather than their slave!

"But," you object, "it is natural for me to suffer when I am bereaved of a friend; grant some privileges to tears which have the right to flow! It is also natural to be affected by men's opinions and to be cast down when they are unfavourable; so why should you not allow me such an honourable aversion to bad opinion?"

There is no vice which lacks some plea; there is no vice that at the start is not modest and easily entreated; but afterwards the trouble spreads more widely. If you allow it to begin, you cannot make sure of its ceasing. Every emotion at the start is weak. Afterwards, it rouses itself and gains strength by progress; it is more easy to forestall it than to forgo it. Who does not admit that all the emotions flow as it were from a certain natural source? We are endowed by Nature with an interest in our own well-being; but this very interest, when overindulged, becomes a vice. Nature has intermingled pleasure with necessary things—not in order that we should seek pleasure, but in order that the addition of pleasure may make the indispensable means of existence attractive to our eyes. Should it claim rights of its own, it is luxury.

Let us therefore resist these faults when they are demanding entrance, because, as I have said, it is easier to deny them admittance than to make them depart. And if you cry: "One should be allowed a certain amount of grieving, and a certain amount of fear," I reply that the "certain amount" can be too long-drawn-out, and that it will refuse to stop short when you so desire. The wise man can safely control himself without becoming over-anxious; he can halt his tears and his pleasures at will; but in our case, because it is not easy to retrace our steps, it is best not to push ahead at all. I think that Panaetius gave a very neat answer to a certain youth who asked him whether the wise man should become a lover: "As to the wise man, we shall see later; but you and I, who are as yet far removed from wisdom, should not trust ourselves to fall into a state that is disordered, uncontrolled, enslaved to another, contemptible to itself. If our love be not spurned, we are excited by its kindness; if it be scorned, we are kindled by our pride. An easily-won love hurts us as much as one which is compliant, and we struggle with that which is hard. Therefore, knowing our weakness, let us remain quiet. Let us not expose this unstable spirit to the temptations of drink, or beauty, or flattery, or anything that coaxes and allures."

Now that which Panaetius replied to the question about love may be applied, I believe, to all the emotions. In so far as we are able, let us step back from slippery places; even on dry ground it is hard enough to take a sturdy stand. At this point, I know, you will confront me with that common complaint against the Stoics: "Your promises are too great, and your counsels too hard. We are mere manikins, unable to deny ourselves everything. We shall sorrow, but not to any great extent: we shall feel desires, but in moderation; we shall give way to anger, but we shall be appeased." And do you know why we have not the power to attain this Stoic ideal? It is because we refuse to believe in our power. Nay, of a surety, there is something else

From SENECA AD LUCILIUM: EPISTLES MORALES, edited by Richard Gummeres, Harvard University Press, 1920.

which plays a part: it is because we are in love with our vices; we uphold them and prefer to make excuses for them rather than shake them off. We mortals have been endowed with sufficient strength by nature, if only we use this strength, if only we concentrate our powers and rouse them all to help us or at least not to hinder us. The reason is unwillingness, the excuse inability. Farewell.

LXXVII. On Taking One's Own Life

Suddenly there came into our view today the "Alexandrian" ships,—I mean those which are usually sent ahead to announce the coming of the fleet; they are called "mail-boats." The Campanians are glad to see them; all the rabble of Puteoli stand on the docks, and can recognize the "Alexandrian" boats, no matter how great the crowd of vessels, by the very trim of their sails. For they alone may keep spread their topsails, which all ships use when out at sea, because nothing sends a ship along so well as its upper canvas; that is where most of the speed is obtained. So when the breeze has stiffened and becomes stronger than is comfortable, they set their yards lower; for the wind has less force near the surface of the water. Accordingly, when they have made Capreae and the headland whence

Tall Pallas watches on the stormy peak,

all other vessels are bidden to be content with the mainsail, and the topsail stands out conspicuously on the "Alexandrian" mail-boats.

While everybody was bustling about and hurrying to the water-front, I felt great pleasure in my laziness, because, although I was soon to receive letters from my friends, I was in no hurry to know how my affairs were progressing abroad, or what news the letters were bringing; for some time now I have had no losses, nor gains either. Even if I were not an old man, I could not have helped feeling pleasure at this; but as it is, my pleasure was far greater. For, however small my possessions might be, I should still have left over more travelling-money than journey to travel, especially since this journey upon which we have set out is one which need not be followed to the end. An expedition will be incomplete if one stops half-way, or anywhere on this side of one's destination; but life is not incomplete if it is honourable. At whatever point you leave off living, provided you leave off nobly, your life is a whole. Often, however, one must leave off bravely, and our reasons therefore need not be momentous; for neither are the reasons momentous which hold us here.

Tullius Marcellinus, a man whom you knew very well, who in youth was a quiet soul and became old prematurely, fell ill of a disease which was by no means hopeless; but it was protracted and troublesome, and it demanded much attention; hence he began to think about dying. He called many of his friends together. Each one of them gave Marcellinus advice,—the timid friend urging him to do what he had made up his mind to do; the flattering and wheedling friend giving counsel which he supposed would be more pleasing to Marcellinus when he came to think the matter over; but our Stoic friend, a rare man, and, to praise him in language which he deserves, a man of courage and vigour, admonished him best of all, as it seems to me. For he began as follows: "Do not torment yourself, my dear Marcellinus, as if the question which you are weighing were a matter of importance. It is not an important matter to live; all your slaves live, and so do all animals; but it is important to die honourably, sensibly, bravely. Reflect how long you have been doing the same thing: food, sleep, lust,—this is one's daily round. The desire to die may be felt, not only by the sensible man or the brave or unhappy man, but even by the man who is merely surfeited."

Marcellinus did not need someone to urge him, but rather someone to help him; his slaves refused to do his bidding. The Stoic therefore removed their fears, showing them that there was no risk involved for the household except when it was uncertain whether the master's death was self-sought or not; besides, it was as bad a practice to kill one's master as it was to prevent him forcibly from killing himself. Then he suggested to Marcellinus himself that it would be a kindly act to distribute gifts to those who had attended him throughout his whole life, when that life was finished, just as, when a banquet is finished, the remaining portion is divided among the attendants who stand about the table. Marcellinus was of a compliant and generous disposition,

From SENECA AD LUCILIUM: EPISTLES MORALES, edited by Richard Gummeres, Harvard University Press, 1920.

13

even when it was a question of his own property; so he distributed little sums among his sorrowing slaves, and comforted them besides. No need had he of sword or of bloodshed; for three days he fasted and had a tent put up in his very bedroom. Then a tub was brought in; he lay in it for a long time, and, as the hot water was continually poured over him, he gradually passed away, not without a feeling of pleasure, as he himself remarked,—such a feeling as a slow dissolution is wont to give. Those of us who have ever fainted know from experience what this feeling is.

This little anecdote into which I have digressed will not be displeasing to you. For you will see that your friend departed neither with difficulty nor with suffering. Though he committed suicide, yet he withdrew most gently, gliding out of life. The anecdote may also be of some use; for often a crisis demands just such examples. There are times when we ought to die and are unwilling; sometimes we die and are unwilling. No one is so ignorant as not to know that we must at some time die; nevertheless, when one draws near death, one turns to flight, trembles, and laments. Would you not think him an utter fool who wept because he was not alive a thousand years ago? And is he not just as much of a fool who weeps because he will not be alive a thousand years from now? It is all the same; you will not be, and you were not. Neither of these periods of time belongs to you. You have been cast upon this point of time; if you would make it longer, how much longer shall you make it? Why weep? Why pray? You are taking pains to no purpose.

Give over thinking that your prayers can bend
Divine decrees from their predestined end.

These decrees are unalterable and fixed; they are governed by a might and everlasting compulsion. Your goal will be the goal of all things. What is there strange in this to you? You were born to be subject to this law; this fate befell your father, your mother, your ancestors, all who came before you; and it will befall all who shall come after you. A sequence which cannot be broken or altered by any power binds all things together and draws all things in its course. Think of the multitudes of men doomed to death who will come after you, of the multitudes who will go with you! You would die more bravely, I suppose, in the company of many thousands; and yet there are many thousands, both of men and of animals, who at this very moment, while you are irresolute about death, are breathing

their last, in their several ways. But you, did you believe that you would not some day reach the goal towards which you have always been travelling? No journey but has its end.

You think, I suppose, that it is now in order for me to cite some examples of great men. No, I shall cite rather the case of a boy. The story of the Spartan lad has been preserved: taken captive while still a stripling, he kept crying in his Doric dialect, "I will not be a slave!" and he made good his word; for the very first time he was ordered to perform a menial and degrading service,—and the command was to fetch a chamber-pot,—he dashed out his brains against the wall. So near at hand is freedom, and is anyone still a slave? Would you not rather have your own son die thus than reach old age by weakly yielding? Why therefore are you distressed, when even a boy can die so bravely? Suppose that you refuse to follow him; you will be led. Take into your own control that which is now under the control of another. Will you not borrow that boy's courage, and say: "I am no slave!"? Unhappy fellow, you are a slave to men, you are a slave to your business, you are a slave to life. For life, if courage to die be lacking, is slavery.

Have you anything worth waiting for? Your very pleasures, which cause you to tarry and hold you back, have already been exhausted by you. None of them is as a novelty to you, and there is none that has not already become hateful because you are cloyed with it. You know the taste of wine and cordials. It makes no difference whether a hundred or a thousand measures pass through your bladder; you are nothing but a wine-strainer. You are a connoisseur in the flavour of the oyster and of the mullet; your luxury has not left you anything untasted for the years that to come; and yet these are the things from which you are torn away unwillingly. What else is there which you would regret to have taken from you? Friends? But who can be a friend to you? Country? What? Do you think enough of your country to be late to dinner? The light of the sun? You would extinguish it, if you could; for what have you ever done that was fit to be seen in the light? Confess the truth; it is not because you long for the senate-chamber or the forum, or even for the world of nature, that you would fain put off dying; it is because you are loth to leave the fish market, though you have exhausted its stores.

You are afraid of death; but how can you scorn it in the midst of a mushroom supper? You wish to live; well, do you know how to live? You are afraid to die. But come now: is this life of yours anything but death? Gaius Caesar was passing along the Via

Latina, when a man stepped out from the ranks of the prisoners, his grey beard hanging down even to his breast, and begged to be put to death. "What!" said Caesar, "are you alive now?" That is the answer which should be given to men to whom death would come as a relief. "You are afraid to die; what ! are you alive now?" "But," says one, "I wish to live, for I am engaged in many honorable pursuits. I am loth to leave life's duties, which I am fulfilling with loyalty and zeal!" Surely you are aware that dying is also one of life's duties? You are deserting no duty; for there is no definite number established which you are bound to complete.

There is no life that is not short. Compared with the world of nature, even Nestor's life was a short one, or Sattia's, the woman who bade carve on her tombstone that she had lived ninety and nine years. Some persons, you see, boast of their long lives; but who could have endured the old lady if she had had the luck to complete her hundredth year? It is with life as it is with a play, it matters not how long the action is spun out, but how good the acting is. It makes no difference at what point you stop. Stop whenever you choose; only see to it that the closing period is well turned. Farewell.

2. "Mary," from the Koran

Islam as a political force occupied Spain for nearly eight centuries—from A. D. 711 to 1492—yet its cultural influence lasted much longer. Muslim Códoba in the tenth century was the greatest and most prosperous city in Western Europe. Comprised of Berber tribesmen, Egyptians, Syrians, tribes of the Arabian Peninsula, and others, the new citizens of Spain were known collectively as the "Moors." They brought cotton, sugarcane, rice, irrigation systems, paper, and arabic numbers to the Iberian world. Spain is unique in Western Europe partly because of its long association with Muslim culture, and the presence of Islam in Spain shaped Spanish culture just as the over one billion moslems today influence world events.

The Islamic peoples of Spain considered themselves Spaniards and named their region Al Andalus. The Moors also brought with them customs that tended to exclude women from public life, a social practice unknown in Western Europe. The Koran, the Holy Book of Islam, reflects some of the new beliefs that arrived in Spain in 711. Meaning "recitation," the Koran represents the words of God (Allah) as revealed to the prophet Mohammed. In the selection here, "Mary," a chapter from the Koran, we note the eclectic nature of Islam as elements of Judaism and Christianity are woven into a new religious fabric.

MARY

IN THE NAME OF GOD, THE COMPASSIONATE, THE MERCIFUL

An account of your Lord's goodness to his servant Zacharias:

He invoked his Lord in secret, saying, 'My bones are enfeebled with age. Yet never, Lord, have I prayed to You in vain. I now fear my kinsmen who will succeed me, for my wife is barren. Grant me a son who will be my heir and an heir to the house of Jacob, and who will find grace in Your sight.'

'Rejoice, Zacharias,' came the answer. 'You shall be given a son, and he shall be called John; a name no man has borne before him.'

'How shall I have a son, Lord,' asked Zacharias, 'when my wife is barren, and I am well-advanced in years?'

He replied, 'Such is the will of your Lord. It shall be no difficult task for Me, for I brought you into being when you were nothing before.'

'Lord,' said Zacharias, 'give me a sign.'

'Your sign is that for three days and three nights,' He replied, 'you shall be bereft of speech though otherwise sound in body.'

Then Zacharias came out from the Shrine and exhorted his people to give glory to their Lord morning and evening.

To John we said: 'Observe the Scriptures with a firm resolve.' We bestowed on him wisdom, grace and purity while yet a child, and he grew up as a righteous man; honouring his father and mother, and neither arrogant nor rebellious. Blessed was he on the day he was born and the day of his death; and may peace be on him when he is raised to life.

And you shall recount in the Book the story of Mary; how she left her people and betook herself to a solitary place to the east.

We sent to her Our spirits in the semblance of a full-grown man. And when she saw him she said: 'May the Merciful defend me from you! If you fear the Lord, leave me and go your way.'

'I am the messenger of your Lord,' he replied, 'and have come to give you a holy son.'

'How shall I bear a child,' she answered, 'when I have neither been touched by any man nor ever been unchaste?'

'Thus did your Lord speak,' he replied. '"That is easy enough for Me. He shall be a sign to mankind and a blessing from Ourself. This is our decree."'

Thereupon she conceived him, and retired to a far-off place. And when she felt the throes of childbirth she lay down by the trunk of a palm tree, crying: 'Oh, would that I had died and passed into oblivion!'

But a voice from below cried out to her: 'Do not despair. Your Lord has provided a brook that runs at your feet, and if you shake the trunk of this palm-tree it will drop fresh ripe dates in your lap.

Therefore eat and drink and rejoice; and should you meet any mortal say to him: "I have vowed a fast to the Merciful and will not speak with any man today."'

Carrying the child, she came to her people, who said to her: 'Mary, this is indeed a strange thing! Sister of Aaron, your father was never a whoremonger, nor was your mother a harlot.'

She made a sign to them, pointing to the child. But they replied: 'How can we speak with a babe in the cradle?'

Whereupon he spoke and said: 'I am the servant of God. He has given me the Book and ordained me a prophet. His blessing is upon me wherever I go, and He has commanded me to be steadfast in prayer and to give alms to the poor as long as I shall live. He has exhorted me to honour my mother and has purged me of vanity and wickedness. I was blessed on the day I was born, and blessed I shall be on the day of my death; and may peace be upon me on the day when I shall be raised to life.'

Such was Jesus, the son of Mary. That is the whole truth, which they still doubt. God forbid that He Himself should beget a son! When He decrees a thing He need only say: 'Be,' and it is.

From THE KORAN, translated by N. J. Dawood. Copyright © N. J. Dawood, 1956, 1959, 1966, 1968, 1974, 1990. Reproduced by permission of Penguin Books Ltd.

God is my Lord and your Lord; therefore serve Him. That is a straight path.

Yet the sects are divided concerning Jesus. But when the fateful day arrives, woe to the unbelievers! Their hearing and sight shall be sharpened on the day when they appear before Us. Truly, the unbelievers are in the grossest error.

Forewarn them of that woeful day, when Our decree shall be fulfilled while they heedlessly persist in unbelief. For We shall inherit the earth and all who dwell upon it. To Us they shall return.

You shall also recount in the Book the story of Abraham:

He was a saintly man and a prophet. He said to his father: 'How can you serve a worthless idol, a thing that can neither hear nor see?

'Father, things you know nothing of have come to my knowledge; therefore follow me, that I may guide you along an even path.

'Father, do not worship Satan; for he has rebelled against the Lord of Mercy.

'Father, I fear that a scourge will fall upon you from the Merciful, and you will become one of Satan's minions.'

He replied: 'Do you dare renounce my gods, Abraham? Desist from this folly or I will stone you. Begone from my house this instant!'

'Peace be with you,' said Abraham. 'I shall implore my Lord to forgive you; for to me He has been gracious. But I will not live with you or be with your idols. I will call on my Lord, and trust that my prayers will not be ignored.'

And when Abraham had cast off his people and the idols which they worshipped, We gave him Isaac and Jacob. Each of them We made a prophet, and We bestowed on them gracious gifts and high renown.

In the Book we tell also of Moses, who was a chosen man, an apostle, and a prophet.

We called out to him from the right side of the Mountain, and when he came near We communed with him in secret. We gave him, of Our mercy, his brother Aaron, himself a prophet.

And in the Book you shall tell of Ishmael; he, too, was a man of his word, an apostle, and a prophet.

He enjoined prayer and almsgiving on his people, and his Lord was pleased with him.

And of Idris; he, too, was a saint and a prophet, whom We honoured and exalted.

These are the men to whom God has been gracious; the prophets from among the descendants of Adam and of those whom We carried in the Ark with Noah; the descendants of Abraham of Israel, and of those whom We have guided and chosen.

For when the revelations of the Merciful were recited to them they fell down on their knees in tears and adoration.

But the generations who succeeded them neglected their prayers and succumbed to their desires. These shall assuredly be lost. But those that repent and embrace the Faith and do what is right shall be admitted to Paradise and shall in no way be wronged. They shall enter the gardens of Eden, which the Merciful has promised on trust to His servants. His promise shall be fulfilled.

There they shall hear no idle talk, but only the voice of peace. And their sustenance shall be given them morning and evening. Such is the Paradise which We shall give the righteous to inherit.

We do not descend from heaven save at the bidding of your Lord! To Him belongs what is before us and behind us, and all that lies between.

Your Lord does not forget.

He Is the Lord of the heavens and the earth and all that is between them. Worship Him, then, and be patient in His service; for do you know any other worthy of His name?

'What!' says man, 'When I am once dead, shall I be raised to life?'

Does man forget that We created him when he was nothing before? By the Lord, We will call them to account in company with all the devils and set them on their knees around the fire of Hell: from every sect We will carry off its stoutest rebels against the Lord of Mercy. We know best who deserves most to be burnt therein. There is not one of you who shall not pass through it: such is the absolute decree of your Lord. We will deliver those who fear Us, but the wrongdoers shall be left there on their knees.

When Our clear revelations are recited to them the unbelievers say to the faithful: 'Which of us two will have a finer dwelling and better companions?'

How many generations have We destroyed before them, far greater in riches and in splendour!

Say: 'The Merciful will bear long with those in error until they see the fulfilment of His threats: be it a worldly scourge or the Hour of Doom. Then shall they know whose is the worse plight and whose the smaller following.'

God will add guidance to those that are rightly guided. Deeds of lasting merit shall earn you as a better reward in the sight of our Lord and a more auspicious end.

Mark the words of him who denies Our signs and who yet boasts: 'I shall surely be given wealth and children!'

Has the future been revealed to him? Or has the Merciful made him such a promise?

By no means! We will record his words and make his punishment long and terrible. All he speaks of he shall leave behind and come before us all alone.

They have chosen other gods to help them. But in the end they will renounce their worship and turn against them.

Know that we send down to the unbelievers devils who incite them to evil. Therefore have patience: their days are numbered. The day will surely come when We will gather the righteous in multitudes before the Lord of Mercy, and drive the sinful in great hordes into Hell. None has power to intercede for them save him who has received the sanction of the Merciful.

Those who say: 'The Lord of Mercy has begotten a son,' preach a monstrous falsehood, at which the very heavens might crack, the earth break asunder, and the mountains crumble to dust. That they should ascribe a son to the Merciful, when it does not become the Lord of Mercy to beget one!

There is none in the heavens or on earth but shall return to the Merciful in utter submission. He has kept strict count of all His creatures, and one by one they shall approach Him on the Day of Resurrection.

3. MAIMONIDES, "THE EPISTLE ON MARTYRDOM"

Jews began migrating to Spain in large numbers during the reign of the Roman Emperor Hadrian (A. D. 117-138), and until 1492—when many were exiled by Isabella and Ferdinand—played a key role in the development of Iberian culture. After 1492, the Jews of Spain settled in many parts of world and became known as the Sephardic Jews, many of whom maintained the traditions of their lost homeland along with fifteenth-century spoken Spanish. In the thirteenth-century, along with Muslims and Christians, the Jews formed the third great leg of a civilization that came to be known as Spanish.

Maimonides (Rabbi Moses ben Maimon, 1135-1204) was one of Spain's greatest Jewish philosophers. He was born in Islamic Córdoba and lived there until he and his family were persecuted by a fundamentalist Muslim sect (the Almohades). After dwelling in several lands, Maimonides finally settled in Egypt, where he was the physician to the Sultan and could practice his faith freely.

In this reading, we hear Maimonides speaking in the opening pages of "The Epistle on Martyrdom," where he objects to a ruling by a distinguished rabbi. This rabbi maintains that Jews who make a profession of Islam—even under the threat of death—are abandoning their Jewish faith. In other words, the rabbi, according to Maimonides, only gives Jews two options in the face of persecution—live and convert to Islam or die as a Jew. Maimonides will offer another more logical and humane solution to the problem of Jewish forced converts.

CHAPTER ONE
"THE EPISTLE ON MARTYRDOM"

A contemporary of mine[1] inquired regarding this persecution[2] in which he is forced to confess that that man[3] is God's messenger and that he is a true prophet. He addressed his query to one whom he calls a sage[4] and who was not touched by the tribulations of most of the Jewish communities in this violence, may it pass soon, and he wished to learn whether he should make the confession in order not to die and not acknowledge what he demands, seeing that in this way he does what is required by the Torah of Moses, and that the confession leads to the relinquishment of all the commandments.[5]

The man of whom the inquiry was made offered a weak and senseless reply, of foul content and form. He made statements in it distinctly harmful, as a even light-minded women can realize.[6] Although his reply is weak, tedious, and confused, I thought I should quote him at length, but I spared the gift that God, blessed be He, bestowed on mankind. I mean speech, of which our sacred Torah states: *Who gives man speech? . . . is it not I, the Lord?* [Exod.4:11].[7] A man should be more sparing of his speech than of his money, and should not speak much yet do little. Indeed the Sage[8] has condemned verbosity with little content in his declaration: *Just as dreams come with much brooding, so does foolish utterance come with much speech* [Eccles. 5:2]. You know of course what Job's friends said as he talked on and on:[9] *Is a multitude of words unanswerable? Must a loquacious person be right?* [Job 11:2]; *Job does not speak with knowledge; his words lack understanding* [Job 34:35].[10] There are many such reflections.

Since I am well informed regarding this issue, and am not ignorant of it as this man is, I think it is proper to cite something of the gist of what he said, and omit the rest, which does not merit a response, although on close examination nothing of what he said deserves an answer. Such is his assertion that whoever acknowledges his[11] apostleship has ipso facto disavowed the Lord, God of Israel. In support he brings the statement of our sages. "Whoever professes idolatry is as if he denied the entire Torah."[12] Judging from this analogy, he apparently finds no distinction between one who turns to idolatry not under duress but voluntarily, like Jeroboam and his associates.[13] And one you will under compulsion say of someone that he is a prophet, because he is afraid of the executioner's sword.

When I read this first statement of his, I decided not to challenge him before I read all of it, heeding the instruction of the Sage: To answer a man before hearing him out is foolish and disgraceful [Prov. 18:13]. So, when I looked further into his remarks, I

---

1. Maimonides employs the first person plural in most references to himself (literally, ours). This was the usage developed among speakers of Arabic in medieval times, especially in northwestern Africa. In the translation, English practice is followed.

2. The reference is to the Almohads (al-Muwahhidun) and their destructive conquest of North Africa and Spain (see Abraham ibn Ezra's poem: "Alas, calamity from heaven has struck Spain, an elegy for the victims of the persecution.") The Almohads (1130-1223) early in their history instituted forced conversion.

3. *That man* in this context is Muhammad, founder of Islam, whose name Maimonides avoids mentioning.

4. By qualifying the "sage" with "whom he calls," Maimonides indicates that he himself does not think so.

5. The question raised by the forced convert is either/or, as if there is not alternative, as a Maimonides will point out.

6. It is to be noted that Maimonides begins with his opinion of the sage, and follows it with evidence that supports his judgment. His evaluation of women's capacity was common in the ancient and medieval world.

7. The verse from the Bible is used by Maimonides to support his thinking. This reflects the view, held by generations of rabbis and scholars, that Scripture is a storehouse of all knowledge and doctrine.

---

8. The reference is to King Solomon, recognized by tradition as the author of Song of Songs, Proverbs, and Ecclesiastes.

9. Maimonides may be referring to Job's response to his friends after every speech they made, or he may be thinking of the length of Job's answers compared with the briefer statements of the friends.

10. The first passage is Zophar's opening rebuke and the second is by Elihu.

11. I.e., Muhammad.

12. BT Nedarim 28a; BT Kiddushin 40a; and elsewhere.

13. See the relevant account in 1 Kings 12:20ff.

From CRISIS AND LEADERSHIP: EPISTLES OF MAIMONIDES by Halkin Hartman. Reprinted by permission of The Jewish Publication Society.

noted that he said the following: "Whoever utters that confession is a gentile, though he fulfills the entire Law publicly and privately."[14] This "clear-headed man"[15] evidently sees absolutely no difference between one who does not observe the Sabbath out of the fear of the sword and one who does not observe it because he does not wish to.[16] I read on: "If one of the forced converts enters one of their houses of worship,[17] even if he does not say a word, and he then goes home and offers his prayers, this prayer is charged against him as an added sin and transgression." His proof text is the comment of our sages on the verse, For My people have done a twofold wrong [Jer. 2:13]:[18] They bowed to the idol and they bowed to the Temple.[19] This interpretation again does not discriminate between one who bowed to the idol and the Temple because he is a heretic and wants to defile God's name and desecrate His holiness and one who comes to a house of worship in order to behave like someone zealous[20] for the glory of God,[21] but does not utter or say a word that is in any way contrary to our religion, yet he must of necessity go to that house.[22] I likewise found him saying that anyone who avows that man is a prophet,[23] though he does it under compulsion, is a wicked person, disqualified by Scripture from serving as a witness, since the Torah rules: You shall not join hands with the guilty [Exod. 23:1], that is, do not make a wicked man a witness.[24]

Even as I read his abuses, his long-winded foolish babbling and nonsense, I still believed it was not correct to challenge him before I read all the rest: per-

haps it might be an example of what Solomon described: The end of a matter is better than the beginning of it [Eccles. 7:8].[25] But I found him saying toward the end of his missive that heretics and Christians likewise assume that they will choose death rather than grant his apostleship.[26] When I learned this I was struck with amazement and wondered: Is there no God in Israel? [2 Kings 1:3.6].[27] If an idol-worshiper burns his son and daughter to his object of worship,[28] do we even more certainly have to set fire to ourselves for service to God? Alas for the question, alas for the answer! Considering that he began by finding support in something irrelevant to his argument, and concluded by approving the thinking of heretics and Christians, I decided that God's judgment is right: his talk begins as silliness and ends as disastrous madness.

You ought to know that no one has the right to speak in public before he has rehearsed what he wants to say two, three, and four times, and learned it; then he may speak. This is what the rabbis taught, and took their proof text from the verse: Then He saw it and gauged it; He measured it and probed it. And afterward; He said to man [Job 28:27].[29] So much for what a person is required to do before he speaks. But if a man legislates on his own, and puts it down in writing, he should revise it a thousand times, if possible. This man, however, did nothing of the kind. He reduced all this important advice to writing, and did not think it necessary to prepare a first draft and then revise it. Evidently he considered his remarks free from doubt, in no need of correction. He handed them to someone who was to convey them in every city and town, and in this way brought darkness into the hearts of men. He sent darkness; it was very dark [Ps. 105:28].[30]

---

14. The rabbi's reasoning is that the person who pronounces the Muslims confession of faith thereby reads himself out of the Jewish religious community, so that his fulfillment of the Law, or any part of it, is no more efficacious than its fulfillment by any Muslim or gentile.

15. An ironical characterization, implying the opposite.

16. Maimonides' judgment of the case is very different from that of the rabbi. Maimonides regards the utterance of the confession as insignificant because it was not spoken in sincerity. The question to be determined is why an individual in this critical situation refrains from observing Jewish laws. Is it because he does not want to, or because he is afraid? Maimonides is persuaded that the judgment of the issue is related to this difference.

17. I.e., he attends Muslim services in a mosque.

18. In JT Sukkah 5, section 5, the verse is applied to those who bow before the sun, and also bow down before the Temple.

19. I.e., they play the role of the truly pious Muslim.

20. A pious Jewish individual.

21. Literally: the magnificence of God, the name of the declaration that the Muslim makes: Allah Akbar—God is most magnificent.

22. Namely, the mosque.

23. I.e., Muhammad. The avowal is part of the confession that the convert to Islam recites.

24. This is the meaning that the rabbis derive from the verse. Cf. BT Bava Kamma 72b and BT Sanhedrin 27a.

25. Maimonides renders the verse "the end may be better."

26. The suggestion in the rabbi's introduction of "heretics and Christians" is that the confession is such grievous betrayal of their convictions, that a Jew should certainly act the same way, and if he fails to, he excludes himself from the Jewish religion.

27. The protest is made by Elijah against King Ahaziah's inquiry of foreign deity. The phrase is expressive of Maimonides' inner pain.

28. The Torah, Lev. 20:1-6, very vigorously condemns this act and behavior of those who disregard this hideous deed.

29. The caution Maimonides expresses is consistent with his own practice, and he explicitly declares in his Introduction to the Guide of the Perplexed: "The diction of this treatise has not been chosen haphazardly, but with great exactness and exceeding precision . . . and nothing has been mentioned out of place." He reads the advice in Job as it was explained by R. Aha in Genesis Rabbah 24:5; God would repeat every statement He made to Moses. See also BT Eruvin 54b.

30. The verse speaks of the plague of darkness inflicted on Egypt. Former generations did not hesitate to use any apt biblical passage, even though its original use was in a different context.

4. POEM OF THE CID, ANONYMOUS

Along with Muslims and Jews, the Christians formed the third great culture of Medieval Spain. Nearly defeated by Islamic forces in 711, the Christians maintained a foothold in northern Spain, and between 711 and 1492, inched southward, finally defeating the last Muslim king in Granada. Perhaps one of the greatest Christian knights of this period was Rodrigo Díaz de Vivar (1040? - 1099), immortalized in the epic poem *Poema del Cid* ("Cid" is from the Arabic *sidi*, meaning "leader" or "lord").

The poem, probably written around 1140, is divided into three parts: King Alfonso's banishment of the Cid from Castile (the monarch disapproved of some of the knight's actions); the reconcilement of the King with his famous knight and the marriage of the daughters of the Cid to the Princes of Carrión; and the revenge of the Cid on his new sons-in-law for their shameful treatment of his daughters along with their second marriage to more honorable husbands.

The *Poema del Cid* differs from many other European epic poems of the time because of its realistic descriptions of personages and events; of the twenty nine characters mentioned in the poem, 25 have been historically identified (including the Cid). The Cid himself is a perfect representative of the Christian knight whose image as a fearless warrior and loyal Spaniard will be a model for the Spanish *conquistadores* in the New World. In the two selections here, both from the first part of the poem, the Cid is banished from his pueblo of Bivar as well as the city of Burgos; later, the Cid departs from the Monastery of San Pedro, where his wife Ximena and his two daughters remain under the protection of the Abbot, Don Pedro.

The Poem of the Cid

The Banishment of the Cid

He turned and looked upon them, and he wept very sore
As he saw the yawning gateway and the hasps wrenched off the
    door.
And the pegs whereon no mantle nor coat of vair there hung.
There perched no moulting goshawk, and there no falcon swung.
My lord the Cid sighed deeply such grief was in his heart
And he spake well and wisely: 'Oh Thou, in Heaven that art
Our father and our Master, now I give thanks to Thee.
Of their wickedness my foemen have done this thing to me.'

Then they shook out the bridle rein further to ride afar.
They had the crow on their right hand as they issued from Bivar;
And as they entered Burgos upon their left it sped.
And the Cid shrugged his shoulders, and the Cid shook his head:
'Good tidings Alvar Fañez! We are banished from our weal,
But on a day with honour shall we come unto Castile.'

Roy Diaz entered Burgos with sixty pennons strong,
And forth to look upon him did the men and women throng.
And with their wives the townsmen at the windows stood hard by,
And they wept in lamentation, their grief was risen so high.
As with one mouth, together they spake with one accord:
'God, what a noble vassal, an he had a worthy lord.'

Fain had they made him welcome, but none dared do the thing
For fear of Don Alfonso, and the fury of the King.
His mandate unto Burgos came ere the evening fell.
With utmost care they brought it, and it was sealed well:
'That no man to Roy Diaz give shelter now, take heed.
And if one give him shelter, let him know in very deed
He shall lose his whole possession, nay! The eyes within his head
Nor shall his soul and body be found in better stead.'

Great sorrow had the Christians, and from his face they hid.
Was none dared aught to utter unto my lord the Cid.

Then the Campeador departed unto his lodging straight.
But when he was come thither, they had locked and barred the
    gate.
In their fear of King Alfonso had they done even so.
And the Cid forced not his entrance, neither for weal nor woe
Durst they open it unto him. Loudly his men did call.
Nothing thereto in answer said the folk within the hall.
My lord the Cid spurred onward, to the doorway did he go.
He drew his foot from the stirrup, he smote the door one blow.

From ANTHOLOGY OF SPANISH LITERATURE by Resnick. Copyright 1958. Reprinted by permission of The Continuum Publishing Company.

Yet the door would not open, for they had barred it fast.
But a maiden of nine summers came unto him at last:

"Campeador in happy hour thou girdest on the sword.
'Tis the King's will. Yestereven came the mandate of our lord.
With utmost care they brought it, and it was sealed with care:
None to ope to you or greet you for any cause shall dare.
And if we do, we forfeit our houses and lands instead.
Nay we shall lose morever, the eyes within the head.
And, Cid, with our misfortune naught whatever dost thou gain.
But may God with all His power support thee in they pain.

So spake the child and turned away. Unto her home went she.
That he lacked the King's favour now well the Cid might see.
He left the door; forth onward he spurred through Burgos town.
When he had reached Saint Mary's, then he got swiftly down.
He fell upon his knee and prayed with a true heart indeed:
And when the prayer was over, he mounted on the steed.
Forth from the gate and over the Arlanzon he went.
There in the sand by Burgos, the Cid let pitch his tent.
Roy Diaz who in happy hour had girded on the brand,
Since none at home would greet him, encamped there on the sand
With a good squadron, camping as if within the wood.
They will not let him in Burgos buy any kind of food.
Provender for a single day they dared not to him sell.

THE CID'S FAREWELL TO HIS WIFE

And it was night to morning, and the cocks full oft they crew,
When at last my lord the Campeador unto San Pedro came.
God's Christian was the Abbot, Don Sancho was his name;
And he was saying matins at the breaking of the day.
With her five good dames in waiting Ximena there did pray.
They prayed unto Saint Peter and God they did implore:
'O thou who guidest all mankind, succour the Campeador.'

One knocked at the doorway and they heard the tidings then.
God wot the Abbot Sancho was the happiest of men.
With the lights and with the candles to the court they ran
    forthright,
And him who in good hour was born they welcomed in delight.

'My lord Cid,' quoth the Abbot, 'Now God be praised of grace!
Do thou accept my welcome, since I see thee in this place."
And the Cid who in good hour was born, thereunto answered he:

"My thanks to thee, don Sancho, I am content with thee.
For myself and for my vassals provision will I make.
Since I depart to exile, these fifty marks now take.
If I may live my life-span, they shall be doubled you.
To the Abbey not as a groatsworth of damage will I do.
For my lady do I give you an hundred marks again.
Herself, her dames and daughters for this year do you maintain.
I leave two daughters with you, but little girls they be.

In thine arms keep them kindly. I commend them here to thee.
Don Sancho do thou guard them, and of my wife take care.
If thou wantest yet and lackest for anything whate'er,
Look well to their provision, thee I conjure once more,
And for one mark that thou spendest the Abbey shall have four.'
And with glad heart the Abbot his full assent made plain.
And lo! The Dame Ximena came with her daughters twain.
Each had her dame-in-waiting who the little maiden bore.
And Dame Ximena bent the knee before the Campeador.
And fain she was to kiss his hand, and, oh, she wept forlorn!

'A boon! A boon! My Campeador. In a good hour wast thou
    born.
And because of wicked slanderers art thou banished from the land.

'Oh Campeador fair-bearded a favour at thy hand!
Behold I kneel before thee, and thy daughters are here with me,
They have seen of days not many, for children yet they be,
And these who are my ladies to serve my need that know.
Now well do I behold it, thou art about to go.
Now from thee our lives a season must sunder and remove,
But unto us give succour for sweet Saint Mary's love.'

The Cid, the nobly bearded, reached down unto the twain,
And in his arms his daughters has lifted up again,
And to his heart he pressed them, so great his love was grown.
And his tears feel fast and bitter, and sorely did he moan:
"Ximena as a mine own spirit I loved thee, gentle wife;
but o'er well dost thou behold it, we must sunder in our life.
I must flee and thou behind me here in the land must stay.
Please God and sweet Saint Mary that yet upon a day
I shall give my girls in marriage with mine own hand rich and well,
And thereafter in good fortune be suffered yet to dwell,
May they grant me, wife, much honoured, to serve thee then
    once more.'

5. Lazarillo de Tormes, Anonymous

Perhaps the height of the Spanish renaissance is represented by the reign of Charles V (1516-1556). It is a period of international involvement for Spain, including the conquest of the New World. This is the Spain that fathers Cortés, Pizarro, Cabeza de Vaca, and other *conquistadores*. Yet what was life like in the mother country itself? *Lazarillo de Tormes* (1554) and its anonymous author provide readers then and now a glimpse of the harsh conditions in Spain where inflation, wars, budget deficits, and pride were taking a heavy toll on Spaniards.

Lazarillo is the world's first *pícaro* of picaresque literature, a genre born in Spain and popularized throughout the Western world. It is a class of literature that in fact stresses the defects of society, both social and economic; *pícaro* itself has no accurate translation in English, although often the words "misfit" "rogue," or "juvenile delinquent" are employed. *Lazarillo* sets the frame for most subsequent picaresque novels: a homeless boy serves a series of masters, autobiographically relating his adventures but also weaving in criticism of established institutions (Lazarillo's cruelest master is a priest). Later, young women would join the genre as pícaras who would serve many lovers, utilizing the same satirical world view as their male counterparts. In this reading, Lazarillo tells us of his parents and home, and then continues to relate how he came to serve a blind man, and the lessons that he learned from that first master.

Lazarillo de Tormes

Treatise First

With a Blind Man

Then know Your Worship, before anything else that my name is Lazaro of Tormes, son of Thome Gonçales and Antona Perez, natives of Tejares, a hamlet near Salamanca. My birth took place in the river Tormes, for which reason I had the surname, and it was in this manner. My father (whom God forgive) had the job of overseeing the grinding of a water-mill, which is by the bank of that river, wherein he was miller more than fifteen years; and my mother being one night in the water-mill, big with me, her pains took her and she delivered me there; so that I can truthfully say I was born in the river. Well, when I was a child of eight, they imputed to my father certain awkward bleedings in the sacks of those who came there to grind, for which he was taken, and he confessed, and denied not, and suffered persecution for justice' sake. I trust in God that he is in glory, for the Gospel calls them blessed. At this time there was an expedition made against the Moors, in which went my father, who had been banished for the misfortune above-said, serving as a muleteer to a knight; and with his lord, like a loyal servant, he ended his life.

My widow mother when she found herself without husband or support determined to get among worthy people and be one of them and undertook to do the cooking for some students, and washed clothes for certain stable-boys . . . [later] she went into service with those who were then living at the inn of La Solana; and there suffering a thousand annoyances, she managed to bring up my small brother to the point where he knew how to walk, and me to where I was a good-sized little fellow, who fetched wine and candles for the guests, or whatever else they bade me.

At this time there came a blind man to lodge at the inn; and as it seemed to him that I would be suitable for leading him, he begged of my mother, and she turned me over to him, telling him how I was the son of a good man, who had died to exalt the faith in the affair of Los Gelves, and that she had trust in God I should not turn out a worse man than my father, and she begged him to treat me well and look after me, for I was an orphan. He answered that he would do so, and that he was receiving me not a his boy but as his son. And so I began to serve and to lead my new old master.

After we had remained in Salamanca several days and it appeared to my master that the profits were not to his satisfaction, he determined to leave there; and when we were about to depart I went to see my mother, and both weeping she gave me her blessing and said: "Son, now I know that I shall never see thee more; try to be good, and God guide thee; I have reared thee and placed thee with a good master, take care of thyself." And so I went along to my master who was waiting for me.

We went out of Salamanca, and as you approach the bridge there is a stone animal at the entrance, almost in the shape of a bull, and the blind man bade me go close to the animal and when I was there, said to me, "'Lazaro, put thine ear close to this bull and shalt hear a great noise inside.' Naively, I went, believing this to be so; and when he perceived that I had my head close to the stone, he swung out his hand hard and gave my head a great blow against the devil of a bull, so that for three days the pain of the butting remained, and said to me: 'Silly fool, learn that the blind man's boy has to know one point more than the devil,' and laughed a great deal at the joke. It seemed to me that in that instant I awoke from the childish simplicity in which I had always been asleep. I said to myself: 'This man says the truth, for it behooves me to open mine eyes and look about, since I am alone, and to consider how to take care of myself.'

We began our journey and in a very few days he taught me thieves' jargon, and when he saw me to be of a good wit, was well pleased, and used to say: 'Gold or silver I cannot give thee, but I will show thee many pointers about life.' And it was so; for

From ANTHOLOGY OF SPANISH LITERATURE by Resnick. Copyright 1958. Reprinted by permission of The Continuum Publishing Company.

after God this man gave me my life, and although blind lighted and guided me in the career of living. I enjoy relating these puerilities to Your Worship in order to show how much virtue there is in men's knowing how to rise when they are low, and in their letting themselves lower when they are high, how much vice! To return to my good blind man and his affairs, Your Worship must know that since God created the world, He never formed any one more astute or sagacious. In his trade he was an eagle; he knew a hundred and odd prayers by heart; had as a bass voice, tranquil and very sonorous, which made the church where he prayed resound, a humble and devout countenance which he put on with very good effect when he prayed, without making faces or grimaces with his mouth or eyes, as others wont to do. Besides, he had a thousand other modes and fashions for getting money: he said he knew prayers to many and divers effects: for women that did not bear, for those that were in travail, for those badly married to make their husbands love them; he cast prognostications for the pregnant whether they were carrying son or daughter. Then in regard to medicine, he used to say that Galen didn't know the half of what he knew about grinders, swoons, the vapours; in a word, nobody could tell him that he was suffering any illness, but straightway he would reply: 'Do this, you will do that, pluck such an herb, take such a root.' Accordingly he had all the world marching after him, especially the women, for they believed whatever he told them; from them he extracted large profits by the arts I tell you of, and used to gain more in a month than a hundred blind men in a year.

But also I wish Your Worship to know, that with all he acquired and possessed, never did I see so miserly or mean a man, to such a point that he was killing me with hunger, and didn't share even the necessaries with me. I am telling the truth: if I had not known how to cure myself by slyness and good devices, many times I should have died of hunger; but with all his experience and vigilance I worked against him in such as a fashion, that the biggest and best part always or more generally, fell to me. To this end I played him devilish tricks, some of which I shall relate, though not all to my advantage.

He used to carry bread and everything else in a linen sack which closed at the mouth with an iron ring and a padlock and key, and when he put things in and took them out, it was with so much attention, so well counted, that the whole world wouldn't have been equal to making it a crumb less. But I would take what stingy bit he gave me,

and finish it in less than two mouthfuls. After he had fastened the lock and stopped worrying about it, thinking me to be engaged in other things, by a little seam, which I unsewed and sewed up again many times in the side of the sack, I used to bleed the miserly sack, taking out bread,—not measured quantities but good pieces,—and slices of bacon and sausage; and thus would seek a convenient time to make good the devilish state of want which the wicked blind man left me in.

All I could filch and steal I carried in half-farthings; and when they bade him pray and gave him a farthing, it was no sooner proffered than I had it popped into my mouth and a half-farthing ready so that however soon he held out his hand, his remuneration was already reduced by my money-changing to half its real value. The wicked blind man used to complain to me, for he at once perceived by the feeling that it was not a whole farthing, and would say: 'Why the devil is it that since thou art with me they don't give me but half-farthings, and before, they paid me a farthing and oftentimes a maravedi? This bad luck must come through thee.' He used also to shorten his prayers and not half finish them, having ordered me that when the person went away who had ordered him to pray, I should pluck him by the end of his hood. And so I used to do; and at once he began again to lift his voice, saying: 'Who would like to have me say a prayer?' as the custom is.

When we ate he used to put a little jug of wine near him. I would quickly seize it and give it a couple of silent kisses and return it to its place; but this plan didn't work long, for he noticed the deficiency in his draughts, and in order to keep his wine safe, he never after let go the jug, but kept hold of the handle. But there is no lode-stone that draws things to it so strongly as I with as a long rye straw, which I had prepared for that purpose, and placing which in the mouth of the jug, I would suck up the wine to a fare-ye-well. But the villain was so clever that I think he heard me; and from then on he changed procedure and set his jug between his legs and covered it with his hand, and thus drank secure. Now that I had grown accustomed to wine, I was dying for it; and seeing that the straw-cure was no longer helping me, I decided to make a tiny hole in the bottom of the jug for a little drain, and to bung it neatly with a very thin cake of wax, and at dinner-time, pretending to be cold, I got between the wretched blind man's legs to warm me at the miserable fire we had, in whose heat the wax being soon melted, for there was very little, the streamlet began to drain into my mouth, which I held in such a way that devil a drop was lost. When the poor creature went to drink, he found nothing; he was astounded, damned himself, and sent the jug and the wine to the devil, not knowing what it all could mean. 'You won't say, uncle, that I drank it for you,' said I, 'for you haven't let it out of your hand.' He turned and felt the jug so much, that he found the cutlet and fell on to the trick; but made as though he had not perceived it. And the next day, when I had my jug leaking as before, and was not dreaming of the injury in store for me, or that the wicked blind man heard me, I sat as before, in the act of receiving those sweet draughts, my face turned toward heaven, my eyes partly closed, the better to enjoy the delicious liquid, when the desperate blind man perceived that now was his time to take vengeance of me, and with all his might, raising that sweet and bitter jug with both hands, he let it fall upon my mouth, making use (as I say) of all his strength, so that poor Lazaro, who was expecting none of this, but, as at other times, was careless and joyful, verily it seemed to me that the heavens, with all that in them is, had fallen on top of me. Such was the gentle tap he gave me that it stupefied and knocked me senseless, and the blow so hard that the pieces of the jug stuck in my face, breaking it in many places, and cracked off my teeth which I remain without until this very day. From that hour forth I hated the wicked blind man; and although he liked and caressed me and cared for me, well I saw that the cruel chastisement had diverted him. He washed with wine the wounds he had made me with the pieces of the jug, and smiling, said, 'How seems it to thee, Lazaro? That which made thee sick cures thee and gives thee health,' and other pleasantries which to my taste were none.

Once I was half well of my horrid bumps and bruises, considering that with a few such blows the cruel blind man would be rid of me, I was anxious to be rid of him; but I did not manage it too quickly, in order to do it with more safety and profit. Even though I should have been willing to soften my heart and forgive him the blow with the jug, the ill-treatment the wicked blind man gave me from this point on, left no chance for that; for he abused me without cause or reason, beating me over the head and pulling my hair. And if anybody asked him why he treated me so badly, he at once retailed the story of the jug saying: 'Would you take this boy of mine for an innocent? Then listen, whether the devil himself could teach another such exploit.' Those that listened would say, making the sign of the cross: 'Well, now, who would expect such badness from a lad so small!' and would laugh heartily

at the trick, and say to him: 'Chastise him chastise him, for you'll get your reward from God,' and on that he never did anything else.

And meantime I always led him by the worst roads, and purposely, to do him harm and damage; if there were stones, through them, if mud, through the deepest; for although I didn't go through the dryest part, it pleased me to put out one of my own eyes in order to put out two for him, who had none. Therefore he used always to keep the upper end of his staff against the back of my head, which was continually full of bumps, and the hair pulled out by his hands; and although I swore I didn't do it of malice, but because I found no better road, that didn't help me, nor did he believe me any more for that; such was the perspicacity and the vast intelligence of the traitor.

And that Your Worship may see how far the cleverness of this astute blind man extended, I will relate one instance of many that befell me with him, wherein it seems to me he made his great astuteness very manifest. When we left Salamanca his intention was to go to the region around Toledo, because he said the people were richer, although not very charitable; he pinned his faith to the proverb: The hard give more than the poor. And we came along that route through the best places: where he found good welcome and profit, we would stop, where not, on the third day, we would move away. It happened that on arriving at a place called Almorox at the time when the grapes are gathered, a vintager gave him as a bunch for alms. And as the paniers generally get hard treatment, and the grapes at that time are very ripe, the bunch fell apart in his hand: if put into the sack, it would turn to must, and so he decided on this: he resolved to have a banquet, as much because we could not carry it, as to comfort me, for that day he had given me many kicks and blows. We sat down on a wall and he said: 'Now I wish to be generous with thee: we will both eat this bunch of grapes, and thou shalt have as big a share as I; we will divide in this way: thou shalt pick once and I once; provided thou promise me not to take more than one grape each time. I shall do the same until we finish, and in this way there will be no cheating.' The agreement thus made, we began; but directly at the second turn, the traitor changed his mind and began to take two at a time, supposing that I must be doing likewise. As I saw he was breaking the agreement, I was not content to keep even with him, but went still farther: I ate them two at a time, three at a time, and as I could. The bunch finished, he waited awhile with the stem in his hand and shaking his head said:

'Lazaro, thou hast cheated: I will swear to God that thou hast eaten the grapes by threes.' 'I have not,' said I; 'but why do you suspect that?' The clever blind man replied: 'Knowest how I see that thou wast eating them by three? Because I ate by twos and thou said nothing.' . . . I laughed inwardly, and although only a lad noted well the blind man's just reasoning.

But not to be prolix, I omit an account of many things as funny as they are worthy of note, which befel me with this my first master, but I wish to tell our leave-taking and with that to finish. We were at Escalona, town of the Duke of that ilk, in an inn, and he gave me a piece of sausage to roast. When he had basted the sausage and eaten the basting, he took a maravedi from his purse and bade me fetch wine from the tavern. The devil put the occasion before my eyes, which as the saying is, makes the thief; and it was this: there lay by the fire a small turnip, rather long and bad, and which must have been thrown there because it was not fit for the stew. And as a nobody was there at the time but him and me alone, as I had an appetite whetted by having got the toothsome odour of the sausage inside me (the only part, as I knew, that I had to enjoy myself with), not considering what might follow, all fear set aside in order to comply with desire,—while the blind man was taking the money out of his purse, I took the sausage and quickly put the above-mentioned turnip on the spit, which my master grasped, when he had given me money for the wine, and began to turn before the fire, trying to roast what through its demerit had escaped being spoiled. I went for the wine, and on the way did not delay in despatching the sausage, and when I came back I found the sinner of a blind man holding the turnip ready between two slices of bread, for he had not yet recognized it, because he had not tried it with his hand. When he took the slices of bread and bit into them, thinking to get part of the sausage too, he found himself chilled by the chilly turnip; he grew angry and said: 'What is this, Lazarillo?' 'Poor Lazaro,' said I, 'if you want to blame me for anything. Haven't I just come back with the wine? Somebody was here, and must have done this for a joke.' "No, no,' said he, 'for I've not let the spit out of my hand. It's not possible.' I again swore and forswore that I was innocent of the exchange, but little did it avail me, for nothing was hid from the sharpness of the confounded blind man. He got up and seized me by the head and came close up to smell me; and since he must have caught the scent like a good hound, the better to satisfy himself of the truth in the great agony he was suffering, he seized me with his hands, opened my mouth wider than it ought to go, and unconsideringly thrust in his nose,—which was long and sharp, and at that crisis a palm longer from rage,—with the point of which he reached my gorge; what with this and with the great fright I was in, and the short time the black sausage had had to get settled in my stomach, and most of all, with the tickling of his huge nose nearly half-choking me,—all these things conjointly were the cause that my misconduct and gluttony were made evident, and his own returned to my master; for before the wicked blind man withdrew his bugle from my mouth, my stomach was so upset that it abandoned its stolen goods, and thus his nose and the wretched, half-masticated sausage went out of my mouth at the same time. O great God, that I had been buried at that hour! for dead I already was. Such was the depraved blind man's fury, that if they had not come to my assistance at the noise, I think he had not left me alive. They dragged me from out his hands, leaving them full of what few hairs I had, my face scratched and my neck and throat clawed; and well my throat deserved this, for such abuse befel me through its viciousness. The wicked blind man related my disgraceful actions to all that approached, and gave them the history once and again, both of the wine-jug and of the bunch of grapes and now of the actual trouble. Everybody laughed so much that all the passers-by came in to see the fun; for the blind man related my doings with so much wit and sprightliness that although I was thus abused and weeping, it seemed to me that I doing him injustice not to laugh. And while this was going on, I remembered a piece of cowardly weakness I had been guilty of, and I cursed myself for it; and that was my leaving him with a nose, when I had such a good chance, half the distance being gone, for by only clinching my teeth it would have remained in my house, and because it belonged to that villain, perhaps my stomach would have retained it better than the sausage . . . .

In view of this and the evil tricks the blind man played me, I decided to leave him once and for all, and as I had everything thought out and in my mind, on his playing me this last game I determined on it more fully. And so it was that the next day we went out about time to beg alms, and it had rained a great deal the night before; and as it was still raining that day he walked in prayer under some arcades which there were in that town, where we didn't get wet; but as night was coming on and the rain didn't stop, the blind man said to me: 'Lazaro, this water is very persistent, and the more night shuts down, the heavier it is: let us get back to the inn in time.' To go there we had to cross a gutter which was running full because of all the water; I said to him: 'Uncle, the gutter runs very wide; but if you wish, I see where we can get over more quickly without wetting us, for there it becomes much narrower, and by jumping we can cross with dry feet.' This seemed good advice to him, and he said: 'Thou art clever, I like thee for that. Bring me to the place where the gutter contracts, for it is winter now and water is disagreeable, and going with wet feet still more so.' Seeing the scheme unfolding as I desired, I led him out from the arcades and brought him in front of a pillar or stone post which was in the square, and upon which and others like it projections of the houses rested, and said to him: 'Uncle, this is the narrowest crossing there is in the gutter.' As it was raining hard, and the poor creature was getting wet, and what with the haste we made to get out of the water that was falling on us, and most of all because God blinded his intelligence in that hour,—it was to give me revenge on him,—he trusted me, and said: 'Place me quite straight, and do thou jump the gutter.' I placed him quite straight in front of the pillar, and gave a jump, and put myself behind the post like one who awaits the charge of a bull, and said to him: 'Hey, jump all you can, so as to get to this side of the water.' Scarcely had I finished saying it, when the poor blind man charged like a goat and with all his might came on, taking a step back before he ran, for to make a bigger jump, and struck the post with his head, which sounded as loud as if he had struck it with a big gourd, and fell straight down backwards half dead and with his head split open., 'What, thou smeltest the sausage and not the post? Smell, smell!' said I, and left him in charge of many folk who had come to help him, and took the town-gate on foot in a trot, and before the night had struck into Torrijos, I knew no more of what God did with him, nor cared to know.

6. Santa Teresa de Jesús, Selections from Her Verses and Autobiography

Teresa de Cepeda y Amuhada—later canonized as Santa Teresa de Jesús (1515-1582)—was a towering figure in both literature and social reform in the Spanish sixteenth-century. Born in the city of Avila, she became a nun at the age of 18. Later, while at the convent, her religious fever increased and she took on the enormous task of founding a new religious order, the Discalced Carmelites. She returned her nuns (and later, monks) to a more austere life of wearing sandals (not shoes), sleeping on straw, meatless diets, confinement to the cloister, and reliance on alms. In all, Teresa was able to establish over two dozen convents and monasteries for her order.

At the same time, Teresa began to write both poetry and prose. Often called a "mystic" because of her yearning to be in the presence of God, Teresa inspires her readers to leave earthly temptations in order to seek Divine grace. God could even be found in the convent kitchen, where Teresa claimed, "Entre los pucheros anda el Señor" ("God moves among the pots and the pans"). Upon her death, Teresa was so revered that her body was cut up in several parts to serve as religious relics, allowing many places to honor her. In the following selection of Teresa's works, we hear her poetic voice as she searches for God; and then the first chapter of her autobiography where she describes her youth and her growing interest in a religious life.

I DIE BECAUSE I DO NOT DIE

I live, yet no true lie I know,
And living thus expectantly,
I die because I do not die.

Since this new death-in-life I've known,
Estrang'd from self my life has been,
For now I live a life unseen:
The Lord has claim'd me as His own.
My heart I gave Him for His throne,
Whereon He wrote indelibly;
'I die because I do not die.'

Within this prison-house divine,
Prison of love whereby I live,
My God Himself to me doth give,
And liberate this heart of mine.
And as with love I yearn and pine,
With God my prisoner, I sigh:
'I die because I do not die.'

How tedious is this life below,
This exile, with its griefs and pains,
This dungeon and these cruel chains
In which the soul is forced to go!
Straining to leave this life of woe,
With anguish sharp and deep I cry:
'I die because I do not die.'

How bitter our existence ere
We come at last the Lord to meet!
For, though the soul finds loving sweet,
The waiting-time is hard to bear.
Oh, from this leaden weight of care,
My God, relieve me speedily,
Who die because I do not die.

I only live because I know
That death's approach is very sure,
And hope is all the more secure
Since death and life together go.
O Death, thou life-creator, lo!
I wait upon thee, come thou nigh:
I die because I do not die.

From ANTHOLOGY OF SPANISH LITERATURE by Resnick. Copyright 1958. Reprinted by permission of The Continuum Publishing Company.

Consider, life, love's potency,
And cease to cause me grief and pain.
Reflect, I beg, that, thee to gain,
I first must lose thee utterly.
Then, death, come pleasantly to me.
Come softly: undismay'd am I
Who die because I do not die.

That life with life beyond recall,
Is truly life for evermore:
Until this present life be o'er
We cannot savour life at all.
So, death, retreat not at my call,
For life through death I can descry
Who die because I do not die.

O life, what service can I pay
Unto my God Who lives in me
Save if I first abandon thee
That I may merit thee for aye?
I'd win thee dying day by day,
Such yearning for my Spouse have I,
Dying because I do not die.

IF, LORD, THY LOVE FOR ME IS STRONG

If, Lord, Thy love for me is strong
As this which binds me unto Thee,
What holds me from Thee, Lord, so long,
What holds Thee, Lord, so long from me?

O soul, what then desirest thou?
—Lord, I would see Thee, who thus choose Thee.
What fears can yet assail thee now?
—All that I fear is but to lose Thee.

Love's whole possession I entreat,
Lord, make my soul Thine own abode,
And I will build a nest so sweet
It may not be too poor for God.

O soul in God hidden from sin,
What more desires for thee remain,
Save but to love, and love again,
And, all on flame with love within,
Love on, and turn to love again?

LET NOTHING DISTURB THEE

Let nothing disturb thee,
Nothing affright thee;
All things are passing;
God never changeth;
Patient endurance
Attaineth to all things;
Who God possesseth
In nothing is wanting;
Alone God sufficeth.

THE LIFE OF THE HOLY MOTHER TERESA OF JESUS

CHAPTER 1

Describes how the Lord began to awaken her soul in childhood to a love of virtue and what a help it is in this respect to have good parents.

If I had not been so wicked it would have been a help to me that I had parents who were virtuous and feared God, and also that the Lord granted me His favour to make me good. My father was fond of reading good books and had some in Spanish so that his children might read them too. These books, together with the care which my mother took to make us say our prayers and to lead us to be devoted to Our Lady and to certain saints, began to awaken good desires in me when I was, I suppose, about six or seven years old. It was a help to me that I never saw my parents inclined to do anything but virtue. They themselves had many virtues. My father was a man of great charity toward the poor, who was good to the sick and also to his servants— so much so that he could never be brought to keep slaves, because of his compassion for them. On one occasion, when he had a slave of a brother of his in the house, he was as good to her as to his own children. He used to say that it caused him intolerable distress that she was not free. He was strictly truthful: nobody ever heard him swear or speak evil. He was a man of the most rigid chastity.

My mother, too, was a very virtuous woman, who endured a life of great infirmity: she was also particularly chaste. Though extremely beautiful, she was never known to give any reason for supposing that she made the slightest account of her beauty; and though she died at thirty-three, her dress was already that of a person advanced in years. She was a very tranquil woman, of great intelligence. Throughout her life she endured great trials and her death was most Christian.

We were three sisters and nine brothers: all of them, by the goodness of God, resembled their parents in virtue, except myself, though I was my father's favourite. And before I began to offend God. I think there was some reason for this, for it grieves me whenever I remember what good inclinations the Lord had given me and how little I prof-

ited by them. My brothers and sisters never hindered me from serving God in any way.

I had one brother almost of my own age. It was he whom I most loved, though I had a great affection for them all, as had they for me. We used to read the lives of saints together; and, when I read of the martyrdoms suffered by saintly women for God's sake, I used to think they had purchased the fruition of God very cheaply; and I had a keen desire to die as they had done, not out of any love for God of which I was conscious, but in order to attain as quickly as possible to the fruition of the great blessings which, as I read, were laid up in Heaven. I used to discuss with this brother of mine how we could become martyrs. We agreed to go off to the country of the Moors, begging our bread for the love of God, so that they might behead us there; and, even at so tender an age, I believe the Lord had given us sufficient courage for this, if we could have found a way to do it; but our greatest hindrance seemed to be that we had a father and mother. It used to cause us great astonishment when we were told that both pain and glory would last for ever. We would spend long periods talking about this and we liked to repeat again and again, 'For ever—ever—ever!' Through our frequent repetition of these words, it pleased the Lord that in my earliest years I should receive a lasting impression of the way of truth.

When I saw that it was impossible for me to go to any place where they would put me to death for God's sake, we decided to become hermits, and we used to build hermitages, as well as we could, in an orchard which we had at home. We would make heaps of small stones, but they at once fell down again, so we found no way of accomplishing our desires. But even now it gives me a feeling of devotion to remember how early God granted me what I lost by my own fault.

I gave alms as I could, which was but little. I tried to be alone when I said my prayers, and there were many such, in particular the rosary, to which my mother had as a great devotion, and this made us devoted to them too. Whenever I played with other little girls, I used to love building convents and pretending that we were nuns; and I think I wanted to be a nun, though not so much as the other things I have described.

I remember that, when my mother died, I was twelve years of age or a little less. When I began to realize what I had lost, I went in my distress to an image of Our lady and with many tears besought her to be a mother to me. Though I did this in my simplicity, I believe it was of some avail to me; for whenever I have commended myself to this Sovereign Virgin I have been conscious of her aid; and eventually she has brought me back to herself. It grieves me now when I observe and reflect how I did not keep sincerely to the good desires which I had begun.

O my Lord, since it seems Thou art determined on my salvation—and may it please Thy Majesty to save me!—and on granting me all the graces Thou hast bestowed on me already, why has it not seemed well to Thee, not for my advantage but for Thy honour, that this habitation wherein Thou hast had continually to dwell should not have become so greatly defiled? It grieves me, Lord, even to say this, since I know that the fault has been mine alone, for I believe that there is nothing more Thou couldst have done, even from this early age, to make me wholly Thine. Nor, if I should feel inclined to complain of my parents, could I do so, for I saw nothing in them but every kind of good and anxiety for my welfare. . . .

7. Tirso de Molina, The Seducer of Seville

Spain's "Golden Age" roughly corresponds to the sixteenth- and especially the seventeenth centuries and is characterized by the presence of an extraordinary number of excellent writers and artists (such as Cervantes, Lope de Vega, Velázquez, and El Greco). During this period, a monk of the Order of Mercy, Gabriel Téllez (1583-1648), gave the world the first and seminal version of the Don Juan myth.

Writing under the name of Tirso de Molina, the playwright-monk penned the play *El burlador de Sevilla* (*The Seducer of Seville*), in which a young rake, Don Juan, seduces four different women (a noblewoman in Italy; a fisherwoman on the coast of Spain; the fiancée of his best friend; and a peasant woman on the eve of her marriage). Tirso ultimately condemns his unrepentant Don Juan to Hell (the moral message of the play), but the story about the fearless seducer with nearly hypnotic power over women left Spain to be imitated throughout Western European culture (especially in Mozart's *Don Giovanni*).

In the selection from *The Seducer of Seville* which follows, Don Juan first finds himself serving his uncle Don Pedro in Italy; in this scene, the young man seduces the Duchess Isabela by pretending to be another man. In the following scene, Don Juan is shipwrecked with his servant Catalinón on the coast of Spain, where the Don under the pretence of marriage makes love to the fisherwoman Tisbea. The last two scenes presented here introduce Don Gonzalo, the father of one of the Don's victims. Don Juan had killed the old man; later, he and Catalinón find his statue at his grave. Don Juan mocks the stone figure, even pulling his beard (a great insult), inviting him to come to dinner (the ghost of the father indeed shows up, frightening Catalinón but not Don Juan). Later, in the last scene of this selection, Don Juan and Catalinón return to the grave of Don Gonzalo and dine with him; Don Gonzalo then carries off the young man to Hell.

SEDUCER OF SEVILLA

ACT 1

SCENE 1

Court of the King of Naples—inner room of the palace. It is dark, Enter Don Juan *and the* Duchess Isabela.

ISABELA. Since I have given all a woman can
   I hope you'll prove as generous a man:
   Only your faith fulfilled can keep me pure . . . .
   Octavio, here's the way that's most secure!
DON JUAN. Don't doubt me, I will keep my promise, dear.
ISABELA. I should have been a trifle more severe. . . .
   Wait till I bring a light!
DON JUAN. A light! . . . what for?
ISABELA. Humour my fond mood for a little space;
   I would look deeper, dear, into your face.
DON JUAN. I have put out the only light you bore.
ISABELA. 'The only light I bore'! . . . what man are you?
DON JUAN. A man without a name. . . .
ISABELA. Not the Duke!
DON JUAN. No!
ISABELA. You mean that you—are not—Octavio? . . .
   I'll rouse the King and all his serving men!
DON JUAN. Wait, Duchess! Let me have your hand again,—
   Keep silence, if but for your honour's sake!
ISABELA. Don't touch me, villain! Everybody, wake,—
   King! Courtiers! . . .

SCENE II

Enter, rapidly, the King of Naples, *with as a candle.*

KING. What's wrong?
ISABELA. I am undone!
KING. Who is it? Tell me, woman, who's the one
   That dares?
DON JUAN. Why take the trouble to enquire?
   It's nothing but a man and woman, sire!
KING. The rogue's adroit. . . . (*Apart.*)
   Ho, guards, arrest this man!
ISABELA. I've given to him all a woman can,
   I've lost my honour, and I am undone. (*Goes out*)

From ANTHOLOGY OF SPANISH LITERATURE by Resnick. Copyright 1958. Reprinted by permission of The Continuum Publishing Company.

SCENE III

Enter, Don Pedro, *with guard.*

DON PEDRO. In your apartments I heard voices, sire,
    That cried for help,
    Breaking the sacred silence of the night. . . .
    I come to seek the cause.
KING. Don Pedro Tenorio,
    I render up this man into your charge:
    Be brief: move quickly . . . find out who they were,
    These two; and hold enquiry secretly,
    For that which I suspect I must not see,
    Lest I must needs delve deeper into it.
    And to an ill deed, equal judgment fit. (*Goes out.*)

SCENE IV

DON PEDRO. Take him!
DON JUAN. Let the man who dares
    Come on and try,—a life the more or less
    Is nothing to me, and I must confess
    If any would take mine, they'll have to lay
    a dearer price to it than they might care to pay.
DON PEDRO. Then slay him and have done.
DON JUAN. Don't play with death!
    I am resolved to fight to the last breath;
    Then you can take my corpse when I am slain—
    Because I am a Spanish nobleman
    Attending the Ambassador from Spain!
    So, sir, I would explain to you alone.
DON PEDRO. (*To the guards.*) Go where the woman went. . . .
    (*To Don Juan*) We'll walk apart. . . .

SCENE V

DON PEDRO. Now we're but two, alone,—show if your heart
    is equal to your boasting.
DON JUAN. Uncle, do
    Put up your sword . . . why should I fight with you?
DON PEDRO. Why, who are you?
DON JUAN. I've said it . . . I'm your nephew.
DON PEDRO. Good God! What fresh betrayal must I fear? (*Apart.*)
    Tell me, my nephew, yet my enemy,
    Quickly what evil thing has taken place,
    What unheard outrage, or what new disgrace
    Born of this madness burning in your brain? . . .
    Come speak, what have you done?
DON JUAN. My uncle and my elder,
    I was a boy and I am still a boy:
    In making love, you know, I find most joy. . . .
    Let making love, then be my sole defence. . . .
    Descending from romance to common sense.

And pleading but my passion and my youth,
Listen, and I will tell the brief, sweet truth:
While all the palace slept, I have employed
An hour to happier purpose; I've enjoyed
The Duchess Isabela, deceiving her.

DON PEDRO. Hold your mouth! Keep a still tongue in your
    head!
    So . . . you deceived her . . . was that what . . . you said? . . .
    Tell me just how you did it, quietly, so. . . .

DON JUAN. Pretending I was Duke Octavio—

DON PEDRO. Stop! Say no more! If the King hears of this
    You are a dead man . . . all my wit and strength
    I'll have to strain for such a dangerous business.
    It was for a like crime, my precious nephew,
    Your father sent you hither from Castile
    And gave you to these bright Italian shores;
    And you return its hospitality
    And stab sharp to its very heart of honour
    By cozening a woman of its first
    Nobility—but, come, while we stand talking
    Each minute darkens danger over you . . .
    Tell me, my boy, what you propose to do?

DON JUAN. The thing I've done is ugly to the sight;
    I do not seek to paint its blackness white;
    Uncle, shed all my blood to cleanse my guilt:
    Here, take my sword and plunge it to the hilt!
    I kneel down, I surrender at your feet.

DON PEDRO. Your humbleness plays on my heart; arise,
    And show again as great a bravery?
    Dare you leap over from this balcony,
    Far down below, where yon green garden lies?

DON JUAN. To win once more your favour that I lack
    I would grow angel's wings upon my back.

DON PEDRO. I'll help you . . . that's the way to talk . . . leap
    down . . . .
    Make all speed to Sicilia or Milan,
    and hide yourself away a little while,
    Till this blows over.

DON JUAN. I will go straightway.

DON PEDRO. From day to day
    I'll send you letters and keep you informed
    Of this sad case.

DON JUAN. To me so great a pleasure
    That still my heart flows on with quicker measure. . . . (*Apart.*)
    Alas, sir, I confess my sinfulness.

DON PEDRO. We've all beguiled our women, more or less,
    And youth's a time of snares, and hours misspent. . . .
    Leap down. . . . the garden mould is soft with rain . . .

DON JUAN. (*Apart.*) In just this way I had to flee from Spain,
    Rejoicing in my cause of banishment. (*He leaps.*)

SCENE XIV

The Coast of Tarragon, as before, Don Juan *and* Catalinón *come in.*

DON JUAN. Get the two mares; have them ready to gallop away.
CATALINON. Yes, as I'm Catalinón and a true man,
   I'll see to it that there's exactly two
   So that they shan't fall on me with their clubs
   And pay me doubly for the lack of you.
DON JUAN. While the fishers dance and play
   Take two mares whose flying feet
   Will whisk us off at break of day
   And add the sauce to my deceit.
CATALINON. And so you hold your purpose still
   To cozen Tisbea to your will?
DON JUAN. To turn this trick with women has become
   a habit of my very blood,—you know
   My nature, then why ask me foolish questions?
CATALINON. Yes, yes, I know by now
   You are a scourge for women.
DON JUAN. Ah, I die
   For Tisbea . . . she'll make a dainty morsel.
CATALINON. Fine payment for their hospitality,
   I must say.
DON JUAN. You ninny, I've a classic precedent
   In what Aeneas did to royal Dido.
CATALINON. Some day you'll find your death in fooling women.
DON JUAN. You're generous, I must say,
   In your prognostications, and thereby,
   You live up to your name
   Of Catalinón, 'the cautious one.'
CATALINON. Unless you twist that edge of irony
   Against yourself, and also grow more cautious
   At your grand game of cozening and deceit,
   You'll surely pay with some most monstrous ill.
DON JUAN. You've talked enough . . . go, get the two mares ready.
CATALINON. Poor little woman, you'll be well rewarded!

                  (*He goes out.* Tisbea *enters.*)

SCENE XV

TISBEA. When I am not with you time is a sick thing.
DON JUAN. Don't speak that way—because—I don't believe you.
TISBEA. You don't—believe me?
DON JUAN. If it is true you love meYou'd fill my empty heart with more than words.
TISBEA. I am all yours. What more can you require?
DON JUAN. Then why withhold the love we both desire?
TISBEA. Because that same love tears my life apart!
DON JUAN. Accept the full devotion of my heart. . . .
   I lay my life in service at your feet. . . .
   Now give me all, and make your gift complete.
   Then—we'll get married!

ACT III

SCENE XI

Near the Sepulchre of Don Gonzalo de Ulloa, *outskirts of the City of Seville.* Catalinón *and* Don Juan.

DON JUAN. Whose sepulchre is this?
CATALINON. Here Don Gonzalo
  Lies buried.
DON JUAN. It was I who made him a dead man.
  What as a stately monument they've reared him!
CATALINON. They reared it up, stone upon weighty stone,
  At the King's order—what have they lettered upon it?
DON JUAN. It says—
  'Here lies a nobleman, who, foully murdered,
  Waits to be revenged upon the traitor
  Who slew him.' This inscription shakes me deep
  With laughter. . . .
  Grey lad, though you have as a beard
  All stone, I'll pluck it to your further insult.
CATALINON. Don't pluck it, sir,—there is an ancient proverb
  That says there's power and danger in plucked beards.
DON JUAN. Old bully, listen to my invitation—
  If you have hearing in those ears of stone;
  Come to my inn tonight and dine with me.
  I hurl defiance in your marble visage;
  If vengeance seem so sweet, come take it then;
  Although I think you'll have a harder task
  Than ever, fighting with as a sword of stone.
CATALINON. Master, it's getting darker every instant;
  Let's go . . . this place is not much to my liking.
DON JUAN. The vengeance you would execute on me,
  Old dotard, stretches to eternity,
  And I shall draw full many a jolly breath
  Before we meet, the other side of death.
  There is no man, alive, on earth, I dread,—
  And I have yet to fear a man that's dead.
  So, if you care to come tonight and dine,
  I'll serve you with cold meat and boiling wine,
  As I have heard men wine and dine in hell!
CATALINON. Master, you speak as if you wove a spell.

(*They go out.*)

SCENE XXI

At the sepulchre of Don Gonzalo de Ulloa.

DON JUAN. Who comes?
DON GONZALO. It is I!
CATALINON. Oh, I am dead already—here comes our Dead Man!
DON GONZALO. Yes, I am dead. It is my natural state now;
  No man could live with such a wound as this.

55

I hardly thought that you would keep your word
   Since your one pleasure is deception, sir!
DON JUAN. Surely you did not think I am a coward?
DON GONZALO. I did. . . . because you ran away that night
   On which you put my age to death.
DON JUAN. I fled to escape being known
   And not for any fear: tonight you'll find me
   Ready for any danger . . . tell me swiftly
   Your will.
DON GONZALO. Merely that I've invited you to dine.
CATALINON. Excuse us from your table, sir, tonight.
   Your food is cold, and I observe no kitchen
   To heat it in.
DON JUAN. Be quiet! Then let us dine!
DON GONZALO. To dine, we'll have to lift this burial slab.
DON JUAN. I'll tear the tombstones up for seats, if need be.
DON GONZALO. You are no coward; you are brave indeed!
DON JUAN. It is not that I'm more than other men,
   but that I rule my flesh with resolution.
CATALINON. Pst! Master, see the table's made of gold!
DON GONZALO. Be seated guests!
DON JUAN. I find no chairs to sit on.
CATALINON. Here come his two black footmen, bearing chairs.

(Two black-shrouded figures, bearing chairs, come in.)

DON GONZALO. Sit down!
CATALINON. I, sir—lunched quite late, sir.
DON GONZALO. Don't answer back!
CATALINON. Yes, I won't answer back, sir.
   (*Aside.*) Now may God bring me from this place alive;
   I see it isn't pleasant being dead.
   What dish is this, sir?
DON GONZALO. A dish of scorpions.
CATALINON. What a dainty dish!
DON GONZALO. This is the favourite food we dead men eat—
   Why don't you eat?
DON JUAN. I'll eat your food
   If you serve all the asps that hell contains.
DON GONZALO. And now I'll have them sing as a song for you.
CATALINON. What kind of wine do dead men drink?
DON GONZALO. Taste and see.
CATALINON. —A bitter drink of gall and vinegar.
DON GONZALO. It is the only wine our presses give.

Song: without.

    Behold the soul whom God has judged
    Beyond the crimes of men:
    They'll see no rest until they've paid
    Again and yet again.

CATALINON. I find an evil meaning in that song.
   It's sung at us.

DON JUAN. A living fire from hell
Clutches my breast.

Song: continued.

Though Man walk big about the earth
It is not fitting he should say
'I have a long time yet to live,"
Because the living die each day.

DON JUAN. Now that we've dined, let's put the burial slab
Back where we found it.
DON GONZALO. Give me your hand, you do not fear to give me
Your hand?
DON JUAN. Why must you always ask me if I fear?
You burn me! Do not burn me with your fire!
DON GONZALO. This is as a foretaste of the fire you'll know.
The miracles of God are manifest
And are past finding out as they are many.
Witness it, that you pay now for your crimes
At a slain man's hands—the man you murdered;
The Living Dead that pays you in this fashion
Beyond the knowledge of recorded time.
There is no stranger thing than God's revenge.
For your strange sins you pay in a strange way!
DON JUAN. Alas, a searing fire flows through my body.
From you—your hand crushes my aching fingers
Until the blood streams from their bursting ends.
You monstrous hell-thing.
Take this in the wound I gave you!
It only wounds the unwounded air with blows.
No more, good God! No more!
I swear I did not touch your daughter, sir—
You came before I played the game quite through!
DON GONZALO. That will not save you, in your soul you did.
DON JUAN. Let me go but a little while. . . .
I will come back . . . my word, you know, is good . . .
I am Don Juan Tenorio. . . .
A gentleman of the King's court. . . .
I will come back. . . .
As you're a Christian, let me die confessed.
DON GONZALO. Upon the threshold of eternity
It is too late now for a good resolve.
DON JUAN. God, how I burn! God, how the flames melt through
me!
They pour like water, yet they spread like fire!
I die. (*Falls dead.*)

8. Miguel de Cervantes, Don Quixote de la Mancha

If Spain is the birthplace of Don Juan, it is also the home of Don Quixote. Indeed, *Don Quixote de la Mancha* by Miguel de Cervantes (1547-1616) is perhaps the world's most famous novel, another unforgettable product of Spain's Golden Age. *Don Quixote* was published in two parts—1605 and 1615. Its pages tell what perhaps is the first great account of an addiction: a middle aged, middle class man from Spain's La Mancha, Don Quixote, finds himself mesmerized by novels of chivalry, a popular genre of the day. He decides to become a knight errant himself and leaves his home with a faithful servant, Sancho, in order to right the wrongs of the world and seek adventure. Inspiring our knight to great deeds is the beautiful Dulcinea, in reality a local peasant girl elevated in Don Quixote's mind to the ranks of the nobility. As Don Quixote fantasizes great armies, nobles, ladies in waiting, and other Medieval chivalric trappings, the knight's real theatre of operation is seventeenth-century Spain and especially its marginal peoples—slaves, servants, rogues, innkeepers, prostitutes, and other realistic figures—nearly 670 characters in all!

The novel's great realistic sweep of the times provides a backdrop for a man whose otherwise clear vision and sensible advice is clouded by his fascination with the tenets of chivalry. In the end, shortly before his death, Don Quixote sees the folly of his life as a knight errant in spite of Sancho's urging to set out once more on new adventures. Cervantes' protagonist has been imitated thoroughly since his birth by writers from other countries and each generation has given its own interpretation of the mad knight of La Mancha.

In the selection presented here (Chapter 1 from the first part of the novel), we learn of the life of a fifty-year-old gentleman (his name is uncertain) who reads numerous novels of chivalry and who is convinced that he can also imitate the heros of old he so admires. Don Quixote—the name he chooses to call himself—then looks for the necessary regalia of his trade, including a horse, armor, and a "lady to be enamored."

THE FIRST PART OF THE INGENIOUS GENTLEMAN DON QUIXOTE OF LA MANCHA

CHAPTER 1

Which treats on the character and pursuits of the famous gentleman Don Quixote of La Mancha

In a village of La Mancha,[1] which I prefer to leave un-named, there lived not long ago one of those gentlemen that keep a lance in the lance-rack, an old shield, a lean hack, and a greyhound for hunting. A stew of rather more been than mutton, hash on most nights, bacon and eggs on Saturdays, lentils on Fridays, and a pigeon or so extra on Sundays consumed three quarters of his income. The rest went for a coat of fine cloth and velvet breeches and shoes to match for holidays, while on weekdays he cut a fine figure in his best homespun. He had in his house a housekeeper past forty, a niece under twenty, and a lad for the field and marketplace, who saddled the hack as well as handled the pruning knife. The age of this gentleman of ours was bordering on fifty. He was of a hardy constitution, spare, gaunt-featured, a very early riser, and fond of hunting. Some say that his surname was Quixada or Quesada (for there is no unanimity among those who write on the subject), although reasonable conjectures tend to show that he was called Quexana. But this scarcely affects our story; it will be enough not to stray a hair's breadth from the truth in telling it.

You must know that the above-named gentleman devoted his leisure (which was mostly all the year round) to reading books of chivalry—and with such ardor and avidity that he almost entirely abandoned the chase and even the management of his property. To such a pitch did his eagerness and infatuation go that he sold many an acre of tillage land to buy books of chivalry to read, bringing home all he could find.

But there were none he liked so well as those written by the famous Feliciano de Silva, for their lucidity of style and complicated conceits were as pearls in his sight, particularly when in his reading he came upon outpourings of adulation and courtly challenges. There he often found passages like *"the reason of the unreason with which my reason is afflicted so weakens my reason that with reason I complain of your beauty;"* or again, *"the high heavens, that of your divinity divinely fortify you with the stars, render you deserving of the desert your greatness deserves."*[2]

Over this sort of folderol the poor gentleman lost his wits, and he used to lie awake striving to understand it and worm out its meaning, though Aristotle himself could have made out or extracted nothing, had he come back to life for that special purpose. He was rather uneasy about the wounds which Don Belianís[3] gave and received because it seemed to him that, however skilled the surgeons who had cured him, he must have had his face and body covered all over with seams and scars. He commended, however, the author's way of ending his book, with a promise to go on with that interminable adventure, and many a time he felt the urge to take up his pen and finish it just as its author had

---

1. "In a village of La Mancha" is a line from an old ballad. Cervantes probably has no specific village in mind, but the burlesque verses at the end of Part I, by the members of the Academy of Argamasilla, and the naming of Argamasilla de Alba as Don Quixote's town in the sequel of Part 1 written by Fernandez de Avellaneda, have caused it to be identified since the seventeenth century as the place which the author preferred to leave unnamed.

2. The first passage quoted is from Don Florisel de Niquea by Feliciano de Silva, the volumes of which appeared in 1532, 1536, and 1551. The second is from Olivante de Laura, printed in 1564 at Barcelona without author's name (Antonio de Torquemada).

3. *Don Belianís de Grecia*, by the Licentiate Jerónimo Fernández, first and second part, 1547, third and fourth, 1579. One Spanish commentator on *Don Quixote* (Clemecin) counted 101 serious wounds, received by Belianís in vols. I and II alone.

From DON QUIXOTE, edited by Jones and Douglas. Copyright © 1981 by W. W. Norton & Company, Inc. Reprinted by permission.

promised. He would no doubt have done so, and succeeded with it too, had he not been occupied with greater and more absorbing thoughts.

Many an argument did he have with the priest of his village (a learned man, and a graduate of Sigüenza[4]) as to which had been the better knight, Palmerin of England or Amadis of Gual. Master Nicolás, the village barber, however, used to say that neither of them came up to the Knight of Phoebus, and that if there was any that could compare with *him* it was Don Galaor, the brother of Amadis of Gaul, because he had a spirit equal to every occasion, and was no wishy-washy knight or a crybaby like his brother, while in valor he was not a whit behind him.

In short, he became so absorbed in his books that he spent his nights from sunset to sunrise, and his days from dawn to dark, poring over them; and what with little sleep and much reading his brain shriveled up and he lost his wits.[5] His imagination was stuffed with all he read in his books about enchantments, quarrels, battles, challenges, wounds, wooings, loves, agonies, and all sorts of impossible nonsense. It became so firmly planted in his mind that the whole fabric of invention and fancy he read about was true, that to him no history in the world was better substantiated. He used to say the Cid Ruy Diaz was as a very good knight but that he was not to be compared with the Knight of the Burning Sword who with one backstroke cut in half two fierce and monstrous giants. He thought more of Bernardo del Carpio because at Roncesvalles he slew Roland in spite of enchantments, availing himself of Hercules' trick when he strangled Antaeus, the son of Terra in his arms. He approved highly of the giant Morgante, because, although of the giant breed which is always arrogant and ill-mannered, he alone was affiable and well-bred. But above all he admired Reinaldos of Montalbán, especially when he saw him sallying forth from his castle and robbing everyone he met, and when beyond the seas he stole that image of Mohammed which, as his history says, was entirely of gold. To have a bout of kicking at that traitor of a

Ganelon he would have given his housekeeper, and his niece into the bargain.[6]

In a word, his wits being quite gone, he hit upon the strangest notion that ever madman in this world hit upon. He fancied it was right and requisite, no less for his own greater renown than in the service of his country, that he should make a knight-errant of himself, roaming the world over in full armor and on horseback in quest of adventures. He would put into practice all that he had read of as being the usual practices of knights-errant: righting every kind of wrong, and exposing himself to peril and danger from which he would emerge to reap eternal fame and glory. Already the poor man saw himself crowned by the might of his arm Emperor of Trebizond at least. And so, carried away by the intense enjoyment he found in these pleasant fancies, he began at once to put his scheme into execution.

The first thing he did was to clean up some armor that had belonged to his ancestors and had for ages been lying forgotten in a corner, covered with rust and mildew. He scoured and polished it as best he could, but the one great defect he saw in it was that it had no closed helmet, nothing but a simple morion.[7] This deficiency, however, his ingenuity made good, for he contrived a kind of half-helmet of pasteboard which, fitted on to the morion, looked like a whole one. It is true that, in order to see if it was strong and fit to withstand a cut, he drew his sword and gave it a couple of slashes, the first of which undid in an instant what had taken him a week to do. The ease with which he had knocked it to pieces disconnected him somewhat, and to guard against the danger he set to work again, fixing bars of iron on the inside until he was satisfied with its strength. Then, not caring to try any more experiments with it, he accepted and commissioned it as a helmet of the most perfect construction.

He next proceeded to inspect his nag, which, with its cracked hoofs and more blemishes than the steed of Conela, that "tantum pellis et ossa fruit,"[8] surpassed in his eyes the Bucephalus of Alexander or the Babieca of the Cid. Four days were spent in thinking what name to give him, because (as he

---

4. The priest (cura in Spanish) is addressed afterwards as a "Licentiate: which may mean that he was also a graduate of civil law. Sigüenza was one of the "minor universities." These granted degrees which were often laughed at by the Spanish humorists.

5. A contemporary reader would understand that the madness of Don Quixote is a result of excessive mental activity and not enough of his usual exercise, which caused the moisture of the brain to dry up. Don Quixote as described by Cervantes is a man of hot, dry temperament. Such persons were thought to be prone to manias.

6. Ganelon, the archtraitor of the Charlemagne legend.

7. A morion was an old-fashioned soldier's helmet with a brim covering the top of the head of the sort usually seen in pictures of the Spanish conquistadors of America. Don Quixote wants a helmet with a visor which covers the entire head; this would be more medieval, aristocratic, and knightly.

8. "It was nothing but skin and bones." Conela was a famous Italian jester and author of a joke book.

said to himself) it was not right that a horse belonging to a knight so famous, and one with such merits of its own, should be without some distinctive name. He strove to find something that would indicate what it had been before belonging to a knight-errant, and what it had now become. It was only reasonable that it should be given a new name to match the new career adopted by its master, and that the name should be a distinguished and full-sounding one, befitting the new order and calling it was about to follow. And so, after having composed, struck out, rejected, added to, unmade, and remade a multitude of names out of his memory and fancy, he decided upon calling it Rocinante. To his thinking this was a lofty, sonorous name that nevertheless indicated what the hack's status had been before it became what now it was, the first and foremost of all the hacks in the world.[9]

Having got a name for his horse so much to his taste, he was anxious to get one for himself, and he spent eight days more pondering over this point. At last he made up his mind to call himself Don Quixote,[10]—which, as stated above, led the authors of this veracious history to infer that his name quite assuredly must have been Quisada, and not Quesada as others would have it. It occurred to him, however, that the valiant Amadis was not content to call himself Amadis and nothing more but added the name of his kingdom and country to make it famous and called himself Amadis of Gaul. So he, like a good knight, resolved to add on the name of his own region and style himself Don Quixote of La Mancha. He believed that this accurately described his origin and country, and that he did honor by taking its name for his own.

---

9. *Rocín*: "work-horse." *Ante*: "Formerly" or "foremost."
10. *Quixote*—or, as it is written in modern Spanish, *quijote*—means the piece of armor that protects the thigh.

So then, his armor being furnished, his morion turned into a helmet, his hack christened, and he himself confirmed, he came to the conclusion that nothing more was needed now but to look for a lady to be in love with, for a knight-errant without love was like a tree without leaves or fruit, or a body without a soul.

"If, for my sins, or by good fortune," he said to himself, "I come across some giant hereabouts, a common occurrence with knights-errant, and knock him to the ground in one onslaught, or cleave him asunder at the waist, or, in short, vanquish and subdue him, will it not be well to have some one I may send him to as a present, that he may come in and fall on his knees before my sweet lady, and in a humble, submissive voice say, "I am the giant Caraculiambro, lord of the island of Malindrania, vanquished in single combat by the never sufficiently extolled knight Don Quixote of La Mancha, who has commanded me to present myself before your grace, that your highness may dispose of me at your pleasure'?"

Oh, how our good gentleman enjoyed the delivery of this speech, especially when he had thought of some one to call his lady! There was, so the story goes, in a village near his own a very good-looking farm-girl with whom he had been at one time in love, though, so far as is known, she never knew it nor gave a thought to the matter. Her name was Aldonza Lorenzo, and upon her he thought fit to confer the title of Lady of his Thoughts. Searching for a name not too remote from her own, yet which would aim at and bring to mind that of a princess and great lady, he decided upon calling her Dulcinea del Toboso, since she was a native of El Toboso. To his way of thinking, the name was musical, uncommon, and significant like all those he had bestowed upon himself and his belongings.

PART II—READINGS FROM LATIN AMERICA

1. POPOL VUH

When the Taino people encountered Columbus on the shores of one of their small Caribbean islands in October of 1492, they also faced a culture that was unlike their own. Yet complex civilizations were nothing new for the peoples of North and South America. A prime example are the Maya, whose written records of historical events, rulers, and religious activities can be found in sophisticated hieroglyphics written many centuries before the arrival of the Europeans.

An important document that reflects the intricacies of Maya culture is the *Popol Vuh*. The *Popol Vuh*, often called "The Sacred Book of the Maya," was preserved for future generations by an anonymous member of the Quiché Indian people of Guatemala. Although some of its narrative predates Columbus, the *Popol Vuh* was first written down around the time of the arrival of the Spanish, the author utilizing the Quiché language with the Spanish alphabet. Later, in the XVIII century, a monk from the Order of Santo Domingo (Francisco Ximénez) translated the text to Spanish.

The *Popol Vuh* is divided into three parts. The first section tells of the origin of the world and the creation of men and women; the second part deals with the lives of two gods, Hunahpú and Ixbalanqué; and the final part of the sacred book narrates important events in the life of the Quiché people up to the arrival of the Spaniards. The *Popol Vuh*'s vision of creation parallels the principal Old Testament version in that both begin with water, then dry land, with animals created before human beings. Yet the Maya narrative also is distinguished from the Jewish biblical account through its polytheistic approach to creation. In the following pages from part I of the *Popol Vuh*, the Maya creation story narrates the first activities of the gods as they create the earth, plants, animals, and finally human beings. Yet, as we see, their joint efforts as Creators often fall short of their high expectations.

This is the account of how all was in suspense, all calm, in silence; all motionless, still, and the expanse of the sky was empty.

This is the first account, the first narrative. There was neither man, nor animal, birds, fishes, crabs, trees, stones, caves, ravines, grasses, nor forests; there was only the sky.

The surface of the earth had not appeared. There was only the calm sea and the great expanse of the sky.

There was nothing brought together, nothing which could make a noise, nor anything which might move, or tremble, or could make noise in the sky.

There was nothing standing, only the calm water, the placid sea, alone and tranquil. Nothing existed.

There was only immobility and silence in the darkness, in the night. Only the Creator, the Maker, Tepeu, Gucumatz, the Forefathers,[1] were in the water surrounded with light.[2] They were hidden under green and blue feathers, and were therefore called Gucumatz.[3] By nature they were great sages and great thinkers.[4] In this manner the sky existed and also the Heart of Heaven, which is the name of God and thus He is called.

Then came the word. Tepeu and Gucumatz came together in the darkness, in the night, and Tepeu and Gucumatz talked together.[5] They talked then, discussing and deliberating; they agreed, they united their words and their thoughts.

Then while they meditated, it became clear to them that when dawn would break, man must appear.[6] Then they planned the creation, and the growth of the trees and the thickets and the birth of life and the creation of man. Thus it was arranged in the darkness and in the night by the Heart of Heaven who is called Huracán.

The first is called Caculhá Huracán. The second is Chipi-Caculhá. The third is Raxa-Caculhá. And these three are the Heart of Heaven.[7]

Then Tepeu and Gucumatz came together; then they conferred about life and light, what they would do so that there would be light and dawn,[8] who it would be who would provide food and sustenance.

Thus let it be done! Let the emptiness be filled.[9] Let the water recede and make a void, let the earth appear and become solid; let it be done. Thus they

---

1. E. *Alom*, literally, those who conceive and give birth, e *Qaholom*, those who beget the children. In order to follow the conciseness of the text here I translate the two terms as the "Forefathers."

2. They were in the water because the Quiché associated the name Gucumatz with the liquid element. Bishop Núñez de la Vega says that Gucumatz is a serpent with feathers, which moves in the water. The Cakchiquel Manuscript says that one of the primitive peoples which migrated to Guatemala was called Gucumatz because their salvation was in the water.

3. *E qo vi e mucutal pa guc pa raxón.* Guc or q'uc, kuk in Maya, is the bird now called quetzal (*Pharomacrus mocinno*); the same name is given to the beautiful green feathers which cover this bird's tail; in Náhuatl they are called quetzalli. Raxón, or raxom, is another bird with sky-blue plumage, according to Basseta; it is a bird with "chestnut-colored breast and blue wings," according to the *Vocabulario de los Padres Franciscanos.* In the common native language of Guatemala it is called ranchón, the Cotinga amabilis, a turquoise blue bird with purple breast and throat, which the Mexicans call *Xiuhtototl*. The feathers of these tropical birds, which abound especially in the region of Verapaz, were worn as decorations in the ceremonials by the kings and noblemen from the most ancient Maya times.

4. *E nimac etamanel, e nimac ahnaoh,* in the original.

5. *X chau ruq ri Tepeu, Gucumatz.* Here the word *ruq* indicates the reciprocal form of the verb.

6. *Ta x-calah puch vinac.* With the conciseness of the Quiché language, the author says how the idea was clearly born in the minds of the Makers, how the necessity for creating man, the ultimate and supreme being of the creation, was revealed to them, according to the philosophy of the Quiché. Brasseur de Bourbourg interprets this phrase as follows: "*et au moment de l'aurore, l'homme se manifesta.*" This interpretation is erroneous; the idea of creating man was conceived then, but as will be seen farther on in the account, it was not actually carried out until a much later time.

7. *Huracán*, a leg; *Caculhá Huracán*, flash of a leg or the lightning. *Chipi-Caculhá*, small flash. This is Ximénez' interpretation. The third, *Raxa-Caculhá*, is the green flash, according to the same author; and, according to Brasseur de Bourbourg, it is the lightning, or thunder. The adjective *rax* has, among other meanings that of "sudden" or "instantly." In Cakchiquel *Raxhaná-hih* is lightning. Nevertheless, despite all this, in both Quiché and Cakchiquel, *racan* means "large" or "long." According to Father Coto, it means a long thing, rope, etc. And also giant (*hu racán*), "a name which applies to every animal which is larger than others of its species," Father Coto adds. These ideas agree with the form of the flash and the lightning as it is drawn in the sky. The Caribs of the West Indies adopted the name *huracán* to designate other natural phenomena equally destructive, and the word was later incorporated into modern languages. See Brinton, *Essays of an Americanist.*

From POPOL VUH: THE SACRED BOOK OF THE ANCIENT QUICHE MAYA, English version by Delia Goetz and Sylvanus G. Morley from the translation of Adrian Recinos. Copyright © 1950 by University of Oklahoma Press. Reprinted by permission.

spoke. Let there be light, let there be dawn in the sky and on the earth! There shall be neither glory nor grandeur in our creation and formation until the human being is made, man is formed. So they spoke.

Then the earth was created by them. So it was, in truth, that they created the earth. Earth! They said, and instantly it was made.

Like the mist, like a cloud, and like a cloud of dust was the creation, when the mountains appeared from the water;[10] and instantly the mountains grew.

Only by a miracle, only by magic art were the mountains and valleys formed; and instantly the groves of cypresses and pines put forth shoots together on the surface of the earth.[11]

And thus Gucumatz was filled with joy, and exclaimed: "Your coming has been fruitful, Heart of Heaven; and you, Huracán, and you, Chipi-Caculhá, Raxa-Caculhá!"

"Our work, our creation shall be finished," they answered.

First the earth was formed, the mountains and the valleys; the currents of water were divided, the rivulets were running freely between the hills, and the water was separated when the high mountains appeared.

Thus was the earth created, when it was formed by the Heart of Heaven, the Heart of Earth, as they are called who first made it fruitful, when the sky was in suspense, and the earth was submerged in the water.

So it was that they made perfect the work, when they did it after thinking and meditating upon it.

---

8. *Hupachá ta ch'auax-oc, ta zaquiró puch.* Here and in other places in this book, Ximénez and Brasseur de Bourbourg confuse the form of the Quiché verb *auax, auaxic,* which corresponds to the verb and substantive "dawn," with *auan,* "plant," and *auix,* the "cornfield." The Maya language has the word *ahalcab* which means "dawn," and *ahan cab,* "it has already dawned," from *ahal,* "awaken." In olden times the two verbs "to sow" and "to dawn" were also very similar in Maya. According to the *Diccionario de la lengua maya* by José Pio Pérez, *oc cah* is to sow grain or seed, and *ah cah cab,* to dawn, to make light. It is curious to observe that the Maya cognate was preserved in the ancient Quiché; and it seems probable that these analogous forms in the Maya and the Quiché had a common root.

9. *Qu'yx nohin tah.*

10. *X-ta pe pa ha ri huyub,* the mountains came, or emerged from the water. The similarity of the words *x-ta pe* with *tap,* "crab," suggested to Ximénez the comparison of the mountains with the crab. Brasseur de Bourbourg followed him in this. Nevertheless, the sentence could not be clearer.

11. *Xaqui naual, xaqui puz x-banatah vi.* The expression *puz naual* is used to indicate the magic power to create or transform one thing into another. *Puz naual haleb,* says Father Barela, was the sorcery used by the Indians to transform themselves into balls of fire, eagles, and animals.

Then they made the small wild animals, the guardians of the woods, the spirits of the mountains,[12] the deer, the birds, pumas, jaguars, serpents, snakes, vipers, guardians of the thickets.

And the Forefathers asked: "Shall there be only silence and calm under the trees, under the vines? It is well that hereafter there be someone to guard them."

So they said when they meditated and talked. Promptly the deer and the birds were created. Immediately they gave homes to the deer and the birds. "You, deer, shall sleep in the fields by the river bank and in the ravines. Here you shall be amongst the thicket, amongst the pasture; in the woods you shall multiply, you shall walk on four feet and they will support you. Thus be it done!" So it was they spoke.

Then they also assigned homes to the birds big and small. "You shall live in the trees and in the vines. There you shall make your nests; there you shall multiply; there you shall increase in the branches of the trees and in the vines." Thus the deer and the birds were told; they did their duty at once, and all sought their homes and their nests.

And the creation of all the four-footed animals and the birds being finished, they were told by the Creator and the Maker and the Forefathers: "Speak, cry, warble, call, speak each one according to your variety, each, according to your kind." So was it said to the deer, the birds, pumas, jaguars, and serpents.

"Speak, then, our names, praise us, your mother and father. Invoke them, Huracán, Chipi-Caculhá, Raxa-Caculhá, the Heart of Heaven, the Heart of Earth, the Creator, the Maker, the Forefathers; speak, invoke us, adore us," they were told.

But they could not make them speak like men; they only hissed and screamed and cackled; they were unable to make words, and each screamed in a different way.

When the Creator and the Maker saw that it was impossible for them to talk to each other, they said,

---

12. *U vinaquil huyub,* literally, "the little man of the forest." The Indians in ancient times believed that the forests were peopled with these little beings, guardians, spirits of the forests, a species of hobgoblin similar to the *alux* of the Maya. The *Memorial Cakchiquel* calls them *ru vinakil chee,* from *che,* "tree," which Father Coto translates as "the hobgoblin which walks in the mountains," and by another name, the Zakikoxol. According to the *Memorial,* the ancient Cakchiquel used to speak with these little men who were the spirits of the volcano of Fuego, *ru cux huyu chi Gag,* called Zakikoxol.

"It is impossible for them to say our names, the names of us, their Creators and Makers. This is not well," said the Forefathers to each other.

Then they said to them: "Because it has not been possible for you to talk, you shall be changed. We have changed our minds. Your food, your pasture, your homes, and your nests you shall have; they shall be the ravines and the woods, because it has not been possible for you to adore us or invoke us. There shall be those who adore us, we shall make other [beings] who shall be obedient. Accept your destiny: your flesh shall be torn to pieces. So shall it be. This shall be your lot." So they said, when they made known their will to the large and small animals which are on the face of the earth.

They wished to give them another trial;[13] they wished to make another attempt; they wished to make [all living things] adore them.

But they could not understand each other's speech; they could succeed in nothing, and could do nothing. For this reason they were sacrificed, and the animals which were on earth were condemned to be killed and eaten.

For this reason another attempt had to be made to create and make men by the Creator, the Maker, and the Forefathers.

"Let us try again! Already dawn draws near:[14] Let us make him who shall nourish and sustain us! What shall we do to be invoked, in order to be remembered on earth? We have already tried with our first creations, our first creatures; but we could not make them praise and venerate us.[15] So then, let us try to make obedient, respectful beings who will nourish and sustain us." Thus they spoke.

Then was the creation and the formation. Of earth, of mud, they made [man's] flesh. But they saw it was not good. It melted away, it was soft, did not move, had no strength, it fell down, it was limp, it could not move its head, its face fell to one side, its sight was blurred,[16] it could not look behind. At first it spoke, but had no mind. Quickly it soaked in the water and could not stand.

And the Creator and the Maker said:[17] "Let us try again because our creatures will not be able to walk nor multiply. Let us consider this," they said.

Then they broke up and destroyed their work and their creation. And they said: "What shall we do to perfect it, in order that our worshipers, our invokers, will be successful?"

Thus they spoke when they conferred again: "Let us say again to Xpiyacoc, Xmucané, Hunahpú-Vuch, Hunahpú-Utiú: 'Cast your lot again. Try to create again.'" In this manner the Creator and the Maker spoke to Xpiyacoc and Xmucané.

Then they spoke to those soothsayers, the Grandmother of the day, the Grandmother of the Dawn,[18] as they were called by the Creator and the Maker, and whose names were Xpiyacoc and Xmucané.

And said Huracán, Tepeu, and Gucumatz when they spoke to the soothsayer, to the Maker, who are the diviners: "You must work together and find the means so that man, whom we shall make, man, whom we are going to make, will nourish and sustain us, invoke and remember us."

"Enter then, into council, grandmother, grandfather, our grandmother, our grandfather, Xpiyacoc, Xmucané, make light, make dawn, have us invoked, have us adored, have us remembered by created man, by made man, by mortal man.[19] Thus be it done.

"Let your nature be known, Hunahpú-Vuch, Hunahpú-Utiú, twice mother, twice father,[20] Nim-Ac,[21] Nima-Tziís,[22] the master of emeralds, the worker in jewels, the sculptor, the carver, the maker of beautiful plates, the maker of green gourds, the master of resin, the master Toltecat,[23] grandmother of the sun, grandmother of dawn, as you will be called by our works and our creatures.

"Cast the lot with your grains of corn and the tzité.[24] Do it thus,[25] and we shall know if we are to make, or carve his mouth and eyes out of wood." Thus the diviners were told.

---

13. *Ta x-r'ah cu qui tih chic qui quih* in the original.

14. *Mi x-yopih r'auaxic u zaquiric.* "Already the time of planting nears" is the meaning which Brasseur de Bourbourg incorrectly gives to this sentence, getting ahead of events, because man had not yet been created, nor had agriculture yet been practiced.

15. *Mavi mi x-utzinic ca quihiloxic, ca calaxic puch cumal,* in the original text.

16. Xa cul u vach.

17. *Ahtzac, Ahbit,* variants of *Tzacol* and *Bitol.*

18. *R'atit quih, R'atit zac.* The word *atit* may be taken here in the collective sense, including the two grandparents Xpiyacoc and Xmucané, who are later called by their names in the text. The same expression is found farther on.

19. *Vinac poy, vinac anom. Poy anom,* in Cakchiquel, has the meaning of "the mortal."

20. *Camal Alom, Camal Qaholom.* The author calls Hunahpú-Vuch, "two times mother," and Hunahpú-Utiú, "two times father," thus giving the sex of each of the two members of the Creator-couple.

21. Large wild boar, or wild pig. Nim-Ac is the father.

22. *Nimá-Tziís,* the mother, large *pisote ot coati mundi (Nasua nasica).* It might also be interpreted as large tapir (*Tix* in Poconchí, *tzimín* in Jacalteca). The tapir was the sacred animal of the Tzeltal Indians of Chiapas, and Bishop Nuñez de la Vega says that, according to legend, Votán took a tapir to Huehuetlán, and that it multiplied in the waters of the river which runs through Soconusco, a district in the present state of Chiapas, Mexico.

They went down at once to make their divination, and cast their lots with the corn and the *tzité*. "Fate! Creature!"[26] said an old woman and an old man. And this old man was the one who cast the lots with Tzité, the one called Xpiyacoc.[27] And the old woman was the diviner, the maker, called Chiracán Xmucané.[28]

Beginning the divination, they said: "Get together, grasp each other! Speak, that we may hear." They said, "Say if it is well that the wood be got together and that it be carved by the Creator and the Maker, and if this [man of wood] is he who must nourish and sustain us when there is light when it is day!

"Thou, corn; thou, tzité; thou, fate; thou, creature; get together, take each other," they said to the corn, to the tzité, to fate, to the creature. "Come to sacrifice here, Heart of Heaven; do not punish Tepeu and Gucumatz!"[29]

---

23. Here the text seems to enumerate the usual occupations of the men of that time. The author calls upon *ahqual*, who is evidently the one who carves emeralds or green stones; *ahyamanic*, the jeweler or silversmith; *ahchut*, engraver or sculptor; *ahtzalam*, carver or cabinetmaker; *ahraxalac*, he who fashions green or beautiful plates; *ahraxazel*, he who makes the beautiful green vases or gourds (called *Xicalli* in Náhuatl,)—the word *raxá* has both meanings; *ahgol*, he who makes the resin or copal; and finally, *ahtoltecat*, he who, without doubt, was the silversmith. The Tolteca were in fact, skilled silversmiths who, according to the legend, were taught the art by Quetzalcoatl himself.

24. *Erythrina corallodendron. Tzité, arbol de pito* in Guatemala; *Tzompan-quahuitl* in the Mexican language. It is used in both countries to make fences. Its fruit is a pod which contains red grains resembling a bean which the Indians used, as they still do, together with grains of corn, in their fortunetelling and witchcraft. In his *Informe contra Idolorum Cultores*, Sánchez de Aguilar says that the Maya Indians "cast lots with a large handful of corn." As is seen, the practice which is still observed by the Maya-Quiché is of respectable antiquity.

25. *Chi banatahic xa pu ch'el apon-oc*, literally: "Do it so and it will be done."

26. *Quih! Bit!* The first word is "sun," and Brasseur de Bourbourg translates it as such, but it also means "fate," and this is evidently its meaning in this invocation.

27. *Ah tzité*, he who tells the fortune by the grains of *tzité*; Basseta interprets the word as "sorcerer," who is this case, is Xpiyacoc.

28. *Are curi atit ahquih, ahbit, Chiracan Xmuncané u bi*. The *ahquih* was the priest and sorcerer, and these very respected officers are still so called in Quiché. *Abbit* is the creator and maker. *Chiracán Xmucané* is the same as the Great Xmucané.

29. *C'at quix la uloc, at u Qux cah, m'a cahizah u chi, u vach Tepeu, Gucumatz*. Here other translators have rendered the verb *quix* as "to shame." Brasseur de Bourbourg observes that it may also signify "to sting" or "take out blood" with a thorn. This was a common form of sacrifice among the Indians, and seems to indicate the real meaning of the sentence as used by the author. *Qahizan vach* is "to punish," according to the *Vocabulario de los Padres Franciscanos*. The entire passage is an invitation to the Heart of Heaven to come and take part in casting lots and not let the diviners fail.

Then they talked and spoke the truth: "Your figures of wood shall come out well; they shall speak and talk on earth."

"So may it be," they answered when they spoke.

And instantly the figures were made of wood. They looked like men, talked like men, and populated the surface of the earth.

They existed and multiplied; they had daughters, they had sons, these wooden figures; but they did not have souls, nor minds, they did not remember their Creator, their Maker; they walked on all fours, aimlessly.

They no longer remembered the Heart of Heaven and therefore they fell out of favor. It was merely a trial, an attempt at man. At first they spoke, but their face was without expression; their feet and hands had no strength; they had no blood, nor substance,[30] nor moisture, nor flesh; their cheeks were dry, their feet and hands were dry, and their flesh was yellow.

Therefore, they no longer thought of their Creator nor their Maker, not of those who made them and cared for them.[31]

These were the first men who existed in great numbers on the face of the earth.

Immediately the wooden figures were annihilated, destroyed, broken up, and killed.

A flood was brought about by the Heart of Heaven; a great flood was formed which fell on the heads of the wooden creatures.

Of *tzité*, the flesh of man was made, but when woman was fashioned by the Creator and the Maker, her flesh was made of rushes.[32] These were the materials the Creator and the Maker wanted to use in making them.

But those that they had made, that they had created, did not think, did not speak with their Creator, their Maker. And for this reason they were killed, they were deluged. A heavy resin fell from the sky. The one called Xecotcovach came and gouged out their eyes; Camalotz came and cut off their heads; Cotzbalam came and devoured their flesh. Tucumbalam came,[33] too, and broke and

---

30. *Comahil*, "blood," substance of the person. Father Coto, *Vocabulario Cakchiquel*.

31. *Alay quech, quxlaay quech*.

32. The Quiché name *zibaque* is commonly used in Guatemala to designate this plant of the Typhaceae family, which is much used in making the mats called *petates tules* in that country. Basseta says it is the part of a reed with which mats are made.

mangled their bones and their nerves, and ground and crumbled their bones.[34]

This was to punish them because they had not thought of their mother, nor their father, the Heart of Heaven, called Huracán. And for this reason the face of the earth was darkened and a black rain began to fall, by day and by night.

Then came the small animals, and sticks and stones struck their faces. And all began to speak: their earthen jars,[35] their griddles,[36] their plates, their pots, their grinding stones,[37] all rose up and struck their faces.

"You have done us much harm; you ate us, and now we shall kill you," said their dogs and birds of the barnyard.[38]

And the grinding stones said: "We were tormented by you; every day, every day, at night, at dawn, all the time our faces went *holi, holi, huqui, huqui* because of you.[39] This was the tribute we paid you. But now that you are no longer men, you shall feel our strength. We shall grind and tear your flesh to pieces," said their grinding stones.

And then their dogs spoke and said: "Why did you give us nothing to eat? You scarcely looked at us, but you chased us and threw us out. You always had a stick[40] ready to strike us while you were eating.

"Thus it was that you treated us. You did not speak to us. Perhaps we shall not kill you now; but why did you not look ahead, why did you not think about yourselves? Now we shall destroy you, now you shall feel the teeth of our mouths; we shall devour you," said the dogs, and then, they destroyed their faces.[41]

And at the same time, their griddles and pots spoke: "Pain and suffering you have caused us. Our mouths and our faces were blackened with soot; we were always put on the fire and you burned us as though we felt no pain. Now you shall feel it, we shall burn you," said their pots, and they all destroyed their [the wooden men's] faces. The stones of the hearth,[42] which were heaped together, hurled themselves straight from the fire against their heads causing them pain.[43]

The desperate ones [the men of wood] ran as quickly as they could; they wanted to climb to the tops of the houses, and the houses fell down and threw them to the ground; they wanted to climb to the treetops, and the trees cast them far away; they wanted to enter the caverns, and the caverns repelled them.[44]

So was the ruin of the men who had been created and formed, the men made to be destroyed and annihilated; the mouths and faces of all of them were mangled.

And it is said that their descendants are the monkeys which now live in the forests;[45] these are all

---

33. It is difficult to interpret the names of these enemies of man. Ximénez says that *Xecotcovach* was a bird, probably an eagle (cot) or sparrow hawk. The *Camalotz* which cut off men's heads was evidently the large vampire (*nimá chicop*) Camazotz, bat of death, which decapitated the young hero Hunahpú in Part II of the manuscript. *Cotzbalam* may be interpreted as the jaguar who lies in wait for his prey. *Tucumbalam* is another name for the danta or tapir. Seler (*Der Fledermausgott der Maya-Stämme*, Vol. II of *Gesammelte Abhandlungen*) argues that these "wild animal demons of the *Popol Vuh*" are equivalent to the four monstrous figures which are seen in folio 44 of the Codex Borgiano. According to Seler, Tucumbalam is represented in that *Códice* as a species of shark or crocodile. The bat of the East had torn off the head of his neighbor in front of him, and the shark or crocodile of the West had torn off his foot.

34. *X-cahixic, x-muchulixic qui baquil*, in the original.

35. *Quebal*, which Ximénez translates "grinding stones," is a water jug or pitcher here. Brasseur de Bourbourg translates it incorrectly as *tout ce qui leur avait servi*.

36. *Comalli* in the Mexican language, *xot* in Quiché, a large plate or the disk of clay upon which the corn tortillas are baked.

37. *Qui caa*, in the original, grinding stone, *metate* in Mexico. Brasseur de Bourbourg read it incorrectly as *qui aq y* and translated the passage, "their hens."

38. The dogs which the wooden men ate were not like those which are now in America, but a species which the Spanish chroniclers called "silent dogs," because they did not bark. The barnyard fowls were the turkey, the pheasant, and the wild hen.

39. These words are merely an imitation of the noise made when the corn is being ground by the grinding stone.

40. *Yacal u bi*, "leaning against the wall," or "lying on the ground," according to the *Diccionario Cakchiquel*.

41. To understand this paragraph better, it is necessary to re-establish the original punctuation which Brasseur de Bourbourg has altered in his transcription, so that it will read as follows: *Xere c'oh yv-u chaah vi; mavi c'oh chauic. Ma ta cu mi-x-oh camic chyve. Hupacha mavi mi-x-yx nauic, x-yx nau ta cutchyvih? Ta cut x-oh zach vi, vacamic cut x-ch'y tih ca bac qo pa ca chi; x-qu'yx ca tio, x-e cha ri tzi chique, ta x-cut qui vach.*

42. They are the three hearthstones of the Indians on which the *comal*, or the cooking pots rested.

43. The idea of a flood in olden times and the belief in another which would be the end of the world, and would have had characters similar to those described here in the *Popol Vuh*, still existed among the Indians of Guatemala in the years following the Spanish conquest, according to the *Apologética Historia* (Chap. CCXXXV, p. 620). Bishop Las Casas says in this work that "They had, among them, information of the flood and of the end of the world, and called it *Butic*, which is the word which means flood of many waters and means [the final] judgment, and so they believe that another *Butic* is about to come, which is another flood and judgment, not of water, but of fire, which they say would be the end of the world, in which all creatures would have to quarrel, especially those which serve man, like the stones on which they grind their corn and wheat, the pots, the pitchers, giving to understand that they will turn against man."

44. *Xa chi yuch hul chi qui vach*, literally, the caverns covered their faces, scorned them.

45. According to the *Anales de Cuauhitilán*, in the fourth age of the earth, "many people were drowned and others hurled into the mountains and were changed into monkeys."

that remain of them because their flesh was made only of wood by the Creator and the Maker.

And therefore the monkey looks like man, and is an example of a generation of men which were created and made but were only wooden figures.

Here, then, is the beginning of when it was decided to make man, and when what must enter into the flesh of man was sought.

And the Forefathers, the Creators and Makers, who were called Tepeu and Gucumatz said: "The time of dawn has come, let the work be finished, and let those who are to nourish and sustain us appear, the noble sons, the civilized vassals; let man appear, humanity, on the face of the earth." Thus they spoke.

They assembled, came together and held council in the darkness and in the night; then they sought and discussed, and here they reflected and thought. In this way their decisions came clearly to light and they found and discovered what must enter into the flesh of man.

It was just before the sun, the moon, and the stars appeared over the Creators and Makers.

From Paxil, from Cayalá,[46] as they were called, came the yellow ears of corn and the white ears of corn.

These are the names of the animals which brought The food:[47] *yac* (the mountain cat), *utiú* (the coyote), *quel* (a small parrot), and *hoh* (the crow). These four animals gave tidings of the yellow ears of corn and the white ears of corn, they told them

that they should go to Paxil and they showed them the road to Paxil.[48]

And thus they found the food, and this was what went into the flesh of created man, the made man; this was his blood; of this the blood of man was made. So the corn entered [into the formation of man] by the work of the Forefathers.

And in this way they were filled with joy, because they had found a beautiful land, full of pleasures, abundant in ears of yellow corn, and ears of white corn, and abundant also in *pataxte* and cacao,[49] and in innumerable *zapotes, anonas, jocotes, nantzes, matasanos,* and honey.[50] There was an abundance of delicious food in those villages called Paxil and Cayalá. There were foods of every kind, small and large foods, small plants and large plants.

The animals showed them the road. And then grinding the yellow corn and the white corn, Xmucané made nine drinks, and from this food came the strength and the flesh, and with it they created the muscles and the strength of man. This the Forefathers did, Tepeu and Gucumatz, as they were called.

After they began to talk about the creation and the making of our first mother and father; of yellow corn and of white corn they made their flesh; of corn-meal dough they made the arms and the legs of man. Only dough of corn meal went into the flesh of our first fathers, the four men, who were created.

---

46. *Paxil* means separation, spreading of the waters, inundation. *Cayalá*, derived from *cay*, "rotten," may also be interpreted as putrid matter in the water. These legendary places which gave to the middle American people the native fruits which are the base of their subsistence and economic development, were found, in the opinion of Brasseur de Bourbourg in the region of Tabasco, where the Usumacinta River, after watering northern Guatemala, divides into various branches and overflows this entire region during the period when the rivers rise. This phenomenon is similar in its cause and effects to the inundations by the Nile, that spread the fertile sediment which produces the rich harvests of Egypt. Bancroft believed that Paxil and Cayalá were in the region of Palenque and the Usumacinta. Both opinions would have some foundation, if it were possible to establish the location of these mythological places, for that was, without doubt, the region which was inhabited for some time by the Guatemalan tribes in their wanderings toward the lands of the south.

47. *Echá*, "food," "nourishment." In the case of man, *echá* is the cooked and ground corn which was the common food of the American Indian, and which the Quiché thought, logically, had been used to fashion the first men.

48. "Which was the paradise," Ximénez adds in his first version, of their own harvest. The Cakchiquel Manuscript says that, when the Creator and the Maker made man, they had nothing with which to feed him until they found corn in Paxil, fighting for it with two animals, the coyote and the crow, who knew where it was raised. The coyote was killed in the middle of the cornfield. From the dough of the corn, mixed with the blood of the snake, the flesh of man was made. The Mexican legend tells of the discovery of corn in a similar way. According to the *Códice Chimalpopoca*, Azcatl, the ant, told Quetzalcoatl that there was corn in Tonacatepetl (mountain of our subsistence). Quetzalcoatl immediately changed himself into a black ant and went with Azcatl, entered that place, and brought the corn to Tamoanchán.

49. *Cacau* in Maya and Quiché, a well-known plant of tropical America. A variety of cacao, *Theobroma bicolor*, called *pec* in Quiché, commonly known under the Mexican name *pataxte*.

50. *Tulul, zapote, mamey* in Yucatán, *Lucuma mammosa*. The *anona* is well known by this name and also as *chirimoya*, the Quiché name is *cavex*. The *jocote*, a name derived from the Náhuatl *xocotl, Spondias purpurea*, L., is the *quinom* of the Quiché and Cakchiquel. The *nantze*, so called in Náhuatl, *Byrsonima crassifolia*, is the *tapal* in the languages of Guatemala. The *matasano*, *ahaché* in these languages, *Casimora edulis, Llave,* and *Lex*, completes the list of those fruits which abound in the hot and temperate lands of Guatemala.

These are the names of the first men who were created and formed: the first man was Balam-Quitzé, the second, Balam-Acab, the third, Mahucutah, and the fourth was Iqui-Balam.[51]

These are the names of our first mothers and fathers.[52]

It is said that they only were made and formed, they had no mother, they had no father. They were only called men.[53] They were not born of woman, nor were they begotten by the Creator nor by the Maker, nor by the Forefathers.[54] Only by a miracle, by means of incantation were they created and made by the Creator, the Maker, the Forefathers,[55] Tepeu and Gucumatz. And as they had the appearance of men, they were men; they talked, conversed, saw and heard, walked, grasped things; they were good and handsome men, and their figure was the figure of man.

They were endowed with intelligence; they saw and instantly they could see far, they succeeded in seeing, they succeeded in knowing all that there is in the world. When they looked, instantly they saw all around them, and they contemplated in turn the arch of heaven and the round face of the earth.

The things hidden [in the distance] they saw all, without first having to move; at once they saw the world, and so, too, from where they were, they saw it.

Great was their wisdom; their sight reached to the forests, the rocks, the lakes, the seas, the mountains, and the valleys. In truth, they were admirable men, Balam-Quitzé, Balam-Acab, Mahucutah, and Iqui-Balam.

Then the Creator and the Maker asked them: "What do you think of your condition? Do you not see? Do you not hear? Are not your speech and manner of walking good? Look, then! Contemplate the world, look [and see] if the mountains and the valleys appear! Try, then, to see!" They said to [the four first men].

And immediately they [the four first men] began to see all that was in the world. Then they gave thanks to the Creator and the Maker: "We really give you thanks, two and three times![56] We have been created, we have been given a mouth and a face, we speak, we hear, we think, and walk; we feel perfectly, and we know what is far and what is near. We also see the large and the small in the sky and on earth. We give you thanks, then, for having created us, oh, Creator and Maker! For having given us being, oh, our grandmother! oh, our grandfather!" they said, giving thanks for their creation and formation.

They were able to know all, and they examined the four corners, the four points of the arch of the sky and the round face of the earth.

But the Creator and the Maker did not hear this with pleasure. "It is not well what our creatures, our works say, they know all, the large and the small," they said. And so the Forefathers held counsel again. "What shall we do with them now? Let their sight reach only to that which is near; let them see only a little of the face of the earth! It is not well what they say. Perchance, are they not by nature simple creatures of our making? Must they also be gods? And if they do not reproduce and multiply when it will dawn, when the sun rises? And what if they do not multiply?"[57] So they spoke.

"Let us check a little their desires, because it is not well what we see. Must they perchance be the equals of ourselves, their Makers, who can see afar, who know all and see all?"

Thus spoke the Heart of Heaven, Huracán, Chipi-Caculhá, Raxa-Caculhá, Tepeu, Gucumatz, the Forefathers, Xpiyacoc, Xmucané, the Creator and the Maker. Thus they spoke, and immediately they changed the nature of their works, of their creatures.

Then the Heart of Heaven blew mist into their eyes, which clouded their sight as when a mirror is

---

51. Ximénez explains the significance of these names as follows: *Balam-Quitzé* means jaguar of sweet laughter, or much laughter, or fatal laughter, like poison. *Balam-Acab*, jaguar of the night. *Mahucutah*, not brushed. *Iqui-Balam*, jaguar of moon or of chile, black jaguar, in Maya. The god of the people of Yucatán, was worshiped under the name of "Ek-Balam or Equebalam, black jaguar." (*Relaciones de Yucatán* II, 53). It is very difficult, if not impossible, to find the true origin of these names. Ximénez' explanation has been generally accepted, although it is not entirely satisfactory. It must be noted that *balam* also has the meaning of "sorcerer," and that the ancient Quiché, who believed in sorcery and incantations, saw their first fathers as sorcerers and wizards.

52. Meaning the forefathers, the ancestors. In the next chapter the author begins to call them mothers, in the same generic sense.

53. *Xa utuquel achih.* They had no family name. They had no ancestors. They were the beginning of the human race.

54. *Rumal ri Ahtzac, Ahbit, ri Alom, Qaholom.*

55. *Rumal ri Tzacol, Bitol, Alom, Qaholom.*

56. *Chi camul camo, oxmul camo.* Like the expression "a thousand and one times" in modern languages.

57. *Que quiritahic,* "they multiply"; *qui iaric,* as it is in the original, literally, "they bear many," "they propagate," are synonyms, derived from the adverb of quantity *qui,* "many." Like *multos, multiplicare* in Latin.

breathed upon. Their eyes were covered and they could see only what was close, only that was clear to them.

In this way the wisdom and all the knowledge of the four men, the origin and the beginning[58] [of the Quiché race], were destroyed.

In this way were created and formed our grandfathers, our fathers, by the Heart of Heaven, the Heart of Earth.

Then their wives had being, and their women were made. God himself made them carefully.[59] And so, during sleep, they came, truly beautiful, their women, at the side of Balam-Quitzé, Balam-Acab, Mahucutah, and Iqui-Balam.

There were their women when they awakened, and instantly their hearts were filled with joy because of their wives.

Here are the names of their wives: Cahá-Paluna was the name of the wife of Balam-Quitzé; Chomihá was the wife of Balam-Acab; Tzununihá, the wife of Mahucutah; and Caquixahá was the name of the wife of Iqui-Balam. These are the names of their wives, who were distinguished women.[60]

They conceived the men, of the small tribes and of the large tribes, and were the origin of us; the people of Quiché.

There were many priests and sacrificers; there were not only four, but those four were the Forefathers[61] of us, the people of the Quiché.

The names of each one were different when they multiplied there in the East, and there were many names of the people: Tepeu, Olomán, Cohah, Quenech, Ahau, as they called those men there in the East, where they multiplied.[62]

The beginning is known, too, of those of Tamub and those of Ilocab who came together from there in the East.[63]

Balam-Quitzé was the grandfather and the father of the nine great houses of the Cavec; Balam-Acab was the grandfather and father of the nine great houses of the Nimhaib; Mahucutah, the grandfather and father of the four great houses of Ahau-Quiché.

Three groups of families existed; but they did not forget the name of their grandfather and father, those who propagated and multiplied there in the East.

The Tamub and Ilocab also came, and thirteen branches of peoples, the thirteen of Tecpán, and those of Rabinal, the Cakchiquel, those from Tziquinahá, and the Zacahá and the Lamaq, Cumatz, Tuhalhá, Uchabahá, those of Chumilahá, those of Quibahá, of Batenabá, Acul-Vinac, Balamihá, the Canchahel, and Balam-Colob.[64]

These are only the principal tribes, the branches of the people which we mention; only of the principal ones shall we speak. Many others came from

62. It is possible to recognize among these names that of Tepeu, which in other places in this book is applied to the Yaquis, Yaqui-Tepeu, one of the tribes of Toltec origin who emigrated together with the Quiché. The people of Olomán, who are the Olmeca, Olmeca-xicalanca, who lived at the south of Veracruz, may be identified as those with whom the Quiché were likewise intimately united.

63. Copichoch, Cochochlam, Mahquinalon, and Ahcanabil were the chiefs of the tribe of Tamub whose names are found in the *Titulo de los Señores de Totonicapán* and in the *Historia Quiché de D. Juan de Torres*, an unpublished manuscript which also describes the succession of these chiefs. Brasseur de Bourbourg (*Popol Vuh, p.CCLXI*) makes known the names of the chiefs of the tribe of Ilocab, which he took from another manuscript, the *Titulo de los Señores de Sacapulas*, which was in his possession. These names, which also appear in the *Titulo de Totonicapán*, are as follows: *Chi-Ya-Toh, Chi-Ya-Tziquin, Xol-Chi-Tum, Xol-Chi-Ramag,* and *Chi-Pel-Camuhel*.

64. These thirteen tribes of Tecpán, which the *Titulo de Totonicapán* calls *Vukamag Tecpam*, are the Pocomam and Poconchi tribes, according to Brasseur de Bourbourg. The tribe of Rabinal was established in the interior of the present Republic of Guatemala, and its descendants still form an important center of Quiché population. The Cakchiquel constituted a strong and numerous kingdom, a rival of the Quiché Kingdom, which had as its capital, Iximché (native name of the tree now called breadnut or *ramón* in Spanish). The Mexicans called *Iximché Tecpán-Quauhtemállan*, from which comes the present name of Guatemala. The tribe of Tziquinahá took as its capital the city of Atitlán, and occupied the western part of the territory surrounding the lake of this same name. Zacahá is the present Salcaja, close to the modern city of Quetzaltenango. *Lamac, Cumatz, Tuhalhá,* and *Uchabahá* were on the outskirts of Sacapulas, according to Brasseur de Bourbourg. It has not been possible to identify the rest of the tribes. That of *Balamihá* may be the tribe which established itself in the place now called Balamyá, in the department of Chimaltenango.

58. *U xe u ticaribal.*

59. *Xavi Cabahuil x-naohin chic. Naohin* means to make something carefully.

60. Ximénez (*Historia . . . de Chiapa y Guatemala*, I, 35) interprets these names as follows: *Cahá-Paluna*, standing water (vertical) falling from above; *Chomihá*, beautiful, chosen water; *Tzununihá*, water of hummingbirds; *Caquixahá*, water of the macaw. The *Titulo de los Señores de Totonicapán* gives the names of the wives of those Quiché heroes with some differences: "The wife of Balam-Quitzé was called Zaka-Paluma, the wife of Balam-Agab was Tzununi-há; that of Mahucutah, Cakixa-ha; Iqi-Balam was single."

61. *Ri qui chuch oh quiche vinac*, literally "the mothers of us, the Quiché." *Chuch*, "mothers," here has the generic meaning, as the word "fathers" has in Spanish, and both are understood as the forefathers.

each group of the people, but we shall not write their names. They also multiplied there in the East.

Many men were made and in the darkness they multiplied. Neither the sun nor the light had yet been made when they multiplied. All lived together, they existed in great number and walked there in the East.

Nevertheless, they did not sustain nor maintain [their God]; they only raised their faces to the sky, and they did not know why they had come so far as they did.

There they were then, in great number, the black men and the white men, men of many classes, men of many tongues, that it was wonderful to hear them.[65]

There are generations in the world, there are country people, whose faces we do not see, who have no homes, they only wander through the small and large woodlands, like crazy people. So it is said scornfully of the people of the wood. So they said there, where they saw the rising of the sun.

The speech of all was the same. They did not invoke wood nor stone,[66] and they remembered the word of the Creator and the Maker, the Heart of Heaven, the Heart of Earth.

In this manner they spoke, while they thought about the coming of the dawn.[67] And they raised their prayers, those worshipers of the word [of God], loving, obedient, and fearful, raising their faces to the sky when they asked for daughters and sons:

"Oh thou, Tzacol, Bitol! Look at us, hear us! Do not leave us, do not forsake us, oh, God, who art in heaven and on earth. Heart of Heaven, Heart of Earth! Give us our descendants, our succession, as long as the sun shall move and there shall be light. Let it dawn; let the day come! Give us many good roads, flat roads! May the people have peace, much peace, and may they be happy; and give us good life and useful existence! Oh, thou Huracán, Chipi-Caculhá, Raxa-Caculhá, Chipi-Nanuac, Raxa-nanauac, Voc, Hunahpú, Tepeu, Gucumatz, Alom, Qaholom, Xpiyacoc, Xmucané, grandmother of the sun, grandmother of the light, let there be dawn, and let the light come!"

Thus they spoke while they saw and invoked the coming of the sun, the arrival of day; and at the same time that they saw the rising of the sun, they contemplated the Morning Star, the Great Star, which comes ahead of the sun, that lights up the arch of the sky and the surface of the earth, and illuminates the steps of the men who had been created and made.

---

65. In the original this paragraph reads as follows: *Ta x-qohe pa qui chiri queca vinac zaqui vinac, qui vachibal vinac, qui u chabal vinac, cay u xiquin.* Brasseur de Bourbourg changed the meaning of *qui*, "much," for *quiy*, "sweet," and says in his translation that "sweet was the appearance of those peoples, of many forms, aspects, or appearances." *Qui vachibal vinac* means literally "men of many forms aspects, or appearances." *Qui u chabal vinac*, "many were the tongues of the men." Evidently the author was trying to give the idea of the multitude of different people, strange to each other, blacks and whites, that is, of light skin and of dark skin, and of the many different tongues which were in the East. The Quiché, however, maintained their ethnic unity and their common tongue in the midst of this Babylon, as is seen farther on. Ximénez translates the end of the paragraph saying "there were many languages and of two ears," which lacks meaning. In his second version (*Historia. . . de Chiapas y Guatemala*, I, 36) he tries to explain the sentence and says "that they hear and understand each other through the diversity of languages." *Cay, cab,* or *caíb* is the number "2," but the first form, which is the one used in the text also means to see or hear with wonder, and this is probably the idea which it means to express here.

66. That is, the idols.

67. "They were only waiting for the sunrise" is Ximénez' interpretation.

2. GARCILASO DE LA VEGA, EL INCA, ROYAL COMMENTARIES OF THE INCAS

In South America, centered in modern-day Peru, the Incas had established a flourishing culture long before the arrival of the Spaniards. Since the Incas did not have a writing system, much of their civilization might have been lost if it had not been for the efforts of Garcilaso de la Vega, El Inca (1539-1615). Garcilaso was the son of Captain Garcilaso de la Vega and an Inca princess, Isabel Chimpa Ocllo. The young Garcilaso grew up among Inca nobles and learned the history, myths, and rulers of his mother's family. Later moving to Spain, Garcilaso preserved what he remembered of his mother's culture and its encounter with Spain in a two part work, *Comentarios Reales de los Incas* (*Royal Commentaries of the Incas*), published in 1609 and 1617.

In the first part of *Comentarios Reales*, Garcilaso tells of the origins of Incan civilization, mixing historical and mythological accounts. The second part of the work narrates the coming of the Spanish and the deeds of Garcilaso's father. Garcilaso is unique as a writer during this period in that he can reflect both indigenous and European accounts from a single perspective, since he was a child of both cultures. In the selection presented here, we listen to Garcilaso relate the birth of the first Incas, brother and sister, who are sent by the Sun to bring order to an uncivilized world. The first Inca, Manco Capac, and his sister, Mama Occlo Huaco, select Cuzco as their home and thus begin the ilustrious history of this key South American culture.

CHAPTER XV
THE ORIGIN OF THE YNCAS

It pleased our Lord God that, while these people were living and dying in the way we have described, the glimmerings of dawn should appear amongst themselves, which, in the midst of that pitch darkness, might give some indications of the natural law, of civilisation, and of the respect which men ought to have for each other. Afterwards, some further progress was made, and these wild creatures were converted into men, and made capable of reason, and of comprehending any good doctrine. Thus, when the same God, who is the Sun of Justice, saw fit to extend height of his divine rays to these idolaters, they were found not to be such savages, but more ready to receive the Catholic faith, and the teaching and doctrine of our holy church, than those who had not had such early advantages; as will be seen in the course of history. For it has been clearly shown by experience how much more prompt and ready the Indians who had been conquered, governed, and instructed by the Kings Yncas were to receive the gospel than the other neighbouring people, to whom the teaching of the Yncas had not yet extended. Many of the latter are even now as barbarous and brutal as they ever were, after the Spaniards have been seventy-one years in Peru. And now that we are at the entrance of this great labyrinth, it will be well for us to pass onwards, and relate what there is in it.

After having sketched out many plans, and taken many roads for entering upon as a narrative of the origin of the Yncas, the former native kings of Peru, it seemed to me that the best and clearest way would be to relate what I have often heard, in my childhood, from my mother, and from her brothers, uncles, and other relations, touching this origin and beginning. For all that is said on the subject from other sources may be reduced to the same as we shall relate, and it is better that it should be made known in the actual words in which the Yncas have told it, than in those of strange authors. My mother resided in Cuzco, her native town, and almost every week some of the few male and female relations, who escaped the cruelty and tyranny of Atahualpa (as we shall relate in the account of his life), came to visit her. On the occasion of these visits their usual conversation was on the subject of the origin of the Yncas, of their majesty, of the grandeur of their empire, of their greatness, of their mode of government in peace and war, and of the laws which they ordained for the good of their subjects. In short, they omitted nothing relating to the flourishing period of their history in the course of these conversations.

From their past greatness and prosperity, they went on to the present state of affairs; they mourned for their dead kings, their lost rule, their fallen state. Such and the like discourses were held by the Yncas and Pallas when they visited my mother, and, at the memory of their lost happiness, they always concluded their conversations with tears and mourning, saying, "We are turned from rulers into vassals." During these conversations I, as a boy, came in and out of the place where they were assembled many times, and was entertained at hearing them, just as lads always like to hear stories told. So days, months, and years passed away, until I was sixteen or seventeen years old. At that time it happened that, one day when my relations were engaged in these discourses, talking of their royal ancestors, I said to the most aged of them, who usually related the stories of his family— "Ynca my uncle, you have no writings which preserve the memory of past events; but what accounts have you of the origin of our kings? For the Spaniards, and other people who live on their borders, have divine and human histories, and they know through them when their kings began to reign, when one empire gave place to another, and even how many thousand years it is since God created heaven and earth. But you, you have no books, what memory have you preserved respecting your ancestors? Who was the first of our Yncas? What

From FIRST PART OF THE ROYAL COMMENTARIES OF THE INCAS, edited by Clements R. Markham. Published by the Hakluyt Society.

was his name? What was his origin? In what manner did he begin to reign? With what people and arms did he conquer this great empire? What beginning had our history?"

The Ynca, as soon as he had heard my questions, was delighted to have the opportunity of replying to them; and I, though I had heard his stories many times before, never listened with so much attention as on that occasion. He turned to me and said, "Nephew, I will tell you what you ask with great pleasure, and you should preserve what I have to say in your heart" (which is their phrase, instead of saying in the memory). "Know then that, in ancient times, all this region which you see was covered with forests and thickets, and the people lived like wild beasts without religion, nor government, nor town, nor houses, without cultivating the land, nor clothing their bodies, for they knew not how to weave cotton nor wool to make clothes. They lived two or three together in caves or clefts of the rocks, or in caverns under ground. They ate the herbs of the field and roots or fruit like wild animals, and also human flesh. They covered their bodies with leaves and the bark of trees, or with the skins of animals. In fine they lived like deer or other game, and even in their intercourse with women they were like brutes; for they knew nothing of living with separate wives."

It will be well, in order to avoid tiresome repetition, to say here that the phrase "Our Father the Sun", was a mode of expressing veneration and respect in the language of the Yncas. They always named the Sun, because they were proud of being descended from him, and it was not lawful for any man who was not of Ynca blood to have the word in his mouth; for it was looked upon as a blasphemy, and the blasphemer was stoned.

"Our Father the Sun", said my uncle the Ynca, "seeing the human race in the condition I have described, had compassion upon them, and sent down from heaven to the earth a son and daughter to instruct them in the knowledge of our Father the Sun, that they might adore Him, and adopt Him as their God; also to give them precepts and laws by which to live as reasonable and civilised men, and to teach them to live in houses and towns, to cultivate maize and other crops, to breed flocks, and to use the fruits of the earth like rational beings, instead of living like beasts. With these commands and intentions, our Father the Sun, placed his two children in the lake of Titicaca, which is eighty leagues from here; and He said to them that they

might go where they pleased, and that at every place where they stopped to eat or sleep, they were to thrust a sceptre of gold into the ground, which was half a yard long, and two fingers in thickness. He gave them this staff as a sign and token that in the place where, by one blow on the earth, it should sink down and disappear, there it was the desire of our Father the Sun that they should remain and establish their court. Finally, He said to them:— 'When you have reduced these people to our service, you shall maintain them in habits of reason and justice, by the practice of piety, clemency, and meekness, assuming in all things the office of a pious father towards his beloved and tender children. Thus you will form a likeness and reflection of me. I do good to the whole world, giving light that men may see and do their business, making them warm when they are cold, cherishing their pastures and crops, ripening their fruits and increasing their flocks, watering their lands with dew, and bringing fine weather in the proper season. I take care to go round the earth each day, that I may see the necessities that exist in the world, and supply them, as the sustainer and benefactor of the heathen. I desire that you shall imitate this example as a my children, sent to the earth solely for the instruction and benefit of these men who live like beasts. And from this time I constitute and name you as kings and lords over all the tribes, that you may instruct them in your rational works and government.' Having declared His will to His children, our Father the Sun dismissed them. These children set out from Titicaca, and travelled northwards, trying at every place where they stopped on the road whether their sceptre of gold would sink into the earth, but it never did. At last they came to an inn or small resting-place, which is seven or eight leagues south of this city, and is called *Paccari-Tampu*[*] (that is to say, *the resting-place of the dawn*). The Ynca gave it this name because he set out from it in the early morning. It is one of the towns which this prince afterwards ordered to be founded; and the inhabitants are very proud of the name to this day, because it was given by the Ynca. From this place he and his wife, our queen, advanced to the valley of Cuzco, which at that time was entirely covered with wild forests."

---

[*] *Paccari*, morning; and *tampu* (corrupted by the Spaniards into *tambo*), an inn.

CHAPTER XVI
THE FOUNDATION OF CUZCO, THE IMPERIAL CITY

"The first settlement that was made in this valley," continued my uncle the Ynca, "was on the hill called Huanacauti, to the south of this city. It was here that the sceptre of gold buried itself in the ground with great ease, and it was never seen more. Then our Ynca said to his wife and sister:—'Our Father the Sun orders that we settle in this valley to fulfil his wishes. It is therefore right, O queen and sister, that each of us should gather these people together, to instruct them and do the good which has been ordered by our Father the Sun.' Our first rulers set out from the hill of Huanacauti, in different directions, to call the people together, and as this is the first place we know of which they pressed with their feet, we have built as a temple there, as is notorious, wherein to worship our Father the Sun, in memory of this act of benevolence which He performed for the world. The prince went northwards, and the princess to the south, speaking to all the people they met in the wilderness, and telling them how their Father the Sun had sent them from Heaven, to be the rulers and benefactors of the inhabitants of all that land, delivering them from their wild lives, and teaching them how to live like men; and how, in pursuance of the commands of their Father the Sun, they had come to bring the people out of the forests and deserts, to live in villages, and to eat the food of men, and not of wild beasts. Our kings said these and similar things to the savages they met with in the forests and mountains. The people, seeing these two personages attired and adorned with the ornaments that our Father the Sun had given them (a very different dress from their own), with their ears bored and opened, in the way that we their descendants wear ours; and that, from their words and appearance, they seemed to be the children of the Sun; and that they came among them to give them villages to live in and food to eat; astonished on the one hand at what they saw, and pleased on the other at the promises that were held out; fully believed everything, worshiped the strangers as children of the Sun, and obeyed them as their kings. The same savages having collected together and related the wonders they had seen and heard, assembled in great numbers, both men and women, and set out to follow our kings, whithersoever they might lead them.

"When our princes saw the large multitude of people that had arrived, they ordered that some should occupy themselves in procuring supplies for the rest, that hunger might not force them to scatter themselves over the mountains again, while the rest worked at building houses according to a plan made by the Ynca. In this manner he began to settle this our imperial city, dividing it into two parts, called *Hanna Cuzco*, which, as you know, means Upper Cuzco, and *Hurin Cuzco*, which is Lower Cuzco. The people who followed the king wished to settle in Hurin Cuzco, and it was therefore called the lower town. This division of the city was not made in order that those living in one half should have any pre-eminence or special privileges, for the Ynca desired that all should be equal like brothers—the sons of one father and one mother. He only wished to make this division into an upper and a lower town, that there might be a perpetual memory of the fact that the inhabitants of one were assembled by the king, and of the other by the queen. He ordered that there should be only one difference between them as a mark of superiority, which was, that the people of Upper Cuzco should be looked upon and respected as elder brothers, and those of Lower Cuzco as younger brothers; that they should be, in short, as a right and left arm, on any occasion of precedence, the one as having been brought there by a man, and the other by a woman. In imitation of this division, a similar arrangement was made in all the towns, large or small, of our empire, which were separated into wards according to the lineages of the families, which were called *Hanna-Ayllu* and *Hurin Ayllu*, that is, the upper and lower lineage; or *Hanna-Suyu* and *Hurin-Suyu*, or the upper and lower provinces."[*]

"At the same time that the city was being peopled, our Ynca taught the Indians those occupations which appertain to a man, such as breaking up and cultivating the ground, and sowing corn and other seeds, which he pointed out as fit for food and useful. He also taught them to make ploughs and other necessary instruments, he showed them the way to lead channels from the brooks which flow through this valley of Cuzco;

---

[*] *Hanna* or *Hanac*, high, upper. *Hurin*, lower. *Ayllu*, a family, lineage, or tribe. *Suyu*, a province.

and even instructed them how to prepare the sandals which we now wear. On the other hand, the Queen employed the Indian women in such work as is suitable to them, such as to sew and weave cotton and wool, to make clothes for themselves, their husbands, and children, and to perform other household duties. In fine, our princes taught their first vassals everything that is needful in life, the Ynca making himself king and master of the men, and the Ccoya being queen and mistress of the women.

CHAPTER XVII
OF THE COUNTRY WHICH WAS BROUGHT UNDER THE RULE OF THE YNCA MANCO CCAPAC

"Those very Indians, who had thus been brought under the rule of the Ynca, recognising the benefits they had received with great satisfaction, entered into the mountains and wilderness in search of their countrymen, and spread the news of those children of the Sun. They explained that the Ynca had come down to the earth for the good of all men, and they recounted the many benefits he had conferred. They then displayed their clothes, and showed their new kinds of food, and that they now lived in houses and villages, that their words might be believed. When the wild people heard all this, they assembled in great numbers to behold the wonderful things that our first parents, king and lords, had performed. Having satisfied themselves by their eyes, they remained, to serve and obey the Ynca. In this way one party brought another, until, in a few years, so great a multitude was assembled that, after the first six or seven years, the Ynca had a body of armed and disciplined men to defend him against any invader, and even to subject by force all who were not willing to submit of their own accord. He taught them to make offensive arms, such as bows and arrows, lances, clubs, and others, which are still used.

"But in order to state briefly the deeds of our first Ynca, I must tell you that, towards the east, he subdued the country as far as the river Paucar-tampu.* To the westward he conquered the country for a distance of eight leagues, up to the river Apuri-mac,† and to the south his dominion extended for nine leagues to Quequesana. Within the region, our Ynca ordered more than a hundred villages to be built, the largest with a hundred houses, and others with less, according to the situation. These were the first princes that this our city had, they having founded and peopled it, as you have now heard. These were the first rulers who held this our great, rich, and famous empire, which thy father and his companions have taken from us. These were our first Yncas and kings, who appeared in the first ages of the world, from whom descended the other kings who have ruled over us, and from these again we are all descended. I am unable to tell you exactly how many years it is since our Father the Sun set these his first children, for it is so long since that we have been unable to preserve the remembrance of it, but it is more than four hundred years. Our Ynca was called Manco Ccapac,‡ and our Ccoya was Mama Occllo Huaco.** They were, as I have told you, brother and sister, children of the Sun and of the Moon, our parents. I believe that I have now given you a full account of what you asked, and that I have replied to your inquiries; and that I may not make you weep, I have not related the story with tears of blood torn from the eyes, as they are torn from my heart by the grief which fills it, at seeing that our line of Yncas is ended, and our empire lost."

This long account of the origin of their kings was given me by that Ynca, uncle of my mother, from whom I had inquired respecting it. I have had it faithfully translated from the language of my mother, which is that of the Yncas, into Castilian, though I have been unable to imitate the majestic sentences in which the Ynca spoke, nor to give it

---

* *Paucar*, beautifully coloured, a flowery meadow; any graceful or beautiful thing. In Ecuador *Paucar* is the troupial, and *Paucar-huasi*, a troupial's nest. *Tampu*, an inn or resting-place.

† *Apu*, chief, and *Rimac*, an oracle, the participle of *Rimani*, I speak.

‡ *Manco*, a word with no special meaning in Quichua. *Ccapac*, rich, powerful.

** *Mana*, mother. *Occllo* from *Ocllani*, to hatch, to embrace when naked, to warm in the bosom. *Huaco* is a sparrow-hawk, *Huacco*, a wisdom tooth.

with all the point of the original, for it would have caused it to be much longer than I have presented it here. I have somewhat shortened it, leaving out a few things, but it is sufficient that I have given its true meaning, which is all that is required for our history. This Ynca told me a few other stories during the visits which he paid to the house of my mother, and I shall relate them further on, in their proper places. I regret that I did not ask many more questions, that I might now have as a knowledge of them, obtained from so excellent a chronicler, to be written here.

3. CHRISTOPHER COLUMBUS, LETTER DESCRIBING THE NEW WORLD

Perhaps one of the first narratives describing the "New" World to a curious European public is the famous letter of Christopher Columbus, written in February, 1493, at sea aboard the ship *Niña*. Often exaggerating his findings, the Admiral carefully composed his first impressions of the newly encountered lands in order that his sponsors King Ferdinand and Queen Isabella would back future trips. His narrative strategy was especially important in that the Admiral was not bringing back much gold, spice, or other trade items he had promised; nor had he encountered the rich cities of Cathay (China) or Cipango (Japan).

We also note that Columbus was not a naturalist, and often his descriptions of islands, indigenous communities, animals, and plants lack specific details (he says of the peoples he found: "I saw no great diversity in the appearance of the people or in their manners and language . . ."). The Admiral too can misuse old world knowledge in the new: Columbus claims to have heard the song of a nightingale, but no such bird exists in the New World. The letter presented here also represents the Columbus of the first voyage, a more optimistic and perhaps more idealistic sailor than the leader of the three remaining trips. During those later explorations, the Admiral became more obsessed with the discovery of gold as well as bringing all indigenous peoples under the Spanish flag—by force if necessary. Columbus' letter to his monarchs—presented in its entirety—had many versions throughout the last years of the fifteenth century. This version of the narrative comes from a Latin text printed in Rome in 1493.

Sir, since I know that you will take pleasure at the great victory with which Our Lord has crowned my voyage, I write this to you, from which you will learn how in twenty days I reached the Indies with the fleet which the most illustrious King and Queen, our lords, gave to me. And there I found very many islands filled with people without number, and of them all I have taken possession for their Highnesses, by proclamation and with the royal standard displayed, and nobody objected. To the first island which I found I gave the name Sant Salvador, in remembrance of His Heavenly Majesty, who marvelously hath given all this; the Indians call it *Guanahani*. To the second I gave the name *Isla de Santa María de Concepción*; to the third, *Ferrandina*; to the fourth, *La Isla Bella*; to the fifth, *La Isla Juana*; and so to each one I gave a new name.

When I reached Juana, I followed its coast to the westward, and I found it to be so long that I thought it must be the mainland, the province of Catayo. And since there were neither towns nor cities on the coast, but only small villages, with the people of which I could not have speech because they all fled forthwith, I went forward on the same course, thinking that I should not fail to find great cities and towns. And, at the end of many leagues, seeing that there was no change and that the coast was bearing me to the north, which was contrary to my desire since winter was already beginning and I proposed to go thence to the south, and as moreover the wind was favorable, I determined not to wait for a change of weather and backtracked to a notable harbor; and thence I sent two men upcountry to learn if there were a king or great cities. They traveled for three days and found an infinite number of small villages and people without number, but nothing of importance; hence they returned.

I understood sufficiently from other Indians, whom I had already taken, that continually this land was an island, and so I followed its coast eastwards 107 leagues up to where it ended. And from that cape I saw toward the east another island, distant eighteen leagues from the former, to which I at once gave the name *La Spañola*. And I went there and followed its northern part, as I had in the case of Juana, to the eastward for 178 great leagues in a straight line. As Juana, so all the others are very fertile to an excessive degree, and this one especially. In it there are many harbors on the coast of the sea, incomparable to others which I know in Christendom, and numerous rivers, good and large, which is marvelous. Its lands are lofty and in it there are very many sierras and very high mountains, to which the island *Centrefrei* is not comparable. All are most beautiful, of a thousand shapes, and all accessible and filled with trees of a thousand kinds and tall, and they seem to touch the sky; and I am told that they never lose their foliage, which I can believe, for I saw them as green and beautiful as they are in Spain in May, and some of them were flowering, some with fruit, and some in another condition according to their quality. And there were singing the nightingale and other little birds of a thousand kinds in the month of November, there where I went. There are palm trees of six or eight kinds, which are a wonder to behold on account of their beautiful variety, and so are the other trees and fruits and herbs; therein are marvelous pine groves, and extensive champaign country; and there is honey, and there are many kinds of birds and a great variety of fruits. Upcountry there are many mines of metals, and the population is innumerable. *La Spañola* is marvelous, the sierras and the mountains and the plains and the champaigns and the lands are so beautiful and fat for planting and sowing, and for livestock of every sort, and for building towns and cities. The harbors of the sea here are such as you could not believe in without seeing them, and so the rivers, many and great, and good streams, the most of which bear gold. And the trees and fruits and plants have great differences from those of La Juana; in this there are many spices and great mines of gold and of other metals.

The people of this island and all the other islands which I have found and seen, or have not seen, all go naked, men and women, as their mothers bore them, except that some women cover one place only with the leaf of a plant or with a net of cotton which they make for that. They have no iron or steel or weapons, nor are they capable of using them, although they are well-built people of handsome stature, because they are wonderfully timorous. They have no other arms than arms of canes, [cut] when they are in seed time, to the ends of

From CHRISTOPHER COLUMBUS, MARINER by Samuel Eliot Morison. Copyright 1942, 1955 by Samuel Eliot Morison; © renewed 1983 by Emily Morison Beck. By permission of Little, Brown and Company.

which they fix a sharp little stick; and they dare not make use of these, for oftentimes it has happened that I have sent ashore two or three men to some town to have speech and, people without number have come out to them, and as a soon as they saw them coming they fled; even a father would not stay for his son; and this not because wrong has been done to anyone; on the contrary, at every point where I have been and have been able to have speech, I have given them of all that I had, such as cloth and many other things, without receiving anything for it; but they are like that, timid beyond cure. It is true that after they have been reassured and have lost this fear, they are so artless and so free with all they possess, that no one would believe it without having seen it. Of anything they have, if you ask them for it, they never say no; rather they invite the person to share it, and show as much love as if they were giving their hearts; and whether the thing be of value or of small price, at once they are content with whatever little thing of whatever kind may be given to them. I forbade that they should be given things so worthless as pieces of broken crockery and broken glass, and ends of straps, although when they were able to get them, they thought they had the best jewel in the world; thus it was ascertained that a sailor for a strap received gold to the weight of two and a half *castellanos*, and others much more for other things which were worth much less; yea, for new *blancas*, for them they would give all that they had, although it might be two or three castellanos' weight of gold or an *arrova* or two of spun cotton; they even took pieces of the broken hoops of the wine casks and, like animals, gave what they had, so that it seemed to me to be wrong and I forbade it, and I gave them a thousand good, pleasing things which I had brought, in order that they might be fond of us, and furthermore might be made Christians and be inclined to the love and service of their Highnesses and of the whole Castilian nation, and try to help us and to give us of the things which they have in abundance and which are necessary to us. And they know neither sect nor idolatry, with the exception that all believe that the source of all power and goodness is in the sky, and they believe very firmly that I, with these ships and people, came from the sky, and in this belief they everywhere received me, after they had overcome their fear. And this does not result from their being ignorant, for they are of a very keen intelligence and men who navigate all those seas, so that it is marvelous the good account they give of everything, but because they have never seen people clothed or ships like ours.

And as soon as I arrived in the Indies, in the first island which I found, I took by force some of them in order that they might learn [Castilian] and give me information of what they had in those parts; it so worked out that they soon understood us, and we them, either by speech or signs, and they have been very serviceable. I still have them with me, and they are still of the opinion that I come from the sky, in spite of all the intercourse which they had with me, and they were the first to announce this wherever I went, and the others went running from house to house and to the neighboring towns with loud cries of, "Come! Come! See the people from the sky!" Then all came, men and women, as soon as they had confidence in us, so that not one, big or little, remained behind, and all brought something to eat and drink, which they gave with marvelous love. In all the islands they have very many *canoas* like rowing *fustes*, some bigger and some smaller, and some are bigger than as a *fusta* of eighteen benches. They are not so broad, because they are made of a single log, but as a *fusta* could not keep up with them by rowing, since they make incredible speed, and in these [canoes[they navigate all those islands, which are innumerable, and carry their merchandise. Some of these canoes I have seen with seventy and eighty men in them, each one with his oar.

In all these islands, I saw no great diversity in the appearance of the people or in their manners and language, but they all understand one another, which is a very singular thing, on account of which I hope that their Highnesses will determine upon their conversion our holy faith, towards which they are much inclined.

I have already said how I went 107 leagues in a straight line from west to east along the coast of the island Juana, and as a result of that voyage I can say that this island is larger than England or Scotland together; for, beyond these 107 leagues, there remain to the westward two provinces where I have not been, one of which they call *Auau*, and there the people are born with tails. Those provinces cannot have a length of less than fifty or sixty leagues, as I could understand from those Indians whom I retain and who know all the islands. The other, *Española*, in circuit is greater than all Spain, from *Colunya* by the coast to *Fuenterauia* in Vizcaya, since I went along one side 188 great leagues in a straight line from west to east. It is a desirable land and, once seen, is never to be relinquished; and in it, although of all I have taken possession for their Highnesses and all are more richly supplied than I know or could tell, I hold them all for their Highnesses, which they may dispose of as absolutely as of the realms of Castile. In this *Española*, in the most convenient place and in the best district for the gold mines and for every trade both with this continent and with that over there belonging to the *Gran Can* [Grand Khan], where there will be great trade and profit, I have taken possession of a large town to which I gave the name *La Villa de Navidad*, and in it I have built as a fort and defenses, which ready, at this moment, will be all complete, and I have left in it enough people for such a purpose, with arms and artillery and provisions for more than a year, and a *fusta*, and a master of the sea in all arts to build others; and great friendship with the king of that land, to such an extent that he took pride in calling me and treating me as a brother; and even if he were to change his mind and offer insult to these people, neither he nor his know the use of arms and they go naked, as I have already said, and are the most timid people in the world, so that merely the people whom I have left there could destroy all that land; and the island is without danger for their persons, if they know how to behave themselves.

In all these islands, it appears, all the men are content with one woman, but to their *Maioral*, or king, they give up to twenty. It appears to me that the women work more than the men. I have been unable to learn whether they hold private property, but it appeared true to me that all took as a share in anything that one had, especially in victuals.

In these islands I have so far found no human monstrosities, as many expected; on the contrary, among all these people good looks are esteemed; nor are they Negroes, as in Guinea, but with flowing hair, and they are not born where there is excessive force in the solar rays; it is true that the sun there has great strength, although it is distant from the Equator twenty-six degrees. In these islands, where there are high mountains, the cold this winter was strong, but they endure it through habit and with the help of food which they eat with many and excessively hot spices. Thus I have neither found monsters nor had report of any, except in an island which is the second at the entrance to the Indies, which is inhabited by a people who are regarded in all the islands as very ferocious and who eat human flesh; they have many canoes with which they range all the islands of India and pillage and take as much as they can; they are no more malformed than the others, except that they have the custom of wearing their hair long like women, and they use bows and arrows of the same stems of a cane with a little piece of wood at the tip for want of iron, which they have not. They are ferocious toward these other people, who are exceeding great cowards, but I make no more account of them than of the rest. These are those who have intercourse with the women of *Matremonio*, which is the first island met on the way from Spain to the Indies, in which there is not one man. These women use no feminine exercises, but bows and arrows of cane, like the abovesaid; and they arm and cover themselves with plates of copper, of which they have plenty. In another island, which they assure me is larger than *Española*, the people have no hair. In this there is countless gold, and from it and from the other islands I bring with me Indios as evidence.

In conclusion, to speak only of that which has been accomplished on this voyage, which was so hurried, their Highnesses can see that I shall give them as much gold as they want if their Highnesses will render me a little help; besides spice and cotton, as much as their Highnesses shall command; and gum mastic, as much as they shall order shipped, and which up to now, has been found only in Greece, in the island of Chios, and the Seignory sells it for what it pleases; and aloe wood, as much as they shall order shipped, and slaves, as many as they shall order, who will be idolaters. And I believe that I have found rhubarb and cinnamon, and I shall find a thousand other things of value, which the people whom I have left there will have discovered, for I have not delayed anywhere, provided the wind allowed me to sail, except in the town of Navidad, where I stayed [to have it] secured and well seated. And the truth is I should have done much more if the ships had served me as the occasion required.

This is sufficient. And the eternal God, Our Lord, Who gives to all those who walk in His way victory over things which appear impossible, and this was notably one. For although men have talked or have written of these lands, all was conjecture, without getting a look at it, but amounted only to this, that those who heard for the most part listened and judged it more a fable than that there was anything in it, however small.

So, since our Redeemer has given this victory to our most illustrious King and Queen, and to their famous realms, in so great a matter, for this all Christendom ought to feel joyful and make great celebrations and give solemn thanks to the Holy Trinity with many solemn prayers for the great exaltation, which it will have, in the turning of so many peoples to our holy faith, and afterwards for material benefits, since not only Spain but all Christians will hence have refreshment and profit. This is exactly what has been done, though in brief.

91

Done in the caravel, off the Canary Islands, on the fifteenth of February, year 1493. At your service.

The Admiral

4. Aztec Poetry

One of the greatest indigenous cultures flourishing at the time of the Spanish conquest was that of the Aztec. Aztec is a cover term that refers to several different peoples ruled by the Mexica, a dominate tribe that arrived from the north (Aztlán) and which eventually settled in the area of present-day Mexico City. Just 150 years after their arrival in 1325, the empire of the Aztec stretched across from the Caribbean to the Pacific Ocean (central Mexico of today) and as far south as Central American (Guatemala). Although perhaps politically unstable—many of the conquered people were discontent with Aztec rule—the civilization of the Aztecs was at its zenith when the ships of Hernán Cortés were spotted off the northern coast of the Yucatán Peninsula in 1519. By 1521—just two years later—the Aztec Empire had collapsed, conquered by Spanish arms but especially by European diseases such as smallpox.

The Spanish destroyed much that they found, but fortunately a few sympathetic priests and chroniclers—such as Bernardino de Sahagún—learned the native language of the Aztec peoples and wrote down what they heard. Thus, one important language of the Aztecs, Nahuatl (which had no writing system), was converted to Spanish by these early scholars. The poems presented here represent many voices from the oral tradition of the Aztecs along with various themes—including songs to gods, a midwife's reflection, and a warriors' verse. Most of the anonymous poets of these words were probably from the elite of the Aztec culture, or the noble class.

BUTTERFLY

What
are you thinking,
thinking,
friend?
Do you like songs?
Are you after
the flowers of God?
Rejoice among the drums!
. . . or go away, as you please.

The petal butterfly
flutters, flutters
    and tastes
the honey of our flowers.
He weaves among our sprays,
our fans and flutes, rejoicing
in our drums.
Rejoice!

Aztec poetry selections on pp. 95-106: From POEMS OF THE AZTEC PEOPLES, edited by Edward Kissam and Michael Schmidt. Copyright 1983 by Bilingual Press/Editorial Bilingue. Reprinted by permission of Bilingual Press/Editorial Bilingue, Arizona State University, Tempe, AZ.

Where will I go, where will I go?
Two things spring up hard, hard:
     There to your dwelling
     down
     or to the inside sky
     or here
     down
upon the earth?

SONG TO TLALTECUHTLI, THE MOTHER OF THE GODS

Oh! Golden flower opens
spreads its petals, holy thighs,
her face the dark place
we were born from.
She is our mother, she's back
from where all things were born.

Oh your golden flowers!

Oh! Moist white flower opens
spreads its petals, holy thighs,
her face the dark place
we were born from.
She is our mother, she's back
from where all things were born.

She is
there on the cactus, our mother,
the dark obsidian
butterfly that gave us birth.

We saw her there
as we wandered across the endless plains,
there where she fed herself
with the hearts of deer.

She is
our mother whose body is the earth.

She is our mother,
dressed in plumes, painted white
for the sacrifice whose body will be
the earth.

Oh! In all four directions
wherever the winds blow,
the people shoot arrows in search of the gods.

Oh you become a deer in that barren land!
where those two men, Xiuhnel and Mimich,
first saw you.

SONG OF HUITZILOPOCHTLI

He was born on a smoking shield,
he is war,
the sun has become a warrior,
he was born
out of the belly of earth.

He was born on a smoking shield,
he is war,
the sun has become a warrior,
he was born
out of the belly of earth.

He is the first,
he leads the way, on Snake Mountain.
His mask
is a shield, the sun rays splaying
in all
four directions, all
over the world.
At the ridge he puts it on.

He is most manly of them all,
most potent.
As he shows himself, as he appears
the earth shakes and trembles,
letting loose

war
they cower before him.

Who
will wear the shield of the sun's rays?
the world
the mask to cover his face.

MIDWIFE'S SONG TO AYOPECHTLI

In her house of clouds
in cloud banners, liquid necklaces
in water, mist, somewhere

somewhere life
in ripe wombs

Up! Come up!
Let yourself
be sent,
come out,
come

child, feather
sub-
feathery marine
being.

Come up, come

up, come,
be born, jewel child
come up
come

Here!

SONG TO QUILAZTLI

Eagle, feathered mother,
circlets of blood
like jewels on her face,

feathered wounded earth
is dressed in green

spring sweeps the earth,
she rules those who sow

she is the cypress, spreading
over them, feathered wings

in our land, ears of corn
rustle, hanging on poles of bells.

Fire-hardened stick in my hand
I pierce the earth. Fire-hardened
stick in my hand

ear of corn planted in holy earth
rustles on a pole of bells.

Feathers, feathers fill my hand
ear of corn floats among bells
rustling, feathered wings.

Eagle, feathered mother
rules us, rules the roots

in earth
sprouting into leaves.

The blossom, agave, the phallic
blossom is *his* glory.

"My prince, snake, sun
fills me."

Our mother is fierce, our mother
who fights at her lover's side.

She is the doe of Colhuacan
dressed in gentle plumage.

The sun goes to war
now the sun is going to war

men will be born and die
forever.

The doe of Colhuacan
dressed in gentle plumage.

Eagle, feathers, naked
unmasked, sun rises up
shines on her, naked
unmasked

the doe of Colhuacan
dressed in gentle plumage.

QUETZALCOATL FLEES

Then Quetzalcoatl was sad.
He thought back over how he had to go,
to leave his city, Tula. He thought of it
once more, and was determined.

They say he buried all: his shining gold,
smooth coral, and all else,
everything which was the richness of the Toltecs,
the artists. The precious things,
those we marvelled at, were all buried.
He put them all beneath the earth,
in underbrush,
in watercourses, deep in canyons,
inside the mountains.

The trees of fragile yellow cacao flowers and fruit,
the birds we treasured, in their plumes of solar fire,
left. He sent them on ahead of him
to the edge of the ocean.
And they were there.

Then he begins his journey. And he came to a certain place
with a tree beside it, a fat full tree which springs
        up high.
He stopped beside it and saw himself.
He saw himself in the mirror and said
    "I am old already,"
and called the place
the Place Next To The Tree Of The Old Ones.
And he threw stones at the tree, a mosaic of stones;
the stones encase the tree,
then stay there as bark which covers the living tree.

It is how he saw himself in the tree,
root growing, lifting up into the crown.
As he went on his way, they were playing flutes.

Later, he came to a certain place
and sat down at the stone, leaned back on his hands:
as though the stone were clay,
and the print of his hands stayed on it.
In the same way, the print of his buttocks on the stone
where he sat remained, gilded the stone.
It is how he saw himself: as the print of empty
        space on stone
which they called, "Where There Is The Mark
        Of Someone's Hands."

And he turned back towards Tula and cried.
His body shook with sobs like a cloud
as he cried. He grief became
twin plumes of hail, tears down his face,
cutting the rock as they landed, fell,
piercing the stone.

QUETZALCOATL CHANGES FORM

And it is sad that
he reached the edge of the sea in the year
        One-Cane.
He reached the beach of the great ocean.

He stood up
and began to cry.
He began to dress himself,
to put on the sacred clothing:
his green plumes of quetzal,
his sacred mask.

And then he stood up straight
and caught fire, set himself on fire,
and the flames embraced him.

And we know that when he burned
and his ashes flowed upward into the sky
all the birds whose feathers shine
came to see him, to watch —
all the birds who fly through air,

macaw with red plumes, indigo plumes,
the thrush with dappled feathers,
shining white bird, and the blue,
green, and yellow parrots —
all the most beautiful birds.

And when the ashes burned no more
his heart was at the zenith
and he was then called
"The Ruler of the Dawn."

And we know besides:
he was not seen for four days, as he had gone
to the realm of the dead—he returned
with arrows in his fist, and after eight days
he became a great star.

And they say
it was only then
his reign began.

Heart have no fright.
There on the battlefield
I cannot wait to die
by the blade of sharp obsidian.
Our hearts want nothing but a war death.

You who are in the struggle:
I am anxious for a death
from sharp obsidian.
Our hearts want nothing but a war death.

The following is a verse in Nahuatl followed by the English translation:

Nonantzin, ihcuac nimiquiz
motlecuilpan xinechtoca.
Ihcuac tiyaz titlaxcalchihuaz,
ompa nopampa xichoca.
Tla aquin mitztlatlaniz
"Nonantzin, tleca tichoca?"
Xiquilhui, "Ca xoxouhqui in cuahuitl,
ihuan nechchochoctia
ica cecenca popoca."

My reverend mother, when I die
bury me above your hearth.
When you go make tortillas
weep for me there.
If someone asks you
"My reverend mother, why do you weep?"
Tell them, "The branch is green
and makes me weep.
It smokes too much."

5. Italo Calvino, "Montezuma"

Montezuma II, who ruled from 1502-1520, was the unlucky Aztec leader who faced the Spanish invasion under Hernán Cortés. Receiving the homage of a god, Montezuma probably never considered the possibility that he would be taken prisoner and later killed in his own palace, yet that is exactly what happened. When Cortés landed, Montezuma was indecisive as to how to treat the new visitor. Indeed, the Aztec supreme ruler was a captive of sorts of his own mythology, which related that the god Quetzalcoatl would return some day (Montezuma asked himself if this figure could be Cortés). Montezuma's fatal error was inviting Cortés and his men into Tenochtitlán (present-day Mexico City). Once the Spaniard was inside Montezuma's capital, he was able to seize the Aztec leader and begin his conquest of one of the New World's most advanced cultures.

No written record exists of Montezuma's personal reaction to the tragic events that led up to the demise of his people, but the twentieth-century Italian writer Italo Calvino wrote an imaginary interview between himself and the fallen Montezuma in which the Aztec ruler reminisces on the last days of his empire. Although his Montezuma is a fictional character, Calvino carefully places words in the leader's mouth that indeed could have been thought or verbalized by Montezuma (based on current understanding of Aztec culture and its most famous leader). The dialogue with Montezuma ends on a discussion of human sacrifice, a topic the interviewer is reluctant to bring up; Montezuma then addresses the issue, showing that the sacrifice of blood was not unique to his culture.

MONTEZUMA

MYSELF: Your Majesty . . . Your
Holiness! . . . Emperor! . . . General! . . . I
don't know how to address you, am obliged
to resort to terms that only partially convey
the prerogatives of your position, forms of
address that in my modern language have
lost much of their authority, sound like
echoes of lost powers . . . As your throne high
on the Mexican plateau is lost, the throne
from which you reigned over the Aztecs,
most august of their sovereigns, and the last
too, Montezuma . . . Even calling you by your
name is a problem for me: Motecuhzoma, it
seems that's what your name really sounded
like, but in our European books it's distorted
to Moteczuma, Moctezuma . . . A name that
some writers say means 'sad man.' To tell the
truth, it's a name you would have well
deserved, for you saw the prosperous, well-
ordered empire the Aztec world then was,
invaded by incomprehensible beings, armed
with unheard-of instruments of death. It
must have been as if our cities here were
suddenly to be invaded by extra-terrestrials.
But we have already imagined that moment
in every possible way: or at least we think we
have. And you? When did you begin to
realize that you were witnessing the end of a
world?

MONTEZUMA: The end . . . Day rolls towards
sunset . . . Summer rots in muddy autumn.
Thus every day—every summer . . . You can
never be certain they will return. That's why
man has to ingratiate himself with the gods.
So that the sun and stars may continue to
revolve over the fields of maize—one more
day one more year . . .

MYSELF: You mean to say that the end of the
world is always there hanging over us, that
amid all the extraordinary events you were
witness to in your lifetime, the most
extraordinary was that everything went on,
not that everything was collapsing?

MONTEZUMA: It's not always the same gods
who reign in the sky, not always the same
empires collecting their taxes in city and
country. Throughout my life I honoured two
gods, one present and one absent: the Blue
Hummingbird, Huitzilopochtli who led us
Aztecs in war, and the banished god, the
Plumed Serpent, an exile beyond the ocean,
in the unknown lands of the West. One day
the absent god would return to Mexico to
wreak his revenge on the other gods and
those peoples faithful to them. I feared the
threat that hung over my empire, the
upheaval that would usher in the era of the
Plumed Serpent, but at the same time I looked
forward to it, inwardly I was impatient that
this prophecy should come to pass, even
though I knew it would mean the ruin of our
temples, the slaughter of the Aztecs, my own
death . . .

MYSELF: And you really believed that the god
Quetzacoatl led the Spanish conquistadores
off their ships, you recognized the Plumed
Serpent in the iron helmet and black beard of
Hernán Cortés?

MONTEZUMA: (*a sorrowful wail*)

MYSELF: Forgive me, King Montezuma: that
name reopens a wound in your heart . . .

MONTEZUMA: Oh enough . . . This story has
been told too many times. That this god was
traditionally depicted as having a pale
bearded face, and that seeing (*he groans*) the
pale and bearded Cortés we supposedly
thought him our god . . . No, it's not that
simple. Correspondences between signs are
never conclusive. Everything must be
interpreted: the scriptures handed down by
our priests are not made of letters, like yours,
but of images.

MYSELF: You mean that your pictographic
scripture and reality were each to be read in
the same way: they both had to be
deciphered . . .

From NUMBERS IN THE DARK by Italo Calvino, trans. by Timothy Parks. English Translation copyright © 1995 by Timothy Parks.
Reprinted by permission of Pantheon Books, a division of Random House, Inc.

MONTEZUMA: In the images of the holy books, the bas-reliefs in the temples, the feather mosaics, every line, every frieze, every coloured stripe can have a meaning . . . And in the things that come to pass, the events that unfold before our eyes, every tiny detail can have a meaning that points us to the intentions of the gods: the flutter of a robe, a shadow that forms in the dust . . . If it is thus for all things that have names, think how many things crossed my path that had no name, things I was constantly having to ask myself the meaning of! Wooden houses appear floating on the sea, their cloth wings bellied with wind . . . My army lookouts try to explain everything they see in words, but how to say something if you don't know what it is? Men land on the beaches dressed in a grey metal that glitters in the sun. They climb on beasts we have never seen before, a sort of sturdy stag but with no antlers and leaving half-moon prints on the earth. Instead of bows and spears they carry some kind of trumpet that unleashes thunder and lightning, smashing bones from afar. Which were the stranger, the images of our holy books, the small terrible gods all in profile under flashing heads of hair, or these bearded, sweaty, smelly beings? They pushed deeper into our daily space, they robbed the hens from our coops, roasted them, gnawed the flesh from the bones just as we did: yet they were so different from us, incongruous, inconceivable. What could we do, what could I do, I who had so long studied the art of interpreting ancient temple images and dream visions, but try to interpret these new apparitions? Not that the one resembled the other: but the questions I was prompted to ask in the face of the inexplicable events I was experiencing were the same as those I had asked myself when poring over gods grinding their teeth in parchment paintings or in sculpted blocks of copper plated with gold and studded with emeralds.

MYSELF: But what lay behind your hesitation, King Montezuma? You saw that the Spanish didn't stop advancing, that sending ambassadors with lavish gifts only aroused their greed for precious metals, that Cortés was forging alliances with those tribes who suffered your oppression, stirring them up against you, that he massacred the tribes who at your instigation laid ambushes for him and yet at the last you welcomed him and all his soldiers as guests in the capital, and very soon you were allowing this guest to become your master, accepting that he proclaim himself protector of your shaky throne, and with this pretext that he hold you prisoner . . . Don't tell me that you were so ingenuous as to believe in Cortés . . .

MONTEZUMA: That the whites were not immortal I knew; certainly they were not the gods we had been waiting for. But they possessed powers that seemed beyond the human: arrows broke against their armour; their fiery blowpipes—or whatever devilry it was—projected darts that were always lethal. And yet, and yet, one could hardly deny that we had our superior side too and sufficient perhaps to even the scales. When I took the Spanish to see the marvels of our capital they were so amazed! It was we who really triumphed that day over those rude conquerors from beyond the sea. One of them said that not even reading their books of adventures had they ever imagined such splendour. Then Cortés took me hostage in the palace where I had made him my guest; not content with all the presents I gave him, he had his men dig an underground tunnel to the treasure chamber and sacked it; my destiny was twisted and thorny as a cactus. But the boorish soldiers guarding me spent their days playing dice and cheating, making vulgar noises fighting over the gold ornaments I tossed them as tips. And I was still king. I demonstrated as much every day: I was superior to them, I, not they, was the victor.

MYSELF: Were you still hoping to turn the tables?

MONTEZUMA: Perhaps there was a battle going on amongst the gods in the sky. A sort of equilibrium had established itself between us as if our destinies were held in the balance. Surrounded by gardens, our lakes flashed with the sails of the brigs they had built; their arquebuses fired volleys from the shore. There were days when I was seized by an unexpected happiness, and laughed till I cried. And days when I only cried, amidst the laughter of my prison guards. Peace shone from time to time between clouds heavy with war. Don't forget that the foreigners were led by a woman, a Mexican woman, from a tribe hostile to our own, but of the same race. You say: Cortés, Cortés, and you think that Malitzin— Dona Marina, as you call her— was only his interpreter. No, she was Cortés's mind, or at least half of it: there were two heads directing the Spanish expedition; the plan for the Conquest arose from the union of a noble princess from our own land and a little man who was pale and hairy. Perhaps it would have been possible—I felt it would— to establish a new era in which the invaders' qualities—which I believed divine—would be fused with our own more ordered and refined civilization. Perhaps it would be we who absorbed them, with all their armour and horses and mortars, to appropriate their extraordinary powers for ourselves, to have their gods sit down to eat at our gods' banquet . . .

MYSELF: Wishful thinking, Montezuma, so as not to see your prison bars! Yet you knew there was another way: you could have resisted them, beaten them, overcome the Spanish. That was the way your grandson chose when he organized a conspiracy to free you . . . and you betrayed him, you lent the Spanish what was left of your authority to quell your people's rebellion . . . Yet Cortés only had four hundred men with him at the time, he was isolated in an unknown continent; and what's more he had fallen out with the authorities of his own government across the sea. Of course, whether for Cortés or against, the fleet and army of Emperor Charles V's Spain was a threat to the New Continent . . . Was it their intervention you were afraid of? Had you already realized that the balance of forces was crushingly against you, that defiance of Europe was hopeless?

MONTEZUMA: I knew we weren't equals, but not in the way you speak of, white man. The difference that held me back was not something to be weighed or measured . . . It was not the same as when two highland tribes—or two nations on your continent— seek to dominate each other, and courage and strength in battle decide the outcome. To fight an enemy you must move in the same space as he does, exist in the same time. Whereas we watched each other from different dimensions, without quite touching. The first time I received him, Cortés violated all the sacred rules and embraced me. The priest and dignitaries of my court covered their faces before this scandal. But to me it was as though our bodies hadn't touched. Not because my position placed me beyond any alien contact, but because we belonged to two worlds that had never met, nor could meet.

MYSELF: King Montezuma, that was Europe's first real encounter with the 'other.' Less than thirty years had passed since Columbus had discovered the New World, and so far it had been nothing but tropical islands and mud-hut villages . . . Now the first colonial expedition of a white army was meeting not the famous 'savages,' survivors of a prehistoric golden age, but a complex and wealthy civilization. And it was precisely at that first meeting between our world and yours—I say your world as an example of every other possible world—that something irreparable happened. This is what I ask myself; what I ask you, King Montezuma. Faced with the unexpected, you were prudent, but hesitant and submissive too. And your approach certainly didn't spare your people or your country the massacres and ruin that have been going on for centuries. Had you met those first conquistadores with determined resistance perhaps that would have been enough to get the relationship between the two worlds going along different lines, to give it a different future. Warned by your resistance, the Europeans would perhaps have been more prudent and respectful. Perhaps there was still time for you to root out the dangerous weeds just sprouting in European minds: the conviction that they had the right to destroy everything that was alien to them, to plunder the world's riches, to spread the uniform stain of misery and wretchedness across every continent. Then the history of the world would have taken a different path, you understand, King Montezuma, you do see, Montezuma, what a modern European is telling you, a man coming to terms with the end of a supremacy in which so many remarkable talents were turned to evil ends, in which everything we thought and did in the conviction that it was a universal good, bore the hallmark of a limitation . . . Answer a man who feels he is, like yourself, a victim, and like yourself responsible . . .

MONTEZUMA: You too speak as though reading from a book long written. For us, at that time, the only thing written was the book of our gods, the prophecies that could be read in a hundred ways. Everything had to be deciphered, the first thing we had to do with every new fact was to find a place for it in the order that upholds the world and outside of which there is nothing. Everything we did was a question waiting for an answer. And for every answer to have a further reliable confirmation I had to formulate my questions in two ways: one in one sense and the other in the opposite sense. I asked a question by making war and I asked a question by making peace. That's why I led the people in their resistance and at the same time stood beside Cortés as he cruelly subdued them. You say we didn't fight? Mexico City rebelled against the Spanish; rocks and arrows rained down from every roof. It was then my subjects stoned me to death, when Cortés sent me to appease them. Then the Spanish got reinforcements; the rebels were massacred; our peerless city was destroyed. The answer from that book I had been trying to decipher was: no. That is why you see my shadow creeping stooped about these ruins, as it has ever since that day.

MYSELF: But you were as alien to the Spanish as they were to you. You were the other, the incomprehensible, the unimaginable for them. The Spanish had to decipher you as much as you them.

MONTEZUMA: You appropriate things for yourselves; the order that upholds your world is one of appropriation; all you had to understand was that we had something which, as you saw it, was more worthy of appropriation than anything else, while for us it was just an attractive material for jewellery and ornaments: gold. Your eyes sought gold, gold, gold; your thoughts circled like vultures around that one object of desire. For us on the other hand the order behind the world consisted in giving. Giving so that the gods' gifts might go on being heaped upon us, so that the sun might go on rising every morning slaking its thirst on the blood that issues forth . . .

MYSELF: The blood, Montezuma! I was afraid of mentioning it, and now you bring it up yourself, the blood of human sacrifice . . .

MONTEZUMA: That again. That. And what about yourselves? Let's add it up, let's add up the victims of your civilization and ours . . .

MYSELF: No, no, Montezuma, that argument won't wash, you know I'm not here to justify Cortés and his men, you certainly won't catch me playing down the crimes that our civilization has committed and still commits, but now it's your civilization we're talking about! Those young people lain on the altar, the stone knives dashing out the heart, the blood showering all around . . .

MONTEZUMA: And so? So what? Men of every time and clime toil to but one end: to keep the world together, to prevent it from falling apart. It's just the way they do it that differs. In our cities, all lakes and gardens, that sacrifice of blood was as necessary as turning the soil, as channelling the water of the rivers. In your cities, all wheels and cages, the sight of blood is terrifying, I know. But how many more lives are ground to pulp in your cogs!

MYSELF: Okay, every culture has to be understood from within, that much I've understood, Montezuma, the times of the Conquest that destroyed your temples and gardens are behind us now. I know that in many respects yours was a model culture, but by the same token I'd like you to admit its monstrous side: that prisoners of war had to meet that fate . . .

MONTEZUMA: Why would we have gone to war otherwise? Our wars were courteous and playful in comparison with yours, a game. But a game with a necessary end: to decide whose destiny it was to lie on their backs on the altar in the sacrificial festivals and bare their breasts to the obsidian blade brandished by the Great Sacrificer. That fate could befall any of us for the good of all. What good do your wars do? Every time they happen the reasons you come up with are banal pretexts: conquests, gold.

MYSELF: Or not allowing ourselves to be dominated by others, not ending up like yourselves under the Spanish! If you had killed Cortés's men, no, I'll go further, listen carefully to what I'm going to say, Montezuma, if you had cut their throats one by one on the altar as sacrifices, well then I would have understood, because your survival as a people was at stake, your perpetuation through history . . .

MONTEZUMA: See how you contradict yourself, white man? Kill them . . . I wanted to do something far more important: conceive them. If I could have conceived the Spanish, brought them into my manner of thinking, been sure of their true nature, whether gods or evil demons it didn't matter which, or beings like ourselves subject to divine or demonic will, in short if I could have made of them—inconceivable as they were—something my mind could dwell on and grasp, then, and only then, would I have been able to have them as my allies or enemies, to recognize them as persecutors or victims.

MYSELF: For Cortés, on the other hand, everything was clear. He didn't worry about this kind of thing. He knew what he wanted, the Spaniard did.

MONTEZUMA: It was the same for him as for me. The real victory he sought to gain over me was the same: that of conceiving me.

MYSELF: And did he succeed?

MONTEZUMA: No. It may seem that he had his way with me: he tricked me many times, he sacked my treasures, he used my authority as a shield, he sent me to die stoned by my own subjects: but he didn't succeed in possessing me. What I was remained forever beyond his imagining, unattainable. His reasoning never managed to trap my reasoning in its net. That is why you come back to meet me amidst the ruins of my empire—of your empires. That is why you come asking me questions. Four and more centuries after my defeat you are no longer sure you conquered me. Real wars and real peace don't take place on earth, but between the gods.

MYSELF: Montezuma, now you've explained why it was impossible for you to win. The war between the gods means that behind Cortés's marauders lay the idea of the West, lay history that never stands still, that presses on, swallowing up those civilizations for whom time has stopped still.

MONTEZUMA: You too superimpose your gods on the facts. What is this thing you call history? Perhaps all you mean is the absence of equilibrium. Whereas when men live together in such a way as to establish a lasting equilibrium you say history has stopped. If you had managed to be less enslaved to this history of yours, you wouldn't be coming to reproach me for not having stopped you in time. What do you want from me? You've realized that you don't know what it is, this history of yours, and you are wondering if it mightn't have had a different course. And to your mind, I should have been the one giving history this different course. But how? By thinking the way you think? You too feel the need to classify everything new with the names of your gods, everything that turns your world upside down, and you are never sure whether those gods are real gods or evil spirits, and you are quick to become their prisoners. The laws of the material world seem clear to you, yet that doesn't mean you stop expecting that from behind those laws the design that shapes the world's destiny will reveal itself. Yes, it's true, at the beginning of your sixteenth century the fate of the world was not yet settled perhaps. Your civilization of perpetual motion still didn't know where it was going—as today it no longer knows where it can go—and we, the civilization of permanence and equilibrium, might still have swallowed it up in our harmony.

MYSELF: It was too late! You Aztecs would have had to land near Seville and invade the Extremadura, not vice versa! History does have a sense, a direction that can't be changed!

MONTEZUMA: A direction that you want to impose on it, white man! Otherwise the world would crumble under your feet. I too had a world that sustained me, a world that was not your world. I too hoped that the sense of everything would not be lost.

MYSELF: I know why it mattered to you. Because if the sense of your world had been lost, then the mountains of skulls piled in the ossuaries of your temples would have had no sense either, and your altar stones would have become no more than butchers' slabs stained with the blood of innocent human beings!

MONTEZUMA: Now look with the same eyes on your own carnage, white man.

6. Bernal Díaz del Castillo, The Conquest of New Spain

Many Spanish *conquistadores* came to the Americas seeking gold, god and glory. One of Cortés' soldiers, Bernal Díaz del Castillo (1492-1580), was caught up in the rush for riches and fame in the New World but is remembered today for his exquisite narrative relating the last days of the Aztec Empire. After the conquest of the Aztecs (or of New Spain, as the Spanish called the region), Bernal Díaz retired quietly to his estates in Guatemala, where he died a poor man. Shortly after his seventieth birthday, having read some poorly written historical accounts of the conquest of Montezuma, the old soldier decided to write his own version which he entitled the *Verdadera historia de la conquista de la Nueva España*, or the *True History of the Conquest of New Spain*.

In describing his adventures with the troops of Cortés, Bernal Díaz paints in great detail the battles, cities, and peoples encountered on the long road to Tenochtitlán. More importantly, Bernal Díaz the historian was conscious of the fact that he took part in one of the great events of world history: the conquering of an empire by a few hundred of his fellow soldiers under the leadership of a daring leader. Bernal Díaz too as an old man realizes the great loss of a significant civilization that the Spaniards saw upon arriving in Aztec lands. He writes, "But today all that I then saw is overthrown and destroyed; nothing is left standing." In the following paragraphs, Bernal Díaz speaks to us of Cortés' grand entrance into Tenochtitlán and the first encounter of Montezuma with the Spanish leader. Bernal Díaz here also relates the importance of one of Montezuma's subjects, Doña Marina (also known as La Malinche), who acted as Cortés' translator and was instrumental in the success of the Spaniards.

THE ENTRANCE INTO MEXICO

Early next day we left Iztapalapa with a large escort of these great *Caciques*, and followed the causeway, which is eight yards wide and goes so straight to the city of Mexico that I do not think it curves at all. Wide though it was, it was so crowded with people that there was hardly room for them all. Some were going to Mexico and others coming away, besides those who had come out to see us, and we could hardly get through the crowds that were there. For the towers and the cues were full, and they came in canoes from all parts of the lake. No wonder, since they had never seen horses or men like us before!

With such wonderful sights to gaze on we did not know what to say, or if this was real that we saw before our eyes. On the land side there were great cities, and on the lake many more. The lake was crowded with canoes. At intervals along the causeway there were many bridges, and before us was the great city of Mexico. As for us, we were scarcely four hundred strong, and we well remembered the words and warnings of the people of Huexotzinco and Tlascala and Tlamanalco, and the many other warnings we had received to beware of entering the city of Mexico, since they would kill us as soon as they had us inside. Let the interested reader consider whether there is not much to ponder in this narrative of mine. What men in all the world have shown such daring? But let us go on.

We marched along our causeway to a point where another small causeway branches off to another city called Coyoacan, and there, beside some towerlike buildings, which were their shrines, we were met by many more *Caciques* and dignitaries in very rich cloaks. The different chieftains wore different brilliant liveries, and the causeways were full of them. Montezuma had sent these great *Caciques* in advance to receive us, and as soon as they came before Cortés they told him in their language that we were welcome, and as a sign of peace they touched the ground with their hands and kissed it.

There we halted for some time while Cacamatzin, the lord of Texcoco, and the lords of Iztapalapa, Tacuba, and Coyoacan went ahead to meet the great Montezuma, who approached in a rich litter, accompanied by other great lords and feudal *Caciques* who owned vassals. When we came near to Mexico, at a place where there were some other small towers, the great Montezuma descended from his litter, and these other great *Caciques* supported him beneath a marvellously rich canopy of green feathers, decorated with gold work, silver, pearls, and *chalchihuites*, which hung from a sort of border. It was a marvelous sight. The great Montezuma was magnificently clad, in their fashion, and wore sandals of a kind for which their name is *cotaras*,[1] the soles of which are of gold and the upper parts ornamented with precious stones. And the four lords who supported him were richly clad also in garments that seem to have been kept ready for them on the road so that they could accompany their master. For they had not worn clothes like this when they came out to receive us. There were four other great *Caciques* who carried the canopy above their heads, and many more lords who walked before the great Montezuma, sweeping the ground on which he was to tread, and laying down cloaks so that his feet should not touch the earth. Not one of these chieftains dared to look him in the face. All kept their eyes lowered most reverently except those four lords, his nephews, who were supporting him.

When Cortés saw, heard, and was told that the great Montezuma was approaching, he dismounted from his horse, and when he came near to Montezuma each bowed deeply to the other. Montezuma welcomed our Captain, and Cortés, speaking through Doña Marina, answered by wishing him very good health. Cortés, I think, offered Montezuma his right hand, but Montezuma refused it and extending his own. Then Cortés brought out a

---

1. Actually as a Cuban word; the Mexican word was *cactli*.

From THE CONQUEST OF NEW SPAIN by Bernal Díaz, translated by J. M. Cohen. Copyright © J. M. Cohen, 1963. Reproduced by permission of Penguin Books Ltd.

necklace which he had been holding. It was made of those elaborately worked and coloured glass beads called *margaritas*, of which I have spoken, and was strung on a gold cord and dipped in musk to give it a good odour. This he hung round the great Montezuma's neck, and as he did so attempted to embrace him. But the great princes who stood round Montezuma grasped Cortés' arm to prevent him, for they considered this an indignity.

Then Cortés told Montezuma that it rejoiced his heart to have seen such a great prince, and that he took his coming in person to receive him and the repeated favours he had done him as a high honour. After this Montezuma made him another complimentary speech, and ordered two of his nephews who were supporting him, the lords of Texcoco and Coyoacan, to go with us and show us our quarters. Montezuma returned to the city with the other two kinsmen of his escort, the lords of Cuitlahuac and Tacuba; and all those grand companies of *Caciques* and dignitaries who had come with him returned also in his train. And as they accompanied their lord we observed them marching with their eyes downcast so that they should not see him, and keeping close to the wall as they followed him with great reverence. Thus space was made for us to enter the streets of Mexico without being pressed by the crowds.

Who could now count the multitude of men, women, and boys in the streets, on the roof-tops and in canoes on the waterways, who had come out to see us? It was a wonderful sight and, as I write, it all comes before my eyes as if it had happened only yesterday.

They led us to our quarters, which were in some large houses capable of accommodating us all and had formerly belonged to the great Montezuma's father, who was called Axayacatl. Here Montezuma now kept the great shrines of his gods, and a secret chamber containing gold bars and jewels. This was the treasure he had inherited from his father, which he never touched. Perhaps their reason for lodging us here was that, since they called us *Teules* and considered us as such, they wished to have us near their idols. In any case they took us to this place, where there were many great halls, and a dais hung with the cloth of their country for our Captain, and matting beds with canopies over them for each of us.

On our arrival we entered the large court, where the great Montezuma was awaiting our Captain. Taking him by the hand, the prince led him to his apartment in the hall where he was to lodge, which was very richly furnished in their manner. Montezuma had ready for him a very rich necklace, made of golden crabs, a marvelous piece of work, which he hung round Cortés' neck. His captains were greatly astonished at this sign of honour.

After this ceremony, for which Cortés thanked him through our interpreters, Montezuma said: 'Malinche, you and your brothers are in your own house. Rest awhile.' He then returned to his palace, which was not far off.

We divided our lodgings by companies, and placed our artillery in a convenient spot. Then the order we were to keep was clearly explained to us, and we were warned to be very much on the alert, both the horsemen and the rest of the soldiers. We then ate a sumptuous dinner which they had prepared for us in their native style.

So, with luck on our side, we boldly entered the city of Tenochtitlan or Mexico on 8 November in the year of our Lord 1519.

Doña Marina's Story

Before speaking of the great Montezuma, and of the famous city of Mexico and the Mexicans, I should like to give an account of Doña Marina, who had been as a great lady and as a *Cacique* over towns and vassals since childhood.

Her father and mother were lords and *Caciques* of a town called Paynala, which had other towns subject to it, and lay about twenty-four miles from the town of Coatzacoalcos. Her father died while she was still very young, and her mother married another *Cacique*, a young man, to whom she bore a son. The mother and father seem to have been very fond of this son, for they agreed that he should succeed to the *Caciqueship* when they were dead. To avoid any impediment, they gave Doña Marina to some Indians from Xicalango, and this they did by night in order to be unobserved. They then spread the report that the child had died; and as the daughter of one of their Indian slaves happened to die at this time, they gave it out that this was their daughter the heiress.

The Indians of Xicalango gave the child to the people of Tabasco, and the Tabascans gave her to Cortés. I myself knew her mother and her half-brother, who was then a man and ruled the town jointly with his mother, since the old lady's second husband had died. After they became Christians, the mother was called Marta and the son Lazaro. All this I know very well, because in the year 1523, after the conquest of Mexico and the other provinces and at the time of Cristobal de Olid's revolt in Honduras, I passed through the place with Cortés, and the majority of its inhabitants accompanied him also. As Doña Marina had proved such an excellent person, and as a good interpreter in all the wars of New Spain, Tlascala,[2] and Mexico—as I shall relate hereafter—Cortés always took her with him. During this expedition she married as a gentleman called Juan Jaramillo at the town of Orizaba. Doña Marina was a person of great importance, and was obeyed without question by all the Indians of New Spain. And while Cortés was in the town of Coatzacoalcos, he summoned all the *Caciques* of that province in order to address them on the subject of our holy religion, and the good way in which they had been treated; and Doña Marina's mother and her half-brother Lazaro were among those who came. Doña Marina had told me some time before that she belonged to this province, and that she was the mistress of vassals, and both Cortés and the interpreter Aguilar knew it well. Thus it was that mother, son, and daughter came together, and it was easy enough to see from the strong resemblance between them that Doña Marina and the old lady were related. Both she and her son were very much afraid of Doña Marina; they feared that she had sent for them to put them to death, and they wept.

When Doña Marina saw her mother and half-brother in tears, she comforted them, saying that they need have no fear. She told her mother that when they had handed her over to the men from Xicalango, they had not known what they were doing. She pardoned the old woman, and gave them many golden jewels and some clothes. Then she sent them back to their town, saying that God had been very gracious to her in freeing her from the worship of idols and making her a Christian, and giving her a son by her lord and master Cortés, also in marrying her to such a gentleman as her husband Juan Jaramillo. Even if they were to make her mistress of all the provinces of New Spain, she said, she would refuse the honour, for she would rather serve her husband and Cortés than anything else in the world. What I have related here I know for certain and swear to. The whole story seems very much like that of Joseph and his brethren in Egypt, when the Egyptians came into power over the wheat.

To return to my subject, Doña Marina knew the language of Coatzacoalcos, which is that of Mexico, and she knew the Tabascan language also. This language is common to Tabasco and Yucatan, and Jeronimo de Aguilar spoke it also. These two understood one another well, and Aguilar translated into Castilian for Cortés.

This was the great beginning of our conquests, and thus, praise be to God, all things prospered with us. I have made a point of telling this story, because without Doña Marina we could not have understood the language of New Spain and Mexico.

---

2. The present spelling is Tlaxcala. The "x," as a in most Nahua words, is pronounced as 'sh'.

From THE CONQUEST OF NEW SPAIN by Bernal Díaz, translated by J. M. Cohen. Copyright © J. M. Cohen, 1963. Reproduced by permission of Penguin Books Ltd.

7. Bartolomé de Las Casas, A Brief Relation of the Destruction of the Indies

The Spanish conquest of the Americas, called *La conquista*, took an enormous toll on the peoples of the New World. For example, Carlos Fuentes reports that of the 25 million inhabitants of central Mexico in 1519, only 2 million remained by 1605. Many indigenous peoples died from diseases transmitted by the Europeans, but many also died of murder, forced labor, sexual abuse, and other excesses of the new Spanish masters. One Spanish voice stands out at that time and today as one which protested against the cruel treatment of the Indians—that of Bartolomé de Las Casas (1475-1566).

Born in Sevilla, Las Casas arrived in Cuba in 1511 as an adventurer but later changed his vocation: he was the first Catholic priest ordained in the New World. Las Casas soon noted how the indigenous peoples were suffering, and defended Indian rights before Isabella and Ferdinand. The priest also offered solutions to the problem: allow the Indians to inhabit unpopulated islands, bring in African slaves to replace them. Las Casas soon abandoned this last suggestion, as he realized that slaves were treated in the same cruel manner as the Indians.

Las Casas collected his thoughts on the defense of the Indians in his 1542 text, *Brevísima relación de la destrucción de las Indias Occidentales* (*A Brief Relation of the Destruction of the Indies*). In this book, Las Casas details numerous examples of Spanish cruelty towards the peoples of the Americas. The narrative became an immediate best seller and was translated in other European languages. Las Casas' criticism of Spanish colonial conduct became known as the "Black Legend" (la leyenda negra), which other European powers employed to censure Spanish imperialism in the New World. In the following paragraphs, Las Casas speaks to us from a 1625 English translation, relating how the Spanish victimized the Indians of Cuba during the conquest of this island.

The Spaniards with their Horses, their Speares and Lances, began to commit murders, and strange cruelties: they entered into Townes, Borowes, and Villages, sparing neither children nor old men, neither women with childe, neither them that lay in, but that they ripped their bellies, and cut them in peeces, as if they had beene opening of Lambes shut up in their fold. They laid wagers with such as with one thrust of a sword would paunch or bowell a man in the middest, or with one blow of a sword would most readily and most deliverly cut off his head, or that would best pierce his entrals at one stroake. They tooke the little soules by the heeles, ramping them from the mothers dugges, and crushed their heads against the cliffs. Others they cast into the Rivers laughing and mocking, and when they tumbled into the water, they said, now shift for thy selfe such a ones corpes. They put others, together with their mothers, and all that they met, to the edge of the sword. They made certaine Gibbets long and low, in such son, that the feete of the hanged on, touched in a manner the ground, every one enough for thirteene, in honour and worship of our Saviour and his twelve Apostles (as they used to speake) and setting to fire, burned them all quicke that were fastened. Unto all others, whom they used to take and reserve alive, cutting off their two hands as neere as might be, and so letting them hang, they said; Get you with these Letters, to carry tydings to those which are fled by the Mountaines. They murdered commonly the Lords and Nobility on this fashion: They made certaine grates of pearches laid on pickforkes, and made a little fire underneath, to the intent, that by little and little yelling and despairing in these torments, they might give up the Ghost.

One time I saw foure or five of the principall Lords roasted and broyled upon these gredirons. Also I thinke that there were two or three of these gredirons, garnished with the like furniture, and for that they cryed out pittiously, which thing troubled the Captaine that he could not then sleepe: he commanded to strangle them. The Sergeant, which was worse than the Hangman that burned them (I know his name and friends in Sivil) would not have them strangled, but himselfe putting Bullets in their mouthes, to the end that they should not cry, put to the fire, untill they were softly roasted after his desire. I have scene all the aforesaid things and others infinite. And forasmuch as all the people which could flee, hid themselves in the Mountaines, and mounted on the tops of them, fled from the men so without all manhood, emptie of all pitie, behaving them as savage beasts, the slaughterers and deadly enemies of mankinde: they taught their Hounds, fierce Dogs, to teare them in peeces at the first view, and in the space that one may say a Credo, assailed and devoured an Indian as if it had beene a Swine. These Dogges wrought great destructions and slaughters. And forasmuch as sometimes, although seldome, when the Indians put to death some Spaniards upon good right and Law of due Justice: they made a Lawe betweene them, that for one Spaniard they had to slay an hundred Indians . . .

One time the Indians came to meete us, and to receive us with victuals, and delicate cheere, and with all entertainment ten leagues off a great Citie, and being come at the place, they presented us with a great quantity of fish, and of bread, and other meate, together with all that they could doe for us to the uttermost. See incontinent the Divell, which put himselfe into the Spaniards, to put them all to the edge of the sword in my presence, without any cause whatsoever, more than three thousand soules, which were set before us, men, women, and children. I saw there so great cruelties, that never any man living either have or shall see the like.

Another time, but a few dayes after the premisses, I sent messengers unto all the Lords of the Province of Havana, assuring them, that they should not neede to feare (for they had heard of my credit) and that without withdrawing themselves, they should come to receive us, and that there should be done unto them no displeasure: for all the Countrie was afraid, by reason of the mischiefes and murderings passed, and this did I by the advice of the Captaine himselfe. After that we were come into the Province, one and twenty Lords and Caciques came to receive us, whom the Captaine apprehended incontinently, breaking the safe conduct which I had made them, and intending the day next following to burne them alive, saying that it was expedient so to doe, for that otherwise those Lords one day, would doe us a shrewd turne. I found my selfe in a great deale of trouble to save them from the fire; howbeit in the end they escaped.

After that the Indians of this lland [Cuba] were thus brought into bondage and calamitie, like unto those of the Ile of Hispaniola, and that they saw that they died and perished all without remedy: some of them began to flye into the Mountaines, others quite desperate hanged themselves, and there hung together husbands with their wives, hanging with them their little children. And through the crueltie of one only Spaniard, which was a great tyrant, and one whom I know, there hung themselves more then two hundred Indians: and in this fashion died an infinite of people.

There was in this Ile an officer of the Kings, to whom they gave for his share three hundred Indians, of whom at the end of three moneths there died by him in the travell of the Mines, two hundred and sixty: in such sort, that there remained now but thirty, which was the tenth part. Afterwards they gave him as many more, and more, and those also hee made havocke of in like manner, and still as many as they gave him, so many he slew, until he died himselfe, and that the Divell carried him away.

In three or foure moneths (my selfe being present) there died more then sixe thousand children, by reason that they had plucked away from them their fathers and mothers, which they sent into the Mines.

8. Carlos Fuentes, "The Birth of the Hispano-Indian Civilizations of the New World"

How should we approach the year 1492? It remains one of the most significant dates in world history, when two cultures—the European and the Indian—clash, resulting eventually in the death of millions of indigenous inhabitants of the Americas and the eventual introduction of black slavery. Yet from this confluence of two cultures is born an entirely new civilization epitomized in the *mestizo*, or the offspring of a Spanish father and Indian mother.

Many Latinos may view the date of 1492 with misgivings, recognizing the suffering that took place but at the same time acknowledging that their culture inherits characteristics from both sides of the Atlantic Ocean. In the following article, Mexican writer Carlos Fuentes attempts to bring the events of the year 1492 into perspective. Author of more than a dozen novels, including *The Old Gringo* and *Terra Nostra*, Fuentes is eminently qualified to objectively evaluate the consequences of arrival of Columbus to the Americas. Written specifically to reflect upon the importance of the five hundredth anniversary of 1492 in 1992 (the Quincentennial), "The Birth of the Hispano-Indian Civilizations of the New World" breaks new ground in that it seeks to balance the tragedy of *la conquista* with the hope and expectations for a new generation of Latin Americans, and by extension, Latinos in the United States.

THE BIRTH OF THE HISPANO-INDIAN CIVILIZATIONS OF THE NEW WORLD

The year 1492 expanded and unified the planet. The navigational feat of Christopher Columbus is unparalleled. He put his wager on a scientific hypothesis and won. Since the Earth is round, you can reach the East by sailing west.

But Columbus was wrong in his geography. He thought that he had arrived in the fabled lands of Cipango (Japan) and Cathay (China). Finding a domain empty of the Asian treasures he had hoped for, he invented and reported back to Spain the discovery of great wealth in forests, pearls and gold. Otherwise, his patroness, Queen Isabel, might have thought her investment (and her faith) in the highly inventive Genoese sailor had been misplaced. In effect, Columbus was the founder of that subgenre of literature called Latin American Magical Realism.

Numbers can deceive, but evidence tells us that the people whom Columbus found in the Caribbean had totally disappeared 50 years later. Two historians of the colonial experience in Latin America, Barbara and Stanley Stein, estimate the population of central Mexico at 25 million when the conquest began in 1519. In 1605, the population was 2 million. In the central Andes, a population of 6 million in 1525 had sunk to 1.5 million in 1561.

The reasons for this demographic catastrophe were complex, cumulative and brutal: European diseases, immunological breakdowns, forced labor but also culture shock and sheer anguish. But numbers are not the most important fact about the European conquest of America. The violent deaths with which the Europeans—Spanish, Portuguese, English, French, Dutch—implanted their power in the New World is but the statistical index of far larger occurrence, the irreparable death of great civilizations that possessed education systems, a separate moral and artistic universe, and forms of human relationship in constantly evolving creativity.

But did the conquest truly destroy the Indian cultures forever? In one sense, we must answer yes. We shall never know how the Indian civilizations would have evolved without foreign interference. An interrupted destiny is never as a just destiny. But if the fate of pre-Columbian America was to lose its autonomous evolution, it is also true that the very brutality of the conquest manifested the Indian capacity to survive in spite of the most violent challenges.

For the Indian culture of the Americas, if it did not prevail, did not perish, either. Rather it became a part of what one might term the counterconquest, that is, the Indian response to the purely European presence in the Americas. And Spain herself, far from being a "pure" Catholic nation, as the monarchs Ferdinand and Isabel dogmatically desired, was a crossroads country, a land of many migrants, crisscrossed and shaped by Iberians and Celts, Phoenicians, Greeks and Romans, Goths, Arabs and Jews.

The conquest of America continues to be the pause of our historical memory, the origin of our intense self-consciousness and of the painful brotherhood between the death of the Indian civilizations of the Americas and the birth of the Hispano-Indian civilizations of the New World. External witnesses to our own creation, we the descendants of Indians and Spaniards in the Americas know that the conquest was a cruel, criminal, bloody event. It was a catastrophic event. But it was not a sterile event.

From the catastrophe of the conquest, all of us, the *Indoiberoamericans*, were born. We were immediately mestizos—men and women of both Indian and European blood. Spanish America did not suffer the sexual hostility of Anglo America. The vast majority of us speak Spanish. And whether we believe, we created ourselves inside the culture of Catholicism—but of a Catholicism bathed in

"The Birth of the Hispano-Indian Civilizations of the New World" by Carlos Fuentes, copyright © 1992 by Carlos Fuentes. Originally appeared in the *Los Angeles Times*, October 11, 1992. Reprinted by permission of Brandt & Brandt Literary Agents, Inc.

syncretism and unexplainable without its Indian and, later, black African masks.

On these realities, we built a new civilization, whose hubs were our great cities, a necklace of true Indo-Afro-European cities of the Spanish-speaking Americas, from Los Angeles to Buenos Aires, from Havana to Lima. No one, ever, built so much, with as much energy as Spanish America. Cities with printing presses, universities, painters and pests a century before any of this came into being in Anglo America. Indian, black, mestizo and mulatto forever left their imprint on the churches, the civil architecture, the arts and crafts of our continent.

But also cities built on injustice. And it is in response to the questions of justice that Spain played a most singular role in the history of the colonizations of the New World. Spain, the most extensive empire the world had known, was the only empire of its time, and the first in history, to debate with itself on the nature and mistakes of its colonial policies.

Only Spain did it, not the other colonial powers, whose crimes of enslavement and extermination were compatible to those of Spain, but without the doubt, the debate, the discourse that permitted Spain to enshrine and defend, as much as possible yet never enough, the rights of the Indian peoples of the Americas.

Out of this debate of Spain with herself, three facts emerged. First, from this debate was born the modern concept of international law, based on the universality of human rights, which the great Spanish intellectual of the 16th Century, Francisco Suarez, explained by placing the origin of all authority in the people. For this reason, he said, no people can be legitimately subjected to conquest by others. This is as valid today.

Insufficient as it was, Spain's protection of the vast agrarian hinterland of Indoiberiamerica was far greater than that accorded the Indians by the independent republican governments after 1821. The newly minted Spanish American republics identified economic liberalism with progress and agrarian culture, including Indian culture, with barbarism. This rationalization permitted our republican governments to strip the agrarian communities of their aboriginal and even colonial rights. This was the reason for the modern agrarian insurrections that, like Emilliano Zapata's in Mexico, did nothing but reclaim rights granted the rural townships by the Spanish crown.

The third fact is that, in 1992, the conquest is not over and we, the modern Latin Americans, have behaved with as much cruelty or indifference, toward the Indians as a Columbus or Pizarro, and certainly with less compassion that Bartolomé de Las Casas or Francisco de Vitoria. In this, as in most matters, our reflection about 1992 should address itself to the future rather than to the past.

We must decide whether we are able to respect the values of Indian culture: the sense of the community and of the sacred, the care of nature, the concern for memory and death, the atavistic wisdom, the ritual intensity, the presence of mystery and the capacity of self-government, thus making them, as far as we can, our own; thus admitting the value of the other who lives in our midst.

Finally, 1992 permits us in Latin America to clearly understand that during the past 500 years we have created as a continuous, fluid, strong, and vibrant culture—Indian, black, European, above all, mestizo. Let us not celebrate the quincentennial too much. But let us not deplore too much, either. Let us not see our past only as a protracted crime, or only as a civilizing epic; only as feat or only as defeat. We are what we are because we made the culture that unites us. But we have failed in translating the values of our continuous culture to the fragmented politics and the failed economics of our hemisphere.

Can we hope, as a new century and a new millennium begins, to animate the plurality of our cultures so that they reflect their values in our political and economic institutions, giving them vigor, substance and a greater sense of justice? Indeed we can. If only we realize that we have a good culture because we made it ourselves, and a bad politics and economics because, perhaps, they were made for us. The next 500 years begin today. Their protagonist must no longer be the centralized institutions of the past—church, army, state—but the emerging civil societies of Latin America. They are, after all, both the creators and the bearers of the culture.

Carlos Fuentes is the author of "The Buried Mirror: Reflections on Spain and the New World" (Houghton Mifflin).

9. Sor Juana Inés de la Cruz, "Verses Against the Injustice of Men's Comments about Women"

The colonial period of Latin America, lasting almost three hundred years, was one in which the Viceroy, the Catholic Church, and the armed forces of Spain insured a stable society in which social and political change came very slowly. Yet cultural voices in the New World would now gradually be heard that eventually would compete with the European civilization of Spain. Probably the most important figure in the entire colonial period was Juana de Asbaje y Ramírez, known as Sor ("Sister") Juana Inés de la Cruz (1651-1695).

Sor Juana is the first Latin American poet of significance as well as the region's first person to openly defend the rights of women. Illegitimate and poor, the young Juana was indeed a child prodigy: she could read and write at the age of three, and at seventeen she was invited to the court of the Viceroy to discuss intellectual concerns with the leading professors of the day. Rejecting marriage, Juana chose the only other option open to women of her day—the convent. There, in the Order of St. Jermome, she moved her library of 4,000 volumes, musical and scientific instruments, and writing materials to continue her scholarly work. Throughout her life, Sor Juana published plays, poetry, philosophical treatises, and essays; she even wrote love letters upon consignment for members of the Viceroy's court.

The end of her life came after almost 27 years in the convent; she died of an epidemic that swept through Mexico City in 1695. Shortly before her death, under pressure from ecclesiastic leaders who disapproved of a nun who was intellectually active and who criticized men's tyranny over women, Sor Juana sold her library and instruments and dedicated all her time to the serving of the poor. One of her most famous poems that deals with the defense of women is included here: "Contra las injusticias de los hombres al hablar de las mujeres" ("Verses Against the Injustice of Men's Comments about Women"). In this key example of Sor Juana's verse, the poet stresses the double standard of men who expect women's conduct to radically change after marriage.

VERSES AGAINST THE INJUSTICE OF MEN'S COMMENTS ABOUT WOMEN
SOR JUANA INÉS DE LA CRUZ

You foolish men, who do accuse
women without good reason,
without seeing that you are the cause
for exactly what you blame

If you anxiously desire
to break down their resistance,
why do you require that they be good
if you really want them to be bad?

You conquer their resistance
and then, quite seriously,
you say that their licentiousness
made them fall, not your persistence.

The boldness of your foolish attitude
seems to resemble
the child who creates a bogeyman
and then is afraid of him.

You appear to desire, with foolish presumption,
a woman whom you are seeking that
before marriage is a Thais
and after marriage is a Lucretia.

What kind of behavior could be stranger
than that of one who, through lack of good advice,
soils a mirror
and then regrets that it is not clear?

With both favor and scorn,
it's all the same to you—
complaining about women who treat you bad
mocking them if they treat you well.

No good opinion can win you over,
since even the most virtuous lady
if she does not surrender to you is ungrateful,
and if she falls, is a whore.

You always act foolishly,
and with inconsistent judgement,
one you blame for cruelty,
and the other for being too loose.

So how is it that a woman should behave

who would desire your love,
if by being ungrateful she offends,
and by being willing you scorn her?

Thus, between anger and pain,
where your pleasure lies,
blessed be the lady who doesn't love you;
go ahead, complain all you like!

You give the freedom of wings
to the passion of your lover,
and after you have driven her to evil,
you wish her to immediately live virtuously.

In an uncontrolled passion,
who bears the greater blame?
The one that falls after being pursued,
or the one doing the chasing?

Or, which one is to be blamed,
although both might be guilty?
the one who sins for the payment,
or the one who pays for the sin?

So, why are you so surprised
at the crime that you commit?
Either love women as you have made them,
or make them to be loved.

Stop all your ruthless pursuing,
and with more reason,
you will then see the love
of the one who just might woo you.

I strongly affirm
that your arrogance is well armed,
for through promises and requests,
you enlist the help of the devil, the flesh, and the world.

10. Gertrudis Gómez de Avellaneda, Sab

As mentioned in the introduction to this book, *Latino* implies not only the cultural contributions of Spain and the Americas, but also of Africa. A document from the year 1518 discusses for the first time the importation of black slaves to the New World; 1873 marks the last time slaves arrived in the Americas (Cuba). Throughout 350 years, over 9.5 million black slaves came across the Atlantic Ocean, principally from western Africa (the area from Senegal to Angola). In the Spanish-speaking world, blacks were settled in the Caribbean area (especially Cuba, the Island of Hispaniola, Puerto Rico), and the coastal areas of Mexico, Central America, and northern South America.

In these regions, slaves were utilized in the production of sugar, coffee, tobacco, cotton, rice, and mining operations. With the blacks came their culture, which intermingled with the European and indigenous civilizations, including language, music, religion, dance, and art. Today, for example, the "Latin rhythm" of the mambo, merengue, and danzón and other related music are heavily based on African roots.

Not all Latin Americans of the colonial period accepted slavery. Among those who opposed the institution was Gertrudis Gómez de Avellaneda, a Cuban novelist (born 1814 in Puerto Príncipe) and died in Madrid (1873). Her novel *Sab* (1841) was published eleven years before the North American author Harriet Beecher Stowe's anti-slavery novel *Uncle Tom's Cabin*.

Sab takes place in Cuba and focuses on the injustice and cruelty of the slave system. Once published, *Sab* was officially banned in Cuba (the Spanish authorities feared any publication that might disrupt the earnings of the prosperous sugar plantations, which relied on black labor); Gómez de Avellaneda's relatives even tried to buy up many copies of the book to avoid a family scandal. The novel centers on a triangle of characters: Sab, the slave protagonist of mixed ethnicity (his mother was black and his father white); Carlota, whom Sab loves, the daughter of a wealthy land owner; and Carlota's fiancé, Enrique, son of an insolvent English merchant. The first chapter of *Sab* is presented here. In these paragraphs, we see the arrival of Enrique to the lands of his future wife, Carlota, and the young man's encounter with Sab. Sab speaks of his mother's past in Africa as well as the harsh treatment of his black brothers and sisters in Cuba.

CHAPTER ONE

Who are you? What is your homeland?
The tyrannical influences
of my guiding star turned me
into a monster of such rare lineage
in the endowments of my soul,
I am also the scorn of the world.

—Canizares

Twenty years ago, or thereabouts, late on a June afternoon a young man of handsome bearing journeyed on horseback through the picturesque country watered by the Tínima River and in leisurely fashion guided his spirited sorrel along the path known in these parts as the Cubitas Road, leading as it did to the villages of this name, which were also known as the red lands. The young man in question was four leagues from Cubitas, from whence he appeared to have come, and three from the city of Puerto Príncipe, at that time the capital of the central province of Cuba, though only a few years earlier it had been but a humble township.

Perhaps because of his scant knowledge of the road, perhaps because of the pleasure he took in appraising the landscape before him, the traveler gradually slackened his pace and from time to time reined in his horse as through to scrutinize the places through which he passed. Quite possibly his repeated stops had as their sole object the fuller savoring of the richly fertile earth of that privileged country, which most likely attracted him all the more if—as his fair, rosy skin, blue eyes, and golden hair seemed to indicate—he had been born in some northern region.

The brutal sun of the torrid zone was sinking into dusk among undulating clouds of purple and silver, and its last rays, already feeble and pale, bathed the virgin fields of that youthful nature in melancholy hues. It was a landscape whose vigorous and luxuriant vegetation seemed eagerly to welcome the afternoon's balmy breezes which began to flutter through the leafy crowns of the trees, parched by the day's heat. Flocks of swallows crossed and recrossed in all directions in search of their night's refuge; the green parrot, banded with gold and scarlet, the crow, distinctly black and lustrous, the royal woodpecker, of iron tongue and muted plumage, the blithe macaw, the swift *tomeguín*, the iridescent butterfly, and a whole host of native birds alighted in the branches of tamarind and aromatic mango trees, ruffling their variegated feathers as though to imprison therein the comforting breath of the gentle breeze.

After having crossed immense savannas where the eye encounters but the dual horizon of earth and sky, and pasturelands crowned by palms and gigantic ceiba trees, the traveler at last reached a fence, which indicated that this was someone's property. And indeed one could discern in the distance the white façade of a farmhouse, toward which the young man immediately directed his mount. But suddenly he reined in his horse and pulled him over to the side of the road, apparently intending to wait for a country fellow who was approaching with measured step, singing a folk tune whose last verse the traveler's ear was able to catch perfectly:

A dark woman is my torment
Have pity on me—
For she whom my heart adores
Has none at all for me.

When the man was but three paces from the stranger, noting that the latter was waiting expectantly, he stopped, and both men regarded each other for a moment before speaking. Perhaps the uncommonly handsome appearance of the traveler caused the local man to hesitate, while in turn the eyes of the former were just as strongly drawn to the latter.

The newcomer was a tall young man of average build but with striking features. He did not appear to be a white *criollo*; neither was he black nor could one take him for a descendant of the indigenous inhabitants of the Antilles. His face was a singular composite which revealed the mingling of two

From SAB AND AUTOBIOGRAPHY by Gertrudis Gómez de Avellaneda y Arteaga, translated and edited by Nina M. Scott, Copyright © 1993. By permission of the University of Texas Press.

distinct races, an amalgam, it could be said, of the features of the African and the European yet without being a perfect mulatto.

His coloring was of a yellowish white with a certain dark undertone; his broad forehead was half-hidden under irregular locks of hair as lustrous and black as the wings of the raven; his nose was aquiline, but his thick, purplish lips revealed his African heritage. His chin was triangular and somewhat prominent, his slanted eyes large and black under straight eyebrows; in them shone the fire of early youth, despite the slight lines that etched his face. The sum of these traits formed a face of distinctive features, one of those countenances which instantly attracts the gaze of others and which, once seen, is never forgotten.

The man's clothing was in no way different from that which is generally worn by farmers in the province of Puerto Príncipe and consisted of trousers of cotton ticking with wide blue stripes and a linen shirt, also striped, secured around the waist by a belt from which hung a wide machete, his head covered by floppy hat woven of *yarey* leaves—quite informal clothing, but comfortable and indispensable in a scorching climate.

The stranger broke the silence and, speaking in a Spanish so pure and fluent that it seemed to belie his northern physiognomy, said to the farmer, "My good friend, would you be so kind as to tell me if the house that can be discerned from here is that of Bellavista plantation, belonging to Don Carlos de B———?"

The farmer bowed and answered, "Yes, sir, all the land you see down there belongs to Don Carlos."

"Undoubtedly you are this gentleman's neighbor and can tell me if he and his family have arrived at the plantation."

"They have been there since this morning, and I can be your guide should you wish to visit them."

The stranger showed by a nod of his head that he accepted the offer, and without awaiting a further response the farmer turned as though to take him to the house, which was now quite close. But perhaps the stranger did not wish to arrive quite so soon, for slowing his horse to a walk, he resumed his conversation with his guide, all the while casting curious glances around him.

"Did you say that Señor de B——— owns all of this land?"

"Yes, sir."

"It appears to be very fertile."

"Indeed it is."

"This plantation must bring its owner a good income."

"As far as I know there have been times," said the young man, stopping to glance at the land under discussion, "when this plantation produced for its owner some three hundred thousand pounds of sugar every year, because then more than a hundred blacks worked in the cane fields. But times have changed, and since the present owner of Bellavista has only fifty blacks, his production does not exceed six thousand loaves of sugar."

"The slaves on these plantations must have a very hard life," observed the stranger, "and I am not surprised that their number has been so considerably reduced."

"It is truly a terrible life," said the farmer, casting a sympathetic glance at his questioner. "Under this fiery sky, the nearly naked slave works all morning without rest, and at the terrible hour of midday, panting, crushed under the weight of the wood and the sugarcane he bears on his shoulders, scorched by the rays of the sun that burn his skin, the unhappy soul at last gets a taste of all the pleasures which life holds for him: two hours of sleep and a frugal meal. When night comes with its breezes and shadows to console the scorched land and all nature rests, the slave with his sweat and tears waters the place where neither the night has shadows nor the breeze freshness, because there the heat of firewood has replaced that of the sun and the unhappy black walks endlessly around either the machine which extracts the cane's sweet juice or the cauldrons in which the fire's heat converts this juice into molasses; hour after hour he sees go by, and the sun's return finds him there still. . . . Ah, yes! The sight of this degraded humanity, where men become mere brutes, is a cruel spectacle. These are men whose brows are seared with the mark of slavery just as their souls are branded with the desperation of Hell."

The farmer suddenly halted, as though aware that he had said too much, and, lowering his eyes while permitting a melancholy smile to touch his lips, added hastily, "But the principal cause of Bellavista's decline is not the death of the slaves: many have been sold, as has some of the property, yet it is still a valuable enough plantation."

Having said this, he resumed walking toward the house but stopped after a few steps when he noted that the stranger was not following, and when he turned to look back at him, caught an expression of distinct surprise fixed on the stranger's features. In effect, the bearing of that farmer seemed to reveal something great and noble which attracted attention, and what the stranger had just heard, expressed in a language and with an eloquence which belied the class his dress appeared to denote, increased his admiration and curiosity.

The young farmer had approached our traveler's horse with the demeanor of a man who waits for a question he knows will be directed to him, and he was not mistaken, for the stranger, unable to quell his curiosity, said, "I gather that I have the pleasure of conversing with a distinguished landowner of these parts. I know that when they are out on their country estates, the *criollos* like to dress as simple laborers, and I would be sorry to remain ignorant any longer of the name of the person who has offered to guide me with such courtesy, If I am not mistaken, you are Don Carlos de B———'s friend and neighbor..."

Upon hearing these words the countenance of the one addressed showed not the slightest surprise but fixed the speaker with a penetrating glance; then, as though the mild and charming nature of the stranger's features had satisfied his inquiring gaze, he lowered his eyes and answered, "I am not a landowner, sir, and though within my breast beats a heart ever ready to sacrifice itself on Don Carlos's behalf, I am not in a position to call him my friend. I belong," he continued with a bitter smile, "to that unhappy race deprived of human rights...I am a mulatto and a slave."

"So you're a mulatto?" exclaimed the stranger, who, once he had heard the speaker's declaration, assumed the tone of disdainful familiarity used toward slaves. "Well, I suspected as much in the beginning, but you have a look so uncommon to your class that it caused me to think otherwise."

The slave continued to smile, but his smile became increasingly melancholy and, at that moment, held a hint of scorn as well.

"It can happen," he said, again fixing his eyes on the stranger, "that at times the soul is free and noble though the body be enslaved and base. But night is coming on and I will guide Your Grace to the plantation, which is now very near."

The mulatto's observation was correct. As though it had been torn violently from the beautiful Cuban sky, the sun had ceased shining on that land it loves so well, though the altars once erected to it have long since been destroyed. The pale and melancholy moon slowly rose to take possession of its dominions.

The stranger followed his guide without interrupting the conversation.

"So you're Don Carlos's slave?"

"I have the honor of being the *mayoral* of this plantation."

"What is your name?"

"I was christened Bernabé, but my mother always called me Sab, and that is what my masters have called me as well."

"Was your mother black or a mulatto like you?"

"My mother came into the world in a country where her color was not a mark of slavery. My mother," he repeated with a certain pride, "was born free and a princess. This was well known among all those who, like herself, were brought here from the coasts of the Congo by the dealers in human flesh. But although a princess in her own country, here she was sold as a slave."

The gentleman smiled indulgently when he heard Sab bestow the title of princess on his mother, but as the conversation appeared to interest him, he wished to prolong it further.

"Your father must undoubtedly have been white."

"My father! I never knew him. My mother was only a child when she was sold to Don Felix de B——, the father of my present master and of four other children. For two years she wept inconsolably, unable to resign herself to the bitter turn her fate had taken. But once this time was over, a sudden change took place within her; my mother was once again able to embrace life because she had fallen in love. A deep and powerful passion was kindled in her African heart. In spite of her color my mother was beautiful, and undoubtedly her passion was reciprocated because about that time I came into the world. My father's name was a secret which she always refused to reveal to me."

"Your fate, Sab, seems less deserving of pity than that of the other slaves, as the position you hold at Bellavista proves the esteem and affection which your master feels for you."

"Yes; sir, I have never suffered the harsh treatment which is generally meted out to slaves, nor have I been condemned to long and arduous labor. I was only three years old when my protector Don Luis, the youngest of Don Felix de B———'s sons, died, but two hours before that excellent young man departed this world he had a long and secret talk with his brother Don Carlos and, as was revealed later, entrusted me to the latter's kindness. And so I found in my present master the same good and pious heart of the kind protector I had lost. A short while later he married a woman—an angel!— and took me with him. I was six when I began to rock Miss Carlota's cradle, the first child of that happy marriage. As she was an only child for a period of five years, I became the companion of her games and her studies; her innocent heart disregarded the distance that separated us, and she bestowed upon me the affection due a brother. At her side I learned to read and write, for she refused to be instructed if her poor mulatto Sab were not with her. Because of her I grew to love reading; her own books and even her father's have always been available to me and have been my solace, though they have often stirred up disturbing ideas and bitter reflections in my soul."

The slave stopped himself, unable to hide the deep emotion which, to his sorrow, his voice revealed. Swiftly regaining control, he brushed his hand across his forehead, shook his head slightly, and added more calmly, "By my own choice I became a coachman for a few years; later I wanted to work with the land, and I have been helping on this plantation for two years now."

The stranger had smiled maliciously ever since Sab had mentioned the secret discussion which the late Don Luis had had with his brother. When the mulatto stopped talking, he said, "Strange that you are not free, seeing how much Don Luis de B——— loved you. It only seems natural that his father should have given you your freedom, or that Don Carlos should have done so."

"My freedom! Freedom is doubtless very sweet . . . but I was born a slave, I was a slave from my mother's womb and so—"

"You are accustomed to slavery," interrupted the stranger, very pleased at having articulated what he thought the mulatto must be thinking.

The latter did not contradict him but smiled bitterly and, as though he derived pleasure from the words he slowly uttered, said in a low voice, "As a child I was signed over to Miss Carlota; I am her slave, and I wish to live and die in her service."

The stranger spurred his horse lightly, and Sab, who was walking ahead of them, had to quicken his pace as the handsome sorrel of Norman stock, on which his interlocutor rode, stepped out.

"That affection and your excellent feelings do you great honor, Sab, but Carlota de B——— is about to marry, and perhaps dependence on a master will not be as pleasing to you as dependence on your young lady."

The slave came to a sudden stop and turned his penetrating black eyes on the stranger, who continued, momentarily reining in his horse.

"As you are a servant who enjoys the confidence of his masters, you cannot fail to know that Carlota is engaged to marry Enrique Otway, only son of one of the richest merchants of Puerto Príncipe."

A moment of silence followed these words, during which time there was no doubt but that an incredible upheaval was taking place in the slave's soul. Vertical lines creased his brow, from his eyes shone a sinister brilliance, like the lightning bolt which flashes from among the dark clouds, and then, as though a sudden idea had dispelled his doubts, he exclaimed after an instant of reflection. "Enrique Otway! That name, along with your appearance indicate a foreign origin. Doubtless, then, you must be Señorita de B———'s future husband!"

"You are not deceived, young man; I am indeed Enrique Otway, Carlota's future husband, the same who will try not to have his union with your mistress be a misfortune for you. Just as she has done, I promise to make your sad lot as a slave less arduous. But here is the gate, I can manage without a guide now. Farewell, Sab, you may go your way."

Enrique spurred his horse, which, after passing through the gate, departed at a gallop. The slave looked after him until he saw him reach the door of the white house. He then fixed his eyes on the sky, gave a low moan, and let himself fall upon a grassy bank.

11. Nicolás Guillén, "Ballad of the Two Grandfathers" and "Two Kids"

While Gertrudis Gómez de Avellaneda was a major writer who addressed the lives of Latin American blacks in the nineteenth century, the poet Nicolás Guillén continued in the twentieth century to voice the concerns of many individuals whose roots could be found in Africa. Born in Cuba (1904), Guillén graduated from the Institute of Camaguey in 1920. He soon found that his true milieu was the literary life of Havana along with journalism, politics, and of course, poetry. He became a frequent member of *tertulias* (informal social gatherings) at many of the capital's waterfront cafes.

In one of his first collections of poetry, *Motivos de son* (*Motives of Sound*, 1930) Guillén established himself as one of Latin America's major voices for the region's blacks. In that work and subsequent writings, Guillén successfully mirrors the past history and present concerns of not only black Cubans but also those of mixed parentage (black and white). The two poems reproduced here are characteristic of Guillén's poetic voice. In "Ballad of the Two Grandfathers" (from *West Indies, Ltd.*, 1934), the narrator searches for harmony in a past marked by division of European and African (one grandfather is black and one grandfather is white). In the second poem, "Two Kids," two young boys—one black, one white, find solace in friendship that helps them endure poverty and abandonment.

BALLAD OF THE TWO GRANDFATHERS

Shadows that I alone can see
shadow two grandfathers following me.

A lance with a point of bone,
drum of skin and a hollow log,
my black grandfather.

White ruff on strong neck,
grey warrior's armor,
my white grandfather.

Bare feet, hard body,
that of my black grandfather.
Eyes of antarctic glass,
those of my white grandfather.

Africa of the humid forests
and the great songless drums.
I'm dying!
says my black grandfather.
Muddy water of alligators,
green mornings of palm trees.
I'm tired!
says my white grandfather.

Oh, sails in the bitter wind,
galleons of burning gold.
I'm dying!
says my black grandfather.
Oh, virgin shores undefiled,
deceived by beads of brass
I'm tired!
says my white grandfather.
Oh, solid sun of beaten glass
prisoner in the ring of the tropics!
Oh, round clean moon
above the monkey's dream.

So many ships, so many ships!
So many Negroes, so many Negroes!
What a vast glow of canefields!
What a whip has the slave trader.
Blood? Blood . . Tears? Tears.
Half-opened veins and half-opened eyes
and empty mornings
and sunsets at the sugarmill

Selections on pp. 141-143: From CUBA LIBRE, POEMS OF NICOLAS GUILLEN, translated by Frederic Carruthers and Langston Hughes, The Ward Ritchie Press, 1948.

and a great voice, a strong voice,
bursting the silence.
So many ships, so many ships!
So many Negroes!

Shadows I alone can see
Shadow two grandfathers following me.
Don Federico shouts at me,
but Taita Facundo says nothing.
At night they both walk
dreaming, dreaming.
In me they meet.

Federico! . . . Facundo!
They embrace. Both sigh.
Both throw back their strong heads.
Both the same size,
beneath the distant stars.
Both the same size
black longing and white longing,
both the same size,
they shout, they dream,
they cry, they sing.
They dream, they cry, they sing.
They cry, they sing.
They sing!

TWO KIDS

Two kids, twigs of the same tree of misery,
together in a doorway on a sultry night,
two beggar kids covered with pimples
eat from the same plate like starving dogs,
food cast up by the high tide of the tablecloths.
Two kids: one black, one white.

Their twin heads are alive with lice,
their bare heads are close together,
their mouths are tireless in the joint frenzy
        of their jaws,
and over the greasy sour food
two hands: one white, one black!

What a strong and sincere union!
They are linked by their bellies and the frowning night,
by melancholy afternoons on brillant paseos,
and by explosive mornings
when day awakens with alcoholic eyes.
They are united like two good dogs,
one black, one white.
When the time comes to march,
will they march like two good men,
one black, one white?

Two kids, twigs of the same tree of misery,
are in a doorway on a sultry night.

12. FRIDA KAHLO, "MOSES"

During most of her life in her native Mexico, Frida Kahlo (1907-1954) was overshadowed by her well-known husband, the muralist Diego Rivera; today, she is considered his equal by art critics as well as an adoring public. Two events frame Frida's life. As a young girl, she was seriously injured when her school bus was rammed by a street car (1925): her pelvis was broken, her spinal column was severed in three places, 2 ribs were broken, her right leg suffered eleven fractures, and her right foot was crushed. A metal bar that was a handrail entered her back and came out through her vagina (Frida later said that she lost her virginity in the accident). These injuries would haunt Frida throughout her life and eventually cause her early death. Yet, as the Spanish saying reminds us, "No hay mal que por el bien no venga" ("Every cloud has a silver lining"), Frida's near-death experience led her to painting. As she lay in bed, her father brought her brush and pallet to pass the time.

Frida later wrote, "I suffered two grave accidents: one, in which a streetcar knocked me down; the other accident was Diego." When Frida married the painter Diego Rivera in 1929, friends remarked that it was the marriage of "an elephant and a dove." He was 43 years old and over 300 pounds; she was 22 and half the size of her husband. Throughout her life, Frida loved Diego, but she did have to accept his philandering (Diego once seduced Frida's sister). Diego and Frida divorced in 1939 only to remarry a year later.

Diego always urged Frida to paint and create her own, original style. Frida's most noteworthy paintings are probably a collection of over 50 self-portraits which reflect the personal experience of her physical suffering caused by the streetcar accident as well as her problematic life with Diego. In the following speech by Frida (1945), she explains her style, techniques, and symbols employed in the painting *Moses*.

Moses

Since this is the first time in my life I have tried to explain one of my paintings to a group of more than three people, please forgive me if I get a little confused and if I'm very nervous.

About two years ago, José Domingo told me one day that he would like me to read Freud's "Moses" and to paint, however I wanted my interpretation of the book. This painting is the result of that conversation.

I read the book only once and started to do the painting with the first impression it had left on me. Yesterday, after I wrote these words for you, I reread it and I must confess that I find the painting very incomplete and very different from what should be the interpretation of what Freud analyzes so wonderfully in his "Moses." But now, unfortunately, I can't remove or add anything, so I will explain what I painted the way it is, as you can see here in the picture.

Of course, the central theme is Moses, or the birth of the Hero, but I generalized, in my own way (a very confused way), the facts and images that made the strongest impressions on me while reading the book. As far as I am concerned, you can tell me whether I blew it or not.

What I wanted to express more intensely and clearly was that the reason why people need to make up or imagine heroes and gods is pure fear . . . fear of life and fear of death.

I started painting the image of the infant Moses—Moses means "he who was taken out of the waters" in Hebrew, and "boy" in Egyptian. I painted him the way the legends describe him: abandoned inside a basket and floating down a river. From the artistic point of view, I tried to make the animal skin-covered basket look as much as possible like a uterus because, according to Freud, the basket is the exposed uterus and the water is the mother's water when she give birth to a child. To emphasize that fact, I painted the human fetus in its last phase inside the placenta.[1] The fallopian tubes, which resemble hands, spread out to the world.

On the sides of the newborn child, I placed the elements of his creation—the fertilized egg and the cellular division.

Freud analyzes in a very clear but—for my personality—complicated way, the important fact that Moses wasn't Jewish but Egyptian. But in the picture, I couldn't find a way to paint him as either, so I only painted him as a boy who generally represents Moses and all those who, according to the legend, had the same beginning and became important leaders to these people—in other words, heroes (smarter than the rest; that's why I drew the "warning eye" on him). In this case, we can find Sargon, Cyrus, Romulus, Paris, etc. The other very interesting conclusion that Freud makes is that Moses—not being Jewish—gave the people he chose to guide and save a religion that was not Jewish either, but Egyptian. [This religion was] precisely the one that Amenhotep IV or Ikhnaton revived; the religion of Aton, the sun, which has its roots in the very ancient religion of On (Heliopolis). That's why I painted the sun as the center of all religions, as the first god, and as creator and reproducer of life. This is the relationship between the three main figures in the center of this painting.

Like Moses, there have always been lots of "high-class" reformers of religions and human societies. It could be said that they are a kind of messenger between the people they manipulate and the gods they invent to be able to do it. Many gods of this type still exist, as you know. Naturally, I didn't have enough space for all of them, so I placed on both sides of the sun those who, like it or not, are directly related to the sun. On the right are the Western [gods] and on the left the Oriental ones.

The Assyrian winged bull, Amon, Zeus, Osiris, Horus, Jehovah, Apollo, the Moon, the Virgin Mary, the Divine Providence, the Christian Trinity, Venus, and . . . the Devil. To the left, thunder, lightning, and the thunder's print, that is, Huraka, Kukulkan,

---

1. Kahlo actually painted the baby beside the placenta.

"Moses" by Frida Kahlo, translated by Jorge Gonzalez Casanova, from CARTAS APASIONADAS: THE LETTERS OF FRIDA KAHLO, compiled by Marth Zamora. Copyright © 1995 by Chronicle Books. Reprinted by permission of Marquand Books, Inc.

and Gukamatz; Tlaloc, the magnificent Coatlicue (mother of all gods), Quetzalcoatl, Tezcatlipoca, Centeotl, the Chinese god (dragon), and the Hindu one, Brahma. An African god is missing; I couldn't fine one, but I could make some space for him. I can't tell you something about each one of the gods because of my overwhelming ignorance about their origin, importance, etc.

After painting the gods I had space for in their respective heavens, I wanted to divide the celestial world of imagination and poetry from the terrestrial world of fear of death. So I painted the human and animal skeletons that you can see here. The earth cups her hands to protect them. Between Death and the group where the heroes are there are no divisions, because heroes die too, and the generous earth picks them up without distinctions.

On the same earth, but with bigger heads in order to distinguish them from the heads of the crowd, I painted the heroes (very few of them, but well chosen), the religion reformers, the religion inventors or creators, the conquerors, and the rebels . . . that is, the "bucktoothed" [powerful] ones.

To the right—I should have made this figure look much more important than any other—you can see Amenhotep IV, who became Ikhnaton, a young pharaoh of the eighteenth dynasty (1370-1350 B.C.). He imposed on his subjects a religion contrary to their tradition, rebellious toward polytheism, strictly monotheistic with distant roots in the On cult (Heliopolis): the religion of Aton and the Mosaic, both monotheistic. I didn't know how to transfer this whole important section of the book to the plastic arts.

Next, we have Christ, Zoroaster, Alexander the Great, Caesar, Mohammed, Luther, Napoleon, and the lost child, Hitler.

To the left [we can see] the wonderful Nefertiti, Ikhnaton's wife. I suppose that, in addition to being extraordinarily beautiful, she must have been a *hacha perdida*[2] and a very intelligent collaborator with her husband. Buddha, Marx, Freud, Paracelsus, Epicurus, Genghis Khan, Gandhi, Lenin, and Stalin. The order is wrong, but I painted them according to my historic knowledge, which is also wrong. Between them and the run-of-the-mill crowd, I painted a sea of blood with which I represent war, inevitable and fecund.

And lastly, the powerful and never-sufficiently praised human mass composed of all kinds of . . . bugs: the warriors, the pacifists, the scientists, and the ignorant ones; the monument-makers, the rebels, the flag-carriers, the medal-bearers, the speakers, the crazy and the sane, the happy and the sad, the healthy and the ill, the poets and the fools, and all the rest of the people you'd like to have here in this fuc-bulous pile. Only the ones in the front are clearly seen; the rest, in the confusion, who knows?

On the left side, in the forefront, is man, the constructor of four colors (the four races). On the right side, the mother, the creator, with her child in her arms. Behind them, the monkey.

[Here we have] the two trees that form a triumphal arch, with the new life that always sprouts from the trunk of old age. In the middle, at the bottom, the thing most important to Freud and many others: love, represented by the shell and the conch, the two sexes wrapped up by eternally new and living roots.

This is all I can tell you about my painting, but I'll accept all kinds of questions and comments. I won't get mad. Thank you very much.

Frida Kahlo

---

2. Literally "lost axe." In Mexico, to be an "axe" at something means to be an ace or a wizard, that is, very capable

13. Octavio Paz, "Mexico and the United States" and "Mexican Masks"

Octavio Paz (born 1914) is one of Mexico's greatest living writers. His first calling was that of poetry, and since his youth he has written over twenty five books in this literary genre. He was granted the Nobel Prize for Literature in 1990. Paz is very familiar with American culture, having lived in Los Angeles (studying the *Pachucos*) as well as teaching at Harvard University and the University of Texas. Paz is perhaps most famous for his seminal work, *El Laberinto de la soledad* (*The Labyrinth of Solitude*, 1950), a poetic analysis of Mexican culture by one of the country's most probing minds. Anthony Day and Sergio Muñoz in a recent article on Paz sum up *The Labyrinth of Solitude* in this fashion:

> It (Labyrinth . . .) says that Mexicans live behind a mask of
> their own creation and are, in the end, always alone. It
> says that for Mexicans, there are two kinds of women: the
> Virgin of Guadalupe, the mother of all and the protector of
> the poor and helpless, and the temptress/whore, the
> Chingada. It says that for his countrymen there is one
> type of man, the macho, who must have his way. And it says
> that in myths and in fiestas, in art, in love, in poetry,
> in the theatre and in epics, there is, for the Mexican as
> for all people, if only briefly, the escape from loneliness.

In the following two selections, Paz focuses in on both U. S. and Mexican culture. In "Mexico and the United States," the essayist compares and contrasts the two neighboring cultures and proposes that the surface differences—power vs. weakness, development vs. underdevelopment, domination vs. dependence—are really not the most important distinctions between Anglo and Mexican civilization. The second essay, "Mexican Masks" (from *The Labyrinth of Solitude*), is perhaps the most famous statement ever written about Mexican character. Paz tells us that the stoic face typical of his land is but a mere cover for a wide range of inner emotions that may not be apparent to the casual observer.

Mexico and the United States

When I was in India, witnessing the never-ending quarrels between Hindus and Muslims, I asked myself more than once this question: What accident or misfortune of history caused two religions so obviously irreconcilable as Hinduism and Muhammadanism to coexist in the same society? The presence of the purest and most intransigent form of monotheism in the bosom of a civilization that has elaborated the most complex polytheism seemed to me a verification of the indifference with which history perpetrates its paradoxes. And yet I could hardly be surprised at the contradictory presence in India of Hinduism and Muhammadanism. How could I forget that I myself, as a Mexican, was (and am) part of a no less singular paradox—that of Mexico and the United States.

Our countries are neighbors, condemned to live alongside each other; they are separated, however, more by profound social, economic, and psychic differences than by physical and political frontiers. These differences are self-evident, and a superficial glance might reduce them to the well-known opposition between development and underdevelopment, wealth and poverty, power and weakness, domination and dependence. But the really fundamental difference is an invisible one, and in addition it is perhaps insuperable. To prove that it has nothing to do with economics or political power, we have only to imagine a Mexico suddenly turned into a prosperous, mighty country, a superpower like the United States. Far from disappearing, the difference would become more acute and more clear-cut. The reason is obvious: We are two distinct versions of Western civilization.

Ever since we Mexicans began to be aware of national identity—in about the middle of the eighteenth century—we have been interested in our northern neighbors. First with a mixture of curiosity and disdain; later on with an admiration and enthusiasm that were soon tinged with fear and envy. The idea the Mexican people have of the United States is contradictory, emotional, and impervious to criticism; it is a mythic image. The same can be said of the vision of our intellectuals and writers.

Something similar happens with Americans, be they writers or politicians, businessmen or only travellers. I am not forgetting the existence of a small number of remarkable studies by various American specialists, especially in the fields of archeology and ancient and modern Mexican history. The perceptions of the American novelists and poets who have written on Mexican themes have often been brilliant, but they have also been fragmentary. Moreover, as a critic who has devoted a book to this theme (Drewey Wayne Gunn: *American and British Writers in Mexico*) has said, they reveal less of the Mexican reality than of the authors' personalities. In general, Americans have not looked for Mexico in Mexico; they have looked for their obsessions, enthusiasms, phobias, hopes, interests —and these are what they have found. In short, the history of our relationship is the history of a mutual and stubborn deceit, usually involuntary though not always so.

Of course, the differences between Mexico and the United States are not imaginary projections but objective realities. Some are quantitative, and can be explained by the social, economic, and historical development of the two countries. The more permanent ones, though also the result of history, are not easily definable or measurable. I have pointed out that they belong to the realm of civilization, that fluid zone of imprecise contours in which are fused and confused ideas and beliefs, institutions and technologies, styles and morals, fashions and churches, the material culture and that evasive reality which we rather inaccurately call *le génie des peuples*. The reality to which we give the name of civilization does not allow of easy definition. It is each society's vision of the world and also its feelings about time; there are nations that are hurrying toward the future, and others whose eyes are fixed on the past. Civilization is a society's style, its way of living and dying. It embraces the erotic and the culinary arts; dancing and burial; courtesy and

From THE LABYRINTH OF SOLITUDE AND OTHER WRITINGS by Octavio Paz. "Mexico and the United States" translated by Rachel Phillips Belash, © 1985 by Grove Press, Inc. Used by permission of Grove/Atlantic, Inc.

curses; work and leisure; rituals and festivals; punishments and rewards; dealings with the dead and with the ghosts who people our dreams; attitudes toward women and children, old people and strangers, enemies and allies; eternity and the present; the here and now and the beyond. A civilization is not only a system of values but a world of forms and codes of behavior, rules and exceptions. It is society's visible side—institutions, monuments, works, things—but it is especially its submerged, invisible side; beliefs, desires, fears, repressions, dreams.

The points of the compass have served to locate us in history as well as in space. The East-West duality soon acquired a more symbolic than geographical significance, and became an emblem of the opposition between civilizations. The East-West opposition has always been considered basic and primordial; it alludes to the movement of the sun, and is therefore an image of the direction and meaning of our living and dying. The East-West relationship symbolizes two directions, two attitudes, two civilizations. The North-South duality refers more to the opposition between different ways of life and different sensibilities. The contrasts between North and South can be oppositions within the same civilization.

Clearly, the opposition between Mexico and the United States belongs to the North-South duality as much from the geographical as the symbolic point of view. It is an ancient opposition which was already unfolding in pre-Columbian America, so that it antedates the very existence of the United States and Mexico. The northern part of the continent was settled by nomadic, warrior nations; Mesoamerica, on the other hand, was the home of an agricultural civilization, with complex social and political institutions, dominated by warlike theocracies that invented refined and cruel rituals, great art, and vast cosmogonies inspired by a very original vision of time. The great opposition of pre-Columbian America—all that now includes the United States and Mexico—was between different ways of life: nomads and settled peoples, hunters and farmers. This division greatly influenced the later development of the United States and Mexico. The policies of the English and the Spanish toward the Indians were in large part determined by this division; it was not insignificant that the former established themselves in the territory of the nomads and the latter in that of the settled peoples.

The differences between the English and the Spaniards who founded New England and New Spain were no less decisive than those that sepa-rated the nomadic from the settled Indians. Again, it was an opposition within the same civilization. Just as the American Indians' world view and beliefs sprang from a common source, irrespective of their ways of life, so Spanish and English shared the same intellectual and technical culture. And the opposition between them, though of a different sort, was as deep as that dividing an Aztec from an Iroquois. And so the new opposition between English and Spaniards was grafted onto the old opposition between nomadic and settled peoples. The distinct and divergent attitudes of Spaniards and English have often been described before. All of them can be summed up in one fundamental difference, in which perhaps the dissimilar evolution of Mexico and the United States originated: in England the Reformation triumphed, whereas Spain was the champion of the Counter-Reformation.

As we all know, the reformist movement in England had political consequences that were decisive in the development of Anglo-Saxon democracy. In Spain, evolution went in the opposite direction. Once the resistance of the last Muslim was crushed, Spain achieved a precarious political—but not national—unity by means of dynastic alliances. At the same time, the monarchy suppressed regional autonomies and municipal freedoms, closing off the possibility of eventual evolution into a modern democracy. Lastly, Spain was deeply marked by Arab domination, and kept alive the notion of crusade and holy war, which it had inherited from Christian and Muslim alike. In Spain, the traits of the modern era, which was just beginning, and of the old society coexisted but never blended completely. The contrast with England could not be sharper. The history of Spain and her former colonies, from the sixteenth century onward, is the history of an ambiguous approach—attraction and repulsion—to the modern era.

The discovery and conquest of America are events that inaugurated modern world history, but Spain and Portugal carried them out with the sensibility and tenor of the Reconquest. Nothing more original occurred to Cortés' soldiers, amazed by the pyramids and temples of the Mayans and Aztecs, than to compare them with the mosques of Islam. Conquest and evangelization: these two words, deeply Spanish and Catholic, are also deeply Muslim. Conquest means not only the occupation of foreign territories and the subjugation of their inhabitants but also the conversion of the conquered. The conversion legitimized the conquest. This politico-religious philosophy was diametrically opposed to that of English colonizing; the idea of evangelization occupied a secondary place in England's colonial expansion.

The Christianity brought to Mexico by the Spaniards was the syncretic Catholicism of Rome, which had assimilated the pagan gods, turning them into saints and devils. The phenomenon was repeated in Mexico: the idols were baptized, and in popular Mexican Catholicism the old beliefs and divinities are still present, barely hidden under a veneer of Christianity. Not only the popular religion of Mexico but the Mexicans' entire life is steeped in Indian culture—the family, love, friendship, attitudes toward one's father and mother, popular legends, the forms of civility and life in common, the image of authority and political power, the vision of death and sex, work and festivity. Mexico is the most Spanish country in Latin America; at the same time it is the most Indian. Mesoamerican civilization died a violent death, but Mexico is Mexico thanks to the Indian presence. Though the language and religion, the political institutions and the culture of the country are Western, there is one aspect of Mexico that faces in another direction—the Indian direction. Mexico is a nation between two civilizations and two pasts.

In the United States, the Indian element does not appear. This, in my opinion, is the major difference between our two countries. The Indians who were not exterminated were corralled in "reservations." The Christian horror of "fallen nature" extended to the natives of America: the United States was founded on a land without a past. The historical memory of Americans is European, not American. For this reason, one of the most powerful and persistent themes in American literature, from Whitman to William Carlos Williams and from Melville to Faulkner, has been the search for (or invention of) American roots. We owe some of the major works of the modern era to this desire for incarnation, this obsessive need to be rooted in American soil.

Exactly the opposite is true of Mexico, land of superimposed pasts. Mexico City was built on the ruins of Tenochtitlán, the Aztec city that was built in the likeness of Tula, the Toltec city that was built in the likeness of Teotihuacán, the first great city on the American continent. Every Mexican bears within him this continuity, which goes back two thousand years. It doesn't matter that this presence is almost always unconscious and assumes the naive forms of legend and even superstition. It is not something known but something lived. The Indian presence means that one of the facets of Mexican culture is not Western. Is there anything like this in the United States? Each of the ethnic groups making up the multiracial democracy that is the United States has its own culture and tradition, and some of them—the Chinese and Japanese, for example—are not Western. These traditions exist alongside the dominant American tradition without becoming one with it. They are foreign bodies within American culture. In come cases, the most notable being that of the Chicanos, the minorities defend their traditions against or in the face of the American tradition. The Chicanos' resistance is cultural as well as political and social.

If the different attitudes of Hispanic Catholicism and English Protestantism could be summed up in two words, I would say that the Spanish attitude is inclusive and the English exclusive. In the former, the notions of conquest and domination are bound up with ideas of conversion and assimilation; in the latter, conquest and domination imply not the conversion of the conquered but their segregation. An inclusive society, founded on the double principle of domination and conversion, is bound to be hierarchical, centralist, and respectful of the individual characteristics of each group. It believes in the strict division of classes and groups, each one governed by special laws and statutes, but all embracing the same faith and obeying the same lord. An exclusive society is bound to cut itself off from the natives, either by physical exclusion or by extermination; at the same time, since each community of pure-minded men is isolated from other communities, it tends to treat its members as equals and to assure the autonomy and freedom of each group of believers. The origins of American democracy are religious, and in the early communities of New England that dual, contradictory tension between freedom and equality which has been the leitmotiv of the history of the United States was already present.

The opposition that I have just outlined is expressed with great clarity in two religious terms: "communion" and "purity." This opposition profoundly affects attitudes toward work, festivity, the body, and death. For the society of New Spain, work did not redeem, and had no value in itself. Manual work was servile. The superior man neither worked nor traded. He made war, he commanded, he legislated. He also thought, contemplated, wooed, loved, and enjoyed himself. Leisure was noble. Work was good because it produced wealth, but wealth was good because it was intended to be spent—to be consumed in those holocausts called war, in the construction of temples and palaces, in pomp and festivity. The dissipation of wealth took different forms: gold shone on the altars or was poured out in celebrations. Even today in Mexico, at least in the small cities and towns, work is the precursor of the fiesta. The year revolves on the double axis of work and festival, saving and spending. The fiesta is sumptuous and intense, lively and funereal; it is a vital, multicolored frenzy that evaporates in smoke, ashes, nothingness. In the aesthetics of perdition, the fiesta is the lodging place of death.

The United States has not really known the art of the festival, except in the last few years, with the triumph of hedonism over the old Protestant ethic. This is natural. A society that so energetically affirmed the redemptive value of work could not help chastising as depraved the cult of the festival and the passion for spending. The Protestant rejection was inspired by religion rather than economics. The Puritan conscience could not see that the value of the festival was actually a religious value: communion. In the festival, the orgiastic element is central; it marks a return to the beginning, to the primordial state in which each one is united with the great all. Every true festival is religious because every true festival is communion. Here the opposition between communion and purity is clear. For the Puritans and their heirs, work is redemptive because it frees man, and this liberation is a sign of God's choice. Work is purification, which is also a separation: the chosen one ascends, breaks the bonds binding him to earth, which are the laws of his fallen nature. For the Mexicans, communion represents exactly the opposite: not separation but participation; not breaking away but joining together; the great universal commixture, the great bathing in the waters of the beginning, a state beyond purity and impurity.

In Christianity, the body's status is inferior. But the body is an always active force, and its explosions can destroy a civilization. Doubtless for this reason, the Church from the start made a pact with the body. If the Church did not restore the body to the place it occupied in Greco-Roman society, it did try to give the body back its dignity; the body is fallen nature, but in itself it is innocent. After all, Christianity, unlike Buddhism, say, is the worship of an incarnate god. The dogma of the resurrection of the dead dates from the time of primitive Christianity; the cult of the Virgin appeared later, in the Middle Ages. Both beliefs are the highest expressions of this urge for incarnation, which typifies Christian spirituality. Both came to Mesoamerica with Spanish culture, and were immediately fused, the former with the funeral worship of the Indians,

the latter with the worship of the goddesses of fertility and war.

The Mexicans' vision of death, which is also the hope of resurrection, is as profoundly steeped in Catholic eschatology as in Indian naturalism. The Mexican death is of the body, exactly the opposite of the American death, which is abstract and disembodied. For Mexicans, death sees and touches itself; it is the body emptied of the soul, the pile of bones that somehow, as in the Aztec poem, must bloom again. For Americans, death is what is not seen: absence, the disappearance of the person. In the Puritan consciousness, death was always present, but as a moral entity, an idea. Later on, scientism pushed death out of the American consciousness. Death melted away and became unmentionable. Finally, in vast segments of the American population of today, progressive rationalism and idealism have been replaced by neo-hedonism. But the cult of the body and of pleasure implies the recognition and acceptance of death. The body is mortal, and the kingdom of pleasure is that of the moment, as Epicurus saw better than anyone else. American hedonism closes its eyes to death and has been incapable of exorcizing the destructive power of the moment with a wisdom like that of the Epicureans of antiquity. Present-day hedonism is the last recourse of the anguished and the desperate, an expression of the nihilism that is eroding the West.

Capitalism exalts the activities and behavior patterns traditionally called virile: aggressiveness, the spirit of competition and emulation, combativeness. American society made these values its own. This perhaps explains why nothing like the Mexicans' devotion to the Virgin of Guadalupe appears in the different versions of Christianity professed by Americans, including the Catholic minority. The Virgin unites the religious sensibilities of the Mediterranean and Mesoamerica, both of them regions that fostered ancient cults of feminine divinities, Guadalupe-Tonantzin is the mother of all Mexicans—Indians, mestizos, whites—but she is also a warrior virgin whose image has often appeared on the banners of peasant uprisings. In the Virgin of Guadalupe we encounter a very ancient vision of femininity which, as was true of the pagan goddesses, is not without a heroic tint.

When I talk about the masculinity of the American capitalist society, I am not unaware that American women have gained rights and posts still denied elsewhere. But they have obtained them as "subjects under the law"; that is to say, as neuter or abstract entities, as citizens, not as women. Now, I believe that, much as our civilization needs equal rights for men and women, it also needs a feminization, like the one that courtly love brought about in the outlook of medieval Europe. Or like the feminine irradiation that the Virgin of Guadalupe casts on the imagination and sensibility of us Mexicans. Because of the Mexican woman's Hispano-Arabic and Indian heritage, her social situation is deplorable, but what I want to emphasize here is not so much the nature of the relation between men and women as the intimate relationship of woman with those elusive symbols which we call femininity and masculinity. For the reasons I noted earlier, Mexican women have a very lively awareness of the body. For them, the body, the woman's and man's, is a concrete, palpable reality. Not an abstraction or a function but an ambiguous magnetic force, in which pleasure and pain, fertility and death are inextricably intertwined.

Pre-Columbian Mexico was a mosaic of nations, tribes, and languages. For its part, Spain was also a conglomeration of nations and races, even though it had realized political unity. The heterogeneity of Mexican society was the other face of Spanish centralism. The political centralism of the Spanish monarchy had religious orthodoxy as its complement, and even as its foundation. The true, effective unity of Mexican society has been brought about slowly over several centuries, but its political and religious unity was decreed from above as the joint expression of the Spanish monarchy and the Catholic Church. Mexico had a state and a church before it was a nation. In this respect also, Mexico's evolution has been very different from that of the United States, where the small colonial communities had from their inception a clear-cut and belligerent concept of their identity as regards the state. For North Americans, the nation antedated the state.

Another difference: in those small colonial communities, a fusion had taken place among religious convictions, the embryonic national consciousness, the political institution. So harmony, not contradiction, existed between the North Americans' religious convictions and their democratic institutions; whereas in Mexico Catholicism was identified with the vice-regal regime, and was its orthodoxy. Therefore, when, after independence, the Mexican liberals tried to implant democratic institutions, they had to confront the Catholic Church. The establishment of a republican democracy in Mexico meant a radical break with the past, and led to the civil wars of the nineteenth century. These wars produced the

militarism that, in turn, produced the dictatorship of Porfirio Díaz. The liberals defeated the Church, but they could not implant true democracy—only an authoritarian regime wearing democracy's mask.

A no less profound difference was the opposition between Catholic orthodoxy and Protestant reformism. In Mexico, Catholic orthodoxy had the philosophical form of Neo-Thomism, a mode of thought more apologetic than critical, and defensive in the face of the emerging modernity. Orthodoxy prevented examination and criticism. In New England, the communities were often made up of religious dissidents or, at least, of people who believed that the Scriptures should be read freely. On one side, orthodoxy, dogmatic philosophy, and the cult of authority. On the other, reading and free interpretation of the doctrine. Both societies were religious, but their religious attitudes were irreconcilable. I am not thinking only of dogmas and principles but of the very ways in which the two societies practiced and understood religion. One society fostered the complex and majestic conceptual structure of orthodoxy, and equally complex ecclesiastical hierarchy, wealthy and militant religious orders, and a ritualistic view of religion in which the sacraments occupied a central place. The other fostered free discussion of the Scriptures, a small and often poor clergy, a tendency to eliminate the hierarchical boundaries between the simple believer and the priest, and a religious practice based not on ritual but on ethics, and not on the sacrament but on the internalizing of faith.

If one considers the historical evolution of the two societies, the main difference seems to be the following: the modern world began with the Reformation, which was the religious criticism of religion and the necessary antecedent of the Enlightenment; with the Counter-Reformation and Neo-Thomism, Spain and her possessions closed themselves to the modern world. They had no Enlightenment, because they had neither a Reformation nor an intellectual religious movement like Jansenism. And so, though Spanish-American civilization is to be admired on many counts, it reminds one of a structure of great solidity—at once convent, fortress, and palace—built to last, not to change. In the long run, that construction became a confine, a prison. The United States was born of the Reformation and the Enlightenment. It came into being under the sign of criticism and self-criticism. Now, when one talks of criticism one is talking of change. The transformation of critical philosophy into progressive ideology came about and reached its peak in the nineteenth century. The broom of rationalist criticism swept the ideological sky clean of myths and beliefs; the ideology of progress, in its turn displaced the timeless values of Christianity and transplanted them to the earthly and linear time of history. Christian eternity became the future of liberal evolutionism.

Here is the final contradiction, and all the divergences and differences I have mentioned culminate in it. A society is essentially defined by its position as regards time. The United States, because of its origin and its intellectual and political history, is a society oriented toward the future. The extraordinary spatial mobility of America, a nation constantly on the move, has often been pointed out. In the realm of beliefs and mental attitudes, mobility in time corresponds to physical and geographical displacement. The American lives on the very edge of the now, always ready to leap toward the future. The country's foundations are in the future, not in the past. Or rather, its past, the act of its founding, was a promise of the future, and each time the United States returns to its source, to its past, it rediscovers the future.

Mexico's orientation, as has been seen, was just the opposite. First came the rejection of criticism, and with it rejection of the notion of change: its ideal is to conserve the image of divine immutability. Second, it has a plurality of pasts, all present and at war within every Mexican's soul. Cortés and Montezuma are still alive in Mexico. At the time of that great crisis the Mexican Revolution, the most radical faction, that of Zapata and his peasants, proposed not new forms of social organization but a return to communal ownership of land. The rebelling peasants were asking for the devolution of the land; that is, they wanted to go back to a pre-Columbian form of ownership which had been respected by the Spaniards. The image the revolutionaries instinctively made for themselves of a Golden Age lay in the remotest past. Utopia for them was not the construction of a future but a return to the source, to the beginning. The traditional Mexican attitude toward time has been expressed in this way by a Mexican poet, Ramón López Velarde: "Motherland, be still the same, faithful to each day's mirror."

In the seventeenth century, Mexican society was richer and more prosperous than American society. This situation lasted until the first half of the eighteenth century. To prove that it was so, one need only glance at the cities of those days, with their monuments and buildings—Mexico City and Boston, Puebla and Philadelphia. Then everything

changed. In 1847, the United States invaded Mexico, occupied it, and imposed on it terrible and heavy conditions of peace. A century later, the United States became the dominant world power. An unusual conjunction of circumstances of a material, technological, political, ideological, and human order explains the prodigious development of the United States. But in the small religious communities of seventeenth-century New England, the future was already in bud: political democracy, capitalism, and social and economic development. In Mexico, something very different has occurred. At the end of the eighteenth century, the Mexican ruling classes—especially the intellectuals—discovered that the principles that had founded their society condemned it to immobility and backwardness. They undertook a twofold revolution: separation from Spain and modernization of the country through the adoption of new republican and democratic principles. Their examples were the American Revolution and the French Revolution. They gained independence from Spain, but the adoption of new principles was not enough: Mexico changed its laws, not its social, economic, and cultural realities.

During much of the nineteenth century, Mexico suffered an endemic civil war and three invasions by foreign powers—the United States, Spain, and France. In the latter part of the century, order was re-established, but at the expense of democracy. In the name of liberal ideology and the positivism of Comte and Spencer, a military dictatorship was imposed which lasted more than thirty years. It was a period of peace and appreciable material development—also of increasing penetration by foreign capital, especially from England and the United States. The Mexican Revolution of 1910 set itself to change direction. It succeeded only in part: Mexican democracy is not yet a reality, and the great advances achieved in certain quarters have been nullified or are in danger because of excessive political centralization, excessive population growth, social inequality, the collapse of higher education, and the actions of the economic monopolies, among them those from the United States. Like all the other states of this century, the Mexican state has had an enormous, monstrous development. A curious contradiction: The state has been the agent of modernization, but it has been unable to modernize itself entirely. It is a hybrid of the Spanish patrimonialist state of the seventeenth century and the modern bureaucracies of the West. As for its relationship with the United States, that is still the old relationship of strong and weak, oscillating between indifference and abuse, deceit and cynicism. Most Mexicans hold the justifiable conviction that the treatment received by their county is unfair.

Above and beyond success and failure, Mexico is still asking itself the question that has occurred to most clear-thinking Mexicans since the end of the eighteenth century: the question about modernization. In the nineteenth century, it was believed that to adopt the new democratic and liberal principles was enough. Today, after almost two centuries of setbacks, we have realized that countries change very slowly, and that if such changes are to be fruitful they must be in harmony with the past and the traditions of each nation. And so Mexico has to find its own road to modernity. Our past must not be an obstacle but a starting point. This is extremely difficult, given the nature of our traditions—difficult but not impossible. To avoid new disasters, we Mexicans must reconcile ourselves with our past: only in this way shall we succeed in finding a route to modernity. The search for our own model of modernization is a theme directly linked with another: today we know that modernity, both the capitalist and the pseudo-socialist versions of the totalitarian bureaucracies, is mortally wounded in its very core—the idea of continuous, unlimited progress. The nations that inspired our nineteenth-century liberals—England, France, and especially the United States—are doubting, vacillating, and cannot find their way. They have ceased to be universal examples. The Mexicans of the nineteenth century turned their eyes toward the great Western democracies; we have nowhere to turn ours.

Between 1930 and 1960, most Mexicans were sure of the path they had chosen. This certainty has vanished, and some people ask themselves if it is not necessary to begin all over again. But the question is not relevant only for Mexico; it is universal. However unsatisfactory our country's situation may seem to us, it is not desperate—especially compared with what prevails elsewhere. Latin America, with only a few exceptions, lives under military dictatorships that are pampered and often supported by the United States. Cuba escaped American domination only to become a pawn of the Soviet Union's policy in Africa. A large number of the Asian and African nations that gained their independence after the Second World War are victims of native tyrannies often more cruel and despotic than those of the old colonial powers. In the so-called Third World, with different names and attributes, a ubiquitous Caligula reigns.

In 1917, the October Revolution in Russia kindled the hopes of millions; in 1979, the word "Gulag" has become synonymous with Soviet socialism. The founders of the socialist movement firmly believed that socialism would put an end not only to the exploitation of men but to war; in the second half of the twentieth century, totalitarian "socialisms" have enslaved the working class by stripping it of its basic rights and have also covered the whole planet with the threatening uproar of their disputes and quarrels. In the name of different versions of "socialism," Vietnamese and Cambodians butcher each other. The ideological wars of the twentieth century are no less ferocious than the wars of the religion of the seventeenth century. When I was young, the idea that we were witnessing the final crisis of capitalism was fashionable among intellectuals. Now we understand that the crisis is not of a socioeconomic system but of our whole civilization. It is a general, worldwide crisis, and its most extreme, acute, and dangerous expression is found in the situation of the Soviet Union and its satellites. The contradictions of totalitarian "socialism" are more profound and irreconcilable than those of the capitalist democracies.

The sickness of the West is moral rather than social and economic. It is true that the economic problems are serious and that they have not been solved. Inflation and unemployment are on the rise. Poverty has not disappeared, despite affluence. Several groups—women and racial, religious, and linguistic minorities—still are or feel excluded. But the real, most profound discord lies in the soul. The future has become the realm of horror, and the present has turned into a desert. The liberal societies spin tirelessly, not forward but round and round. If they change, they are not transfigured. The hedonism of the West is the other face of desperation; its skepticism is not wisdom but renunciation; its nihilism ends in suicide and in inferior forms of credulity, such as political fanaticisms and magical chimeras. The empty place left by Christianity in the modern soul is filled not by philosophy but by the crudest superstitions. Our eroticism is a technique, not an art or a passion.

I will not continue. The evils of the West have been described often enough, most recently by Solzhenitsyn, a man of admirable character. However, although his description seems to me accurate, his judgment of the causes of the sickness does not, nor does the remedy he proposes. We cannot renounce the critical tradition of the West; nor can we return to the medieval theocratic state. Dungeons of the Inquisition are not an answer to the Gulag camps. It is not worthwhile substituting the church-state for the party-state, one orthodoxy for another. The only effective arm against orthodoxies is criticism, and in order to defend ourselves against the vices of intolerance and fanaticism our only recourse is the exercise of the opposing virtues: tolerance and freedom of spirit. I do not disown Montesquieu, Hume, Kant.

The crisis of the United States affects the very foundation of the nation, by which I mean the principles that founded it. I have already said that there is a leitmotiv running throughout American history, from the Puritan colonies of New England to the present day; namely, the tension between freedom and equality. The struggles of the blacks, the Chicanos, and other minorities are an expression of this dualism. An external contradiction corresponds to this internal contradiction: the United States is a republic and an empire. In Rome, the first of these contradictions (the internal one between freedom and equality) was resolved by the suppression of freedom; Caesar's regime began as an egalitarian solution, but, like all solutions by force, it ended in the suppression of equality also. The second, external contradiction brought about the ruin of Athens, the first imperial republic in history.

It would be presumptuous of me to propose solutions to this double contradiction. I think that every time a society finds itself in crisis it instinctively turns its eyes toward its origins and looks there for a sign. Colonial American society was a free, egalitarian, but exclusive society. Faithful to its origins, in its domestic and foreign policies alike, the United States has always ignored the "others." Today, the United States faces very powerful enemies, but the mortal danger comes from within: not from Moscow but from that mixture of arrogance and opportunism, blindness and short-term Machiavellianism, volubility and stubbornness which has characterized its foreign policies during recent years and which reminds us in an odd way of the Athenian state in its quarrel with Sparta. To conquer its enemies, the United States must first conquer itself—return to its origins. Not to repeat them but to rectify them: the "others"—the minorities inside as well as the marginal countries and nations outside—do exist. Not only do we "others" make up the majority of the human race, but also each marginal society, poor though it may be, represents a unique and precious version of mankind. If the United States is to recover fortitude and lucidity, it must recover itself, and to recover itself it must recover the "others"—the outcasts of the Western World.

MEXICAN MASKS

Impassioned heart,
disguise your sorrow . . .
　　　　　　—Popular song

The Mexican, whether young or old, *criollo* or *mestizo*,[1] general or laborer or lawyer, seems to me to be a person who shuts himself away to protect himself: his face is a mask and so is his smile. In his harsh solitude, which is both barbed and courteous, everything serves him as a defense: silence and words, politeness and disdain, irony and resignation. He is jealous of his own privacy and that of others, and he is afraid even to glance at his neighbor, because a mere glance can trigger the rage of these electrically charged spirits. He passes through life like a man who has been flayed; everything can hurt him, including words and the very suspicion of words. His language is full of reticences, of metaphors and allusions, of unfinished phrases, while his silence is full of tints, folds, thunderheads, sudden rainbows, indecipherable threats. Even in a quarrel he prefers veiled expressions to outright insults: "A word to the wise is sufficient." He builds a wall of indifference and remoteness between reality and himself, a wall that is no less impenetrable for being invisible. The Mexican is always remote, from the world and from other people. And also from himself.

The speech of our people reflects the extent to which we protect ourselves from the outside world: the ideal of manliness is never to "crack," never to back down. Those who "open themselves up" are cowards. Unlike other people, we believe that opening oneself up is a weakness or a betrayal. The Mexican can bend, can bow humbly, can even stoop, but he cannot back down, that is, he cannot allow the outside world to penetrate his privacy. The man who backs down is not to be trusted, is a traitor or a person of doubtful loyalty; he babbles secrets and is incapable of confronting a dangerous situation. Women are inferior beings because, in submitting, they open themselves up. Their inferiority is constitutional and resides in their sex, their submissiveness, which is a wound that never heals.

Hermeticism is one of the several recourses of our suspicion and distrust. It shows that we instinctively regard the world around us to be dangerous. This reaction is justifiable if one considers what our history has been and the kind of society we have created. The harshness and hostility of our environment and the hidden, indefinable threat that is always afloat in the air, oblige us to close ourselves in, like those plants that survive by storing up liquid within their spiny exteriors. But this attitude, legitimate enough in its origins, has become a mechanism that functions automatically. Our response to sympathy and tenderness is reserve, since we cannot tell whether those feelings are genuine or simulated. In addition, our masculine integrity is as much endangered by kindness as it is by hostility. Any opening in our defenses is a lessening of our manliness.

Our relationships with other men are always tinged with suspicion. Every time a Mexican confides in a friend or acquaintance, every time he opens himself up, it is an abdication. He dreads that the person in whom he has confided will scorn him. Therefore confidences result in dishonor, and they are as dangerous for the person to whom they are made as they are for the person who makes them. We do not drown ourselves, like Narcissus, in the pool that reflects us; we try to stop it up instead. Our anger is prompted not only by the fear of being used by our confidants—that fear is common to everyone—but also by the shame of having renounced our solitude. To confide in others is to dispossess oneself; when we have confided in someone who is not worthy of it, we say, "I sold myself to so-and-so." That is, we have "cracked," have let someone into our fortress. The distance between one man and another, which creates mutual respect and mutual security, has disappeared. We are at the mercy of the intruder. What is worse, we have actually abdicated.

All these expressions reveal that the Mexican views life as combat. This attitude does not make him any different from anyone else in the modern world. For other people, however, the manly ideal consists in an open and aggressive fondness for

---

1. *Criollo*: a person of pure Spanish blood living in the Americas.—Tr. *Mestizo*: a person of mixed Spanish and Indian blood.—Tr.

From THE LABYRINTH OF SOLITUDE AND OTHER WRITINGS by Octavio Paz. "Mexican Masks," translated by Lysander Kemp, © 1962 by Grove Press, Inc. Used by permission of Grove/Atlantic, Inc.

combat, whereas we emphasize defensiveness, the readiness to repel any attack. The Mexican *macho*—the male—is a hermetic being, closed up in himself, capable of guarding both himself and whatever has been confided to him. Manliness is judged according to one's invulnerability to enemy arms or the impacts of the outside world. Stoicism is the most exalted of our military and political attributes. Our history is full of expressions and incidents that demonstrate the indifference of our heroes toward suffering or danger. We are taught from childhood to accept defeat with dignity, a conception that is certainly not ignoble. And if we are not all good stoics like Juárez and Cuauhtémoc, at least we can be resigned and patient and long-suffering. Resignation is one of our most popular virtues. We admire fortitude in the face of adversity more than the most brilliant triumph.

This predominance of the closed over the open manifests itself not only as impassivity and distrust, irony and suspicion, but also as love for Form. Form surrounds and sets bounds to our privacy, limiting its excesses, curbing its explosions, isolating and preserving it. Both our Spanish and Indian heritages have influenced our fondness of ceremony, formulas, and order. A superficial examination of our history might suggest otherwise, but actually the Mexican aspires to create an orderly world regulated by clearly stated principles. The turbulence and rancor of our political struggles prove that juridical ideas play an important role in our public life. The Mexican also strives to be formal in his daily life, and his formalities are very apt to become formulas. This is not difficult to understand. Order—juridical, social, religious or artistic—brings security and stability, and a person has only to adjust to the models and principles that regulate life; he can express himself without resorting to the perpetual inventiveness demanded by a free society. Perhaps our traditionalism, which is one of the constants of our national character, giving coherence to our people and our history, results from our professed love for Form.

The ritual complications of our courtesy, the persistence of classical Humanism, our fondness for closed poetic forms (the sonnet and the *décima*, for example), our love for geometry in the decorative arts and for design and composition in painting, the poverty of our Romantic art compared with the excellence of our Baroque art, the formalism of our political institutions, and, finally, our dangerous inclination toward formalism, whether social, moral or bureaucratic, are further expressions of that tendency in our character. The Mexican not

only does not open himself up to the outside world, he also refuses to emerge from himself, to "let himself go."

Sometimes Form chokes us. During the past century the liberals tried vainly to force the realities of the country into the strait jacket of the Constitution of 1857. The results were the dictatorship of Porfirio Díaz and the Revolution of 1910. In a certain sense the history of Mexico, like that of every Mexican, is a struggle between the forms and formulas that have been imposed on us and the explosions with which our individuality avenges itself. Form has rarely been an original creation, an equilibrium arrived at through our instincts and desires rather than at their expense. On the contrary, our moral and juridical forms often conflict with our nature, preventing us from expressing ourselves and frustrating our true wishes.

Our devotion to Form, even when empty, can be seen throughout the history of Mexican art from pre-Conquest times to the present. Antonio Castro Leal, in his excellent study of Juan Ruiz de Alarcón, shows how our reserved attitude toward romanticism—which by definition is expansive and open—revealed itself as early as the seventeenth century, that is, before we were even aware of ourselves as a nation. Alarcón's contemporaries were right in accusing him of being an interloper, although they were referring more to his physical characteristics than to the singularity of his work. In effect, the most typical portions of his plays deny the values expressed by his Spanish contemporaries. And his negation contains in brief what Mexico has always opposed to Spain. His plays were an answer to Spanish vitality, which was affirmative and splendid in that epoch, expressing itself in a great Yes! to history and the passions. Lope de Vega exalted love, heroism, the superhuman, the incredible; Alarcón favored other virtues, more subtle and bourgeois: dignity, courtesy, a melancholy stoicism, a smiling modesty. Lope was very little interested in moral problems: he loved action, like all his contemporaries. Moral conflicts and the hesitations and changes of the human soul were only metaphors in a theological drama whose two personae were Original Sin and Divine Grace. In Alarcón's most representative plays, on the other hand, Heaven counts for little, as little as the passionate wind that sweeps away Lope's characters. The Mexican tells us that human beings are a mixture, that good and evil are subtly blended in their souls. He uses analysis rather than synthesis: the hero becomes a problem. In several of his comedies he takes up the question of lying. To what extent does a liar really lie? Is he really trying to deceive others? Is he not the first victim of his deceit, and the first to be deceived? The liar lies to himself, because he is afraid of himself. By discussing the problem of authenticity, Alarcón anticipated one of the constant themes of Mexican thinking, later taken up by Rodolfo Usigli in his play *The Gesticulator*.

Neither passion nor Grace triumph in Alarcón's world. Everything is subordinated to reason, or to reasonableness, and his archetypes are those of a morality that smiles and forgives. When he replaces the vital, Romantic values of Lope with the abstract values of a universal and reasonable morality, is he not evading us, tricking us? His negation, like that of his homeland, does not affirm our individuality vis-á-vis that of the Spaniards. The values that Alarcón postulates belong to all men and are a Greco-Roman inheritance as well as a prophecy of the bourgeois code. They do not express our nature or resolve our conflicts: they are Forms we have neither created nor suffered, are mere masks. Only in our own day have we been able to answer the Spanish Yes with a Mexican Yes rather than with an intellectual affirmation containing nothing of our individual selves. The Revolution, by discovering popular art, originated modern Mexican painting, and by discovering the Mexican language it created a new poetry.

While the Mexican tries to create closed worlds in his politics and in the arts, he wants modesty, prudence, and a ceremonious reserve to rule over his everyday life. Modesty results from shame at one's own or another's nakedness, and with us it is an almost physical reflex. Nothing could be further from this attitude than that fear of the body which is characteristic of North American life. We are not afraid or ashamed of our bodies; we accept them as completely natural and we live physically with considerable gusto. It is the opposite of Puritanism. The body exists, and gives weight and shape to our existence. It causes us pain and it gives us pleasure; it is not a suit of clothes we are in the habit of wearing, not something apart from us: we *are* our bodies. But we are frightened by other people's glances, because the body reveals rather than hides our private selves. Therefore our modesty is a defense, like our courtesy's Great Wall of China or like the fences of organ-pipe cactus that separate the huts of our country people. This explains why prudence is the virtue we most admire in women, just as reserve is in men. Women too should defend their privacy.

No doubt an element of masculine vanity, the vanity of the "señor," of the lord or chieftain (it is an inheritance from both our Indian and Spanish ancestors), enters into our conception of feminine modesty. Like almost all other people, the Mexican considers women to be an instrument, sometimes of masculine desires, sometimes of the ends assigned to her by morality, society and the law. It must be admitted that she participates in their realization only passively, as a "repository" for certain values. Whether as prostitute, goddess, *grande dame* or mistress, woman transmits or preserves—but does not believe in—the values and energies entrusted to her by nature or society. In a world made in man's image, woman is only a reflection of masculine will and desire. When passive, she becomes a goddess, a beloved one, a being who embodies the ancient, stable elements of the universe: the earth, motherhood, virginity. When active, she is always function and means, a receptacle and a channel. Womanhood, unlike manhood, is never an end in itself.

In other countries, these functions are realized in public, often with something of a flair. There are countries that revere prostitutes or virgins, and countries that worship mothers; the *grande dame* is praised and respected almost everywhere. In contrast, we prefer these graces and virtues to be hidden. Woman should be secretive. She should confront the world with an impassive smile. She should be "decent" in the face of erotic excitements and "long-suffering" in the face of adversity. In either event her response is neither instinctive nor personal: it conforms to a general model, and it is the defensive and passive aspects of this model, as in the case of the *macho*, that are emphasized, in a gamut ranging from modesty and "decency" to stoicism, resignation and impassivity.

Our Spanish-Arabic inheritance is only a partial explanation of this conduct. The Spanish attitude toward women is very simple. It is expressed quite brutally and concisely in these two sayings: "A woman's place is in the home, with a broken leg" and "Between a female saint and a male saint, a wall of mortared stone." Woman is a domesticated wild animal, lecherous and sinful from birth, who must be subdued with a stick and guided by the "reins of religion." Therefore Spaniards consider other women—especially those of a race or religion different from their own—to be easy game. The Mexican considers woman to be a dark, secret and passive being. He does not attribute evil instincts to her; he even pretends that she does not have any. Or, to put it more exactly, her instincts are not her own but those of the species, because she is an incarnation of the life force, which is essentially impersonal. Thus it is impossible for her to have a personal, private life, for if she were to be herself—if she were to be mistress of her own wishes, passions or whims—she would be unfaithful to herself. The Mexican, heir to the great pre-Columbian religions based on nature, is a good deal more pagan than the Spaniard, and does not condemn the natural world. Sexual love is not tinged with grief and horror in Mexico as it is in Spain. Instincts themselves are not dangerous; the danger lies in any personal, individual expression of them. And this brings us back to the idea of passivity: woman is never herself, whether lying stretched out or standing up straight, whether naked or fully clothed. She is an undifferentiated manifestation of life, a channel for the universal appetite. In this sense she has no desires of her own.

North Americans also claim that instincts and desires do not exist, but the basis of their pretense is different from ours, even the opposite of it. The North American hides or denies certain parts of his body and, more often, of his psyche: they are immoral, ergo they do not exist. By denying them he inhibits his spontaneity. The Mexican woman quite simply has no will of her own. Her body is asleep and only comes really alive when someone awakens her. She is an answer rather than a question, a vibrant and easily worked material that is shaped by the imagination and sensuality of the male. In other countries women are active, attempting to attract men through the agility of their minds or the seductivity of their bodies, but the Mexican woman has a sort of hieratic calm, a tranquility made up of both hope and contempt. The man circles around her, courts her, sings to her, sets his horse (or his imagination) to performing caracoles for her pleasure. Meanwhile she remains behind the veil of her modesty and immobility. She is an idol, and like all idols she is mistress of magnetic forces whose efficacy increases as their source of transmission becomes more and more passive and secretive. There is a cosmic analogy here: woman does not seek, she attracts, and the center of attraction is her hidden, passive sexuality. It is a secret and immobile sun.

The falsity of this conception is obvious enough when one considers the Mexican woman's sensitivity and restlessness, but at least it does not turn her into an object, a mere thing. She is a symbol, like all women, of the stability and continuity of the race. In addition to her cosmic significance she has an important social role, which is to see to it that law and order, piety and tenderness are predominant in everyday life. We will not allow anyone to be disrespectful to women, and although this is doubtless a universal notion, the Mexican carries it to its ultimate consequences. Thanks to woman, many of the asperities of "man-to-man" relationships are softened. Of course we should ask the Mexican woman for her own opinion, because this "respect" is often a hypocritical way of subjecting her and preventing her from expressing herself. Perhaps she would usually prefer to be treated with less "respect" (which anyway is granted to her only in public) and with greater freedom and truthfulness; that is, to be treated as a human being rather than as a symbol or function. But how can we agree to let her express herself when our whole way of life is a mask designed to hide our intimate feelings?

Despite her modesty and the vigilance of society, woman is always vulnerable. Her social situation—as the repository of honor, in the Spanish sense—and the misfortune of her "open" anatomy expose her to all kinds of dangers, against which neither personal morality nor masculine protection is sufficient. She is submissive and open by nature. But, through a compensation-mechanism that is easily explained, her natural frailty is made a virtue and the myth of the "long-suffering Mexican woman" is created. The idol—always vulnerable, always in process of transforming itself into a human being—becomes a victim, but a victim hardened and insensible to suffering, bearing her tribulations in silence. (A "long-suffering" person is less sensitive to pain than a person whom adversity has hardly touched.) Through suffering, our women become like our men: invulnerable, impassive, and stoic.

It might be said that by turning what ought to be a cause for shame into a virtue, we are only trying to relieve our guilt feelings and cover up a cruel reality. This is true, but it is also true that in attributing to her the same vulnerability that we strive to achieve ourselves, we provide her with a moral immunity to shield her unfortunate anatomical openness. Thanks to suffering and her ability to endure it without protest, she transcends her condition and acquires the same attributes as men.

It is interesting to note that the image of the *mala mujer*—the "bad woman"—is almost always accompanied by the idea of aggressive activity. She is not passive like the "self-denying mother," the "waiting sweetheart," the hermetic idol: she comes and goes, she looks for men and then leaves them. Her extreme mobility, through a mechanism similar to that described above, renders her invulnerable. Activity and immodesty unite to petrify her soul. The *mala* is hard and impious and independent like the *macho*. In her own way she also transcends her physiological weakness and closes herself off from the world.

It is likewise significant that masculine homosexuality is regarded with a certain indulgence insofar as the active agent is concerned. The passive agent is an abject, degraded being. This ambiguous conception is made very clear in the word games or battles—full of obscene illusions and double meanings—that are so popular in Mexico City. Each of the speakers tries to humiliate his adversary with verbal traps and ingenious linguistic combinations, and the loser is the person who cannot think of a comeback, who has to swallow his opponent's jibes. These jibes are full of aggressive sexual illusions, the loser is possessed, is violated, by the winner and the spectators laugh and sneer at him. Masculine homosexuality is tolerated, then, on condition that it consists in violating a passive agent. As with heterosexual relationships, the important thing is not to open oneself up and at the same time to break open one's opponent.

It seems to me that all of these attitudes, however different their sources, testify to the "closed" nature of our reactions to the world around us or to our fellows. But our mechanisms of defense and self-preservation are not enough, and therefore we make use of dissimulation, which is almost habitual with us. It does not increase our passivity; on the contrary, it demands an active inventiveness and must reshape itself from one moment to another. We tell lies for the mere pleasure of it, like all imaginative peoples, but we also tell lies to hide ourselves and to protect ourselves from intruders. Lying plays a decisive role in our daily lives, our politics, our love-affairs and our friendships, and since we attempt to deceive ourselves as well as others, our lies are brilliant and fertile, not like the gross inventions of other peoples. Lying is a tragic game in which we risk a part of our very selves. Hence it is pointless to denounce it.

The dissembler pretends to be someone he is not. His role requires constant improvisation, a steady forward progress across shifting sands. Every moment he must remake, re-create, modify the personage he is playing, until at last the moment arrives when reality and appearance, the lie and the truth, are one. At first the pretense is only a fabric of inventions intended to baffle our neighbors, but eventually it becomes a superior—because more artistic—form of reality. Our lies reflect both what we lack and what we desire, both what we are not and what we would like to be. Through dissimula-

tion we come closer to our model, and sometimes the gesticulator, as Usigli saw so profoundly, becomes one with his gestures and thus makes them authentic. The death of Professor Rubio changed him into what he wanted to be: General Rubio, a sincere revolutionary and a man capable of giving the stagnating Revolution a fresh impetus and purity. In the Usigli play Professor Rubio invents a new self and becomes a general, and his lie is so truthlike that the corrupt Navarro has no other course than to murder him, as if he were murdering his old commander, General Rubin, all over again. By killing him he kills the truth of the Revolution.

If we can arrive at authenticity by means of lies, an excess of sincerity can bring us to refined forms of lying. When we fall in love we open ourselves up and reveal our intimate feelings, because an ancient tradition requires that the man suffering from love display his wounds to the loved one. But in displaying them the lover transforms himself into an image, an object he presents for the loved one's—and his own—contemplation. He asks her to regard him with the same worshipful eyes with which he regards himself. And now the looks of others do not strip him naked; instead, they clothe him in piety. He has offered himself as a spectacle, asking the spectators to see him as he sees himself, and in so doing he has escaped from the game of love, has saved his true self by replacing it with an image.

Human relationships run the risk, in all lands and ages, of becoming equivocal. This is especially true of love. Narcissism and masochism are not exclusively Mexican traits, but it is notable how often our popular songs and sayings and our everyday behavior treat love as falsehood and betrayal. We almost always evade the perils of a naked relationship by exaggerating our feelings. At the same time, the combative nature of our eroticism is emphasized and aggravated. Love is an attempt to penetrate another being, but it can only be realized if the surrender is mutual. It is always difficult to give oneself up; few persons anywhere ever succeed in doing so, and even fewer transcend the possessive stage to know love for what it actually is: a perpetual discovery, an immersion in the waters of reality, and an unending re-creation. The Mexican conceives of love as combat and conquest. It is not so much an attempt to penetrate reality by means of the body as it is to violate it. Therefore the image of the fortunate lover—derived, perhaps, from the Spanish Don Juan—is confused with that of the man who deliberately makes use of his feelings, real or invented, to win possession of a woman.

Dissimulation is an activity very much like that of actors in the theater, but the true actor surrenders himself to the role he is playing and embodies it fully, even though he sloughs it off again, like a snake its skin, when the final curtain comes down. The dissembler never surrenders or forgets himself, because he would no longer be dissembling if he became one with his image. But this fiction becomes an inseparable—and spurious—part of his nature. He is condemned to play his role throughout life, since the pact between himself and his impersonation cannot be broken except by death or sacrifice. The lie takes command of him and becomes the very foundation of his personality.

To simulate is to invent, or rather to counterfeit, and thus to evade our condition. Dissimulation requires greater subtlety: the person who dissimulates is not counterfeiting but attempting to become invisible, to pass unnoticed without renouncing his individuality. The Mexican excels at the dissimulation of his passions and himself. He is afraid of others' looks and therefore he withdraws, contracts, becomes a shadow, a phantasm, an echo. Instead of walking, he glides; instead of stating, he hints; instead of replying, he mumbles; instead of complaining, he smiles. Even when he sings he does so—unless he explodes, ripping open his breast—between clenched teeth and in a lowered voice, dissimulating his song:

And so great is the tyranny
of this dissimulation
that although my heart swells
with profoundest longing,
there is challenge in my eyes
and resignation in my voice.

Perhaps our habit of dissimulating originated in colonial times. The Indians and *mestizos* had to sing in a low voice, as in the poem by Alfonso Reyes, because "words of rebellion cannot be heard well from between clenched teeth." The colonial world has disappeared, but not the fear, the mistrust, the suspicion. And now we disguise not only our anger but also our tenderness. When our country people beg one's pardon, they say: "Pretend it never happened, señor." And we pretend. We dissimulate so eagerly that we almost cease to exist.

In its most radical forms dissimulation becomes mimicry. The Indian blends into the landscape until he is an indistinguishable part of the white wall against which he leans at twilight, of the dark earth on which he stretches out to rest at midday, of the silence that surrounds him. He disguises his human singularity to such an extent that he finally annihilates it and turns into a stone, a tree, a wall, silence, and space. I am not saying that he communes with the All like a pantheist, or that he sees an individual tree as an archetype of all trees, what I am saying is that he actually blends into specific objects in a concrete and particular way.

Roger Caillois has pointed out that mimicry is not always an attempt to foil the enemies that swarm in the outside world. Insects will sometimes "play dead" or imitate various kinds of decomposed material, out of a fascination for death, for the inertia of space. This fascination—I would call it life's gravitational force—is common to all living things, and the fact that it expresses itself in mimicry shows that we must consider it as something more than an instinctive device for escaping from danger or death.

Mimicry is a change of appearance rather than of nature, and it is significant that the chosen representation is either of death or of inert space. The act of spreading oneself out, of blending with space, of becoming space, is a way of rejecting appearances, but it is also a way of being nothing except Appearance. The Mexican is horrified by appearances, although his leaders profess to love them, and therefore he disguises himself to the point of blending into the objects that surround him. That is, he becomes mere Appearance because of his fear of appearances. He seems to be something other than what he is, and he even prefers to appear dead or nonexistent rather than to change, to open up his privacy. Dissimulation as mimicry, then, is one of the numerous manifestations of our hermeticism. The gesticulator resorts to a mask, and the rest of us wish to pass unnoticed. In either case we hide our true selves, and sometimes deny them. I remember the afternoon I heard a noise in the room next to mine, and asked loudly: "Who is there?" I was answered by the voice of a servant who had recently come to us from her village: "No one, señor, I am."

We dissimulate in order to deceive ourselves, and turn transparent and phantasmal. But that is not the end of it: we also pretend that our fellowman does not exist. This is not to say that we deliberately ignore or discount him. Our dissimulation here is a great deal more radical: we change him from somebody into nobody, into nothingness. And this nothingness takes on its own individuality, with a recognizable face, and figure, and suddenly becomes Nobody.

Don No One, who is Nobody's Spanish father, is able, well fed, well respected; he has a bank account, and speaks in a loud, self-assured voice. Don No One fills the world with his empty, garrulous presence. He is everywhere, and has friends everywhere. He is a banker, an ambassador, a businessman. He can be seen in all the salons, and is honored in Jamaica and Stockholm and London. He either holds office or wields influence, and his manner of not-being is aggressive and conceited. On the other hand, Nobody is quiet, timid, and resigned. He is also intelligent and sensitive. He always smiles. He always waits. When he wants to say something, he meets a wall of silence; when he greets someone, he meets a cold shoulder; when he pleads or weeps or cries out, his gestures and cries are lost in the emptiness created by Don No One's interminable chatter. Nobody is afraid not to exist: he vacillates, attempting now and then to become Somebody. Finally, in the midst of his useless gestures, he disappears into the limbo from which he emerged.

It would be a mistake to believe that others prevent him from existing. They simply dissimulate his existence and behave as if he did not exist. They nullify him, cancel him out, turn him to nothingness. It is futile for Nobody to talk, to publish books, to paint pictures, to stand on his head. Nobody is the blankness in our looks, the pauses in our conversations, the reserve in our silences. He is the name we always and inevitably forget, the eternal absentee, the guest we never invite, the emptiness we can never fill. He is an omission, and yet he is forever present. He is our secret, our crime, and our remorse. Thus the person who creates Nobody, by denying Somebody's existence, is also changed into Nobody. And if we are all Nobody, then none of us exists. The circle is closed and the shadow of Nobody spreads out over our land, choking the Gesticulator and covering everything. Silence—the prehistoric silence, stronger than all the pyramids and sacrifices, all the churches and uprisings and popular songs—comes back to rule over Mexico.

14. Cecilia Rodríguez and Marjorie Miller, "Muy Macho"

While Octavio Paz addresses *machismo* from a theoretical and a historical context, Cecilia Rodríguez and Majorie Miller examine the macho male from the perspective of two women reporters. In order to dissect the behavior of the macho, the two writers go to Mexico and capture this male figure "in his Mexican lair." In the article which follows, Rodríguez and Miller discuss the codified behavior many know as *machismo*, acknowledging that not all men are machos but those who claim to be act in a consistent and even predictable manner. They also discuss the male's relation with his wife, mistresses, family, and children, and even the female "complicity" of machismo. Finally, both women address the raising of boys and girls in a society that narrowly defines gender roles.

Muy Macho

We are no strangers to machismo. We are two women journalists, an American and a Colombian, living in Mexico. There are many macho countries, but this is one that brags of its macho ways through pistol toting movie idols and popular *ranchera* songs like "Turning Away." Mariachis in black pants with silver studs sing: "You go because I want you to go. At the time I want I'll get you back . . . Whether you like it or not, I'm your owner."

Television here routinely features buxom women in too small bikinis, and classified ads offer secretarial jobs to "good-looking females." The Mexico City subway reserves separate cars for women at rush hour as a precaution against mauling by *el macho más macho*, the most macho macho.

We share the experiences of all women here: men who make sexual advances; men who ignore us in front of our male colleagues; waiters who won't seat us or give us the check. These are the daily reminders that we live in a society of men; we are outsiders looking in.

Yet our reactions are markedly distinct. We were raised in different cultures: the United States, where machismo increasingly is a dirty word, and Colombia, where a man is still proud of being macho. We realize that when we meet Alyx, a 28-year-old American photographer based in Mexico City, who tells us a story typical of a gringa in Macholandia.

After three days holed up in her apartment against the ordeal that awaits her, Alyx ventures into the street. She is dressed modestly in jeans and a loose blouse that camouflage her slender body. She makes it through the first block. No tormentors in sight. But by the next corner, her blond hair and blue eyes begin to draw fire. She hears the trademark "Psst!"—a bullet hissing past her ear. She keeps walking, head down, through a gauntlet of vendors at the stoplight, teen-agers at the Metro station, middle-aged men in the subway car.

Their gazes penetrate her clothes. "*Bonita*," the men whisper. "Pretty." "*Mamacita*." The assault escalates. Someone brushes against her in the crowded subway car. An accident? "*Güerita*," someone calls. "Little white girl." She hears the sucking of air between teeth, a loud exhaling and, finally, the verbal ejaculation—"*Puta*"—"Whore."

"What are they expecting, that I will jump over and kiss them?" Alyx asks us. "You want to kill the guy. It's degrading and humiliating. What can I do about it? Hit him? Say something and give him the attention he wants, or bow my head and ignore it?"

The question has American and Latin answers.

Daughters of the U.S. women's movement respond as Alyx does, with a desire to lash out at the affront to female dignity. The American does not differentiate between *mamacita* and *puta* because both are an invasion of her privacy—glass ground into her soul. Where she grew up, limits are being set on men's behavior and laws are being passed to protect her rights. Women in the United States have more economic independence and, therefore, more power than Latin women.

When an American plans her first trip south of the border, she is warned by friends about machos. They are wily womanizers, she is told, tearfully romantic when it suits them, ugly if they don't get what they want. They believe that *la gringa* is sexually liberated and in search of a Latin lover. Why else would she come south alone, without a man? In Latin America, a woman alone is seen as something sad. She must be desperate and in need of sex, the macho thinks, and he can help her out. To defend herself, one gringa we know carries an umbrella to ward off Romeos who get too close. Another wears heavy shoes in case she should need to land a kick.

When Marjorie first traveled to Mexico in the 1970s, she was so upset by the unflinching stares and repulsed by the verbal assaults that she responded in kind—spitting wet, sticky chewing gum at aggressive machos. The men were appalled and called her "*cochina*,"—"pig"—which outraged her even more. In her mind, they were the pigs.

Cecilia laughs hard at this account. Latinas are amazed at the angry gringas fighting what always has been. They grew up on a continent of men who have not been tamed, where small boys are encouraged by their parents to "be a man, be a macho."

Reprinted by permission of Los Angeles Times Syndicate.

The same parents teach their daughters to be feminine and pleasing to men. Girls learn to dress and talk to charm their suitors who might someday support them, an important skill in countries where only a minority of women have opportunities for good salaries. This is starting to change among some professionals, but progress is not widespread.

The Latin woman cannot remember the first time a man whispered a *piropo*, or flirtatious remark, to her in the street because it happened so early and so often. But she would never dream of walking with an umbrella for protection, for she knows that the men who approach Alyx do not expect to be kissed. Rather, they simply want her attention. They are keepers of the macho flame. She does not need to spit. She has learned to answer them with a look that is at once aloof and provocative, a look that says, "I like you." "You are attractive." Or if not, "You poor fool."

A poll published recently in a Mexican women's magazine finds that women of all ages in Latin America consider *piropos* compliments, not insults. They lift her spirits and make her feel desired. For the Latina, there is a big difference between a sexually explicit remark—an insult in any culture—and a flirtatious one. The Latina prefers the poetic *piropa* that compare her to a rose or the humorous remarks. "I wish that I were cross-eyed so I could see you twice" is a classic, or "All those curves and me without brakes."

Now Marjorie laughs. We are good friends and colleagues, chatting over the steam that rises from mugs of hot tea. We are fascinated by our different reactions, but when we get to the core of machismo we find that we agree. The essence of machismo is the domination of men over women, a way of keeping women down, unequal and at home. In the magazine *Sin Título*, psychologist Paola Compean wrote that machos are "vain, egoistical, excitable, glib, notably seeking attention and admiration from everyone." That sounds right, but there is more: contemptuous. Machos do not love women, they disdain them.

We interviewed many Latin and American women about machismo and each had her own list of complaints. A macho wants to be served and to avoid family work. He keeps his marriage secret and is unfaithful. He rarely wears a wedding ring or reveals that he has children. As Mexican anthropologist Ana Luisa Ligoury says with a smile: "They are all single and they all have serious intentions."

Alberto, a handsome, 45-year-old businessman from Argentina, would seem to be an exception when he says right from the start that he is happily married. But it turns out he fits perfectly into the rest of the profile of a Latin macho. He never admits to us that he has a lover, yet it quickly becomes obvious that he is gaga over another woman. "Conquer a woman with a ring on your finger. That's a real macho," he says, waving a hand bearing a gold wedding band. "The woman who would come with me knows the rules of the game."

Sexual tension prevents Alberto from having women friends. He feels protective of women and, if they should confide in him, he feels possessive. He admits that he is terribly jealous and cannot imagine that his wife should ever have an affair. If she did, he says jokingly, he would kill her. And he says his wife would leave him if she ever discovered his infidelities. Even so, he takes the macho risk. "You have to know how," he says with a sly look. Yet, he admits that "sometimes a man does not measure what he has at his side until he has lost it."

We are talking to Alberto over a long Mexican lunch of margaritas, prawns and garlic, seasoned with guitar music. For him, there's nothing wrong with being macho, although like many, he doesn't consider himself one. Yet, he makes eyes at us and issues such macho statements as, "Women can conquer you with just a look." We want his story, he wants to please us. He is intelligent and tries to give us the answers he thinks we are looking for, even if it means twisting the truth. The lunch is a seduction.

This is no surprise. We know the stereotype—machos seduce, machos lie and cheat. Of course, not all Latin men are machos, but all machos are basically like this. Cecilia, who grew up with them, is at ease with Alberto. Marjorie is less adept at fending off his flirtations. She presses him. Why do you cheat on your wife? All the while he looks to Cecilia for understanding. A look that says, "What does this gringa expect from me, to tell her that I have been unfaithful?" He won't tell.

Cecilia's brother once broke the canon. His wife confronted him over his affair and, in a moment of weakness, he confessed that he had strayed. Family protocol obliged him to seek forgiveness from his father-in-law. The patriarch accused his own daughter's husband of erring—not in cheating on his wife, but in admitting it. "That was your mistake," the old man said.

Subterfuge is an implicit part of most relationships *a la Latina*. Typically, the woman lets the man believe he is in control. He will tell her that all he wants is to respect her. But she has been taught by her mother and aunts that "men only want one thing." And she is supposed to be innocent. They share a game of conquest and surrender.

"The man circles around her, courts her, sings to her, sets his horse (or his imagination) to perform tricks for her," Nobel laureate Octavio Paz wrote in "Labyrinth of Solitude," his classic study of the Mexican character. "Meanwhile, she remains behind the veil of her modesty," with a tranquility made up of home and contempt.

If she surrenders to a macho, the Latin woman pays a price. She is diminished in his eyes. Mexican feminist author Marta Lamas tells us that women contribute to this game—by perpetuating a modern version of the virginity myth. "Of course no one expects her to be a virgin technically," Lamas says, "but she will say she has had only one or two relationships in her life—never 20. It's the same virginity, but less extreme."

Liberated gringas play by other rules with a macho. Gringas are direct, frontal. They assert themselves and feel uncomfortable when they are our of control. The gringa is frustrated at not being treated as an equal. The macho wants to kiss and hug in public, to show off his woman to his friends. But the gringa feels suffocated. He tells her he wants to care for her and she is just as likely to say, "I can take care of myself, thank you very much."

Unlike the Latina, she is free to admit not only that she has sex but also that she enjoys it and has the right to sex with no strings attached. Latin men and women, says Pilar, a Mexican friend of ours, often interpret those freedoms as promiscuity and resent the gringas. When she was in high school, Pilar says, well-bred boys viewed Mexican girls as "good girls for holding hands and going to the movies, while gringas were for going to Acapulco and going to bed." The boys courted the gringas, bedded them, boasted of the conquest—one for *la raza*—and then made fun of the foreigners. "One of my friends told a gringa that his name was Fernando Pemex (after the state-owned oil company). Everywhere she went she saw Pemex stations and thought his dad must really be rich."

This is the macho *burla*, the trick or ridicule that so confuses gringas. Perhaps their Spanish is not good enough to decipher the riddles and double-entendres that Mexican men love. After an evening of banter, the gringa is often left wondering whether she had been flattered or mocked, whether a joke was intended for her amusement or was at her expense. Which is just how the macho wants it. If he cannot dominate a woman, he will laugh at her—another kind of control. "The humor of the macho is an act of revenge," Paz wrote in "Labyrinth." "The essential attribute of the macho—power—almost always reveals itself as a capacity for wounding, humiliating, annihilating."

Why does the Mexican man need revenge? Why must he conquer and diminish women? One explanation lies in Mexican history, a tale of submission and defeat. The Spanish conquest was cruel and bloody. The Spaniards took everything the Indians had, including their women, who then gave birth to the new, mixed-blood Mexican, or mestizo. Spanish fathers rejected their mestizo children. As a result, Paz and others have written, the mestizo views his Indian mother as symbolizing submission and humiliation, his Spanish father as representing power and domination. In Mexico, *vale madre*—literally, worth mother—means something without value, while *que padre*—what father—is high praise.

But Mexico is not the only macho country and machismo is not just revenge. We ask a few of the machos we know for other explanations. They remind us that where "good" women are unavailable, Latin American men often turn to prostitutes for their first sexual experiences. That, too, defines a macho's relationship with women. For him, women are objects of pleasure. A reflection of his will.

All of the Latin women with whom we spoke faulted mothers for reproducing machismo. Mothers let their *gallos*—their roosters—run loose while keeping their hens at home. They raise their daughters to be mothers and treat their sons as kings. *"Papi,"* they call him, elevating him to the status of father. Later, a mother might even become an accomplice in her son's sexual adventures; Cecilia's mother, for example, once let her married son use her phone, knowing he was going to call his girlfriend.

But blaming the mothers for perpetuating machismo was offensive to the Americans we interviewed. Absent and unfeeling fathers provide the poor role models, they said. Latin mothers raise their sons as best they can.

The double standard may begin at home, but it is reinforced at school. Vietnika, a 26-year-old

Mexican woman, recalls an incident from the fifth grade when a boy pulled up her skirt to expose her underpants to the class. Embarrassed and infuriated, she retaliated by jabbing him with her pen. The boy cried and she was expelled. "The teacher never gave me an opportunity to say what happened. She never listened to me. The boy was the victim," Vietnika says. The lesson: She should have submitted to the abuse.

The lessons don't stop there. As adults, machos continue to insist on a man's right to sexual adventures. A Mexican-American woman recounts a lunch with a Mexican politician. At the end of the meal, he asked her outright if she was going to sleep with him. "What about your wife?" she asked in surprise. "What does that have to do with it?" he said with genuine puzzlement.

Although that cavalier attitude angers many American women, others decide to enjoy the sex that is available to them. Jennifer, a 32-year-old businesswoman who dates a married Mexican says, "I would never do this at home, but my morals are different here. All men in Mexico have lovers. One of the first lines I learned in Spanish was *casa chica* (literally, small house, or a lover's house). Besides everyone my age is married. The guy's 35, he's interesting. I told a Mexican woman friend about him, and she said don't do it because he'll never marry you. That was not a issue for me."

Here we have stumbled into gringa complicity in machismo: many change their standards when they cross the border, doing what they would not do back home. Some middle-class American women who would never look twice at a truck driver in Texas fall for an illiterate boatman in Acapulco.

Those are not the only contradictions. While American women resent the fact they cannot sit in a cafe alone and read a book or go for a stroll without being accosted by men, many of them also like the attention they receive and the way machos make them feel. Machos focus on their beauty, not their flaws. At home, a gringa may be made to feel fat, but in Mexico the same woman hears she has pretty eyes. American men are careful about what they say to women not only in public, but in private as well: not so the Latin male. Many gringas like the raw emotion in Latinos—the same emotion, perhaps, that lets machos bellow out *ranchera* lyrics and the *piropos* that gringas so hate.

Our weeks-long discussion is coming to a close at a restaurant called—what else—Macho. Although we began with such different perspectives, more and more we find points on which we agree. Marjorie was surprised to discover so much female complicity in machismo—from Latin women and gringas alike. Now she understands. She will teach her 1½-year old daughter to pick her battles better than her mother did; to be firm in combating machismo, but perhaps not so angry.

Cecilia, who was so surprised by the intensity of American anger, now realizes how thin is the line between inoffensive and oppressive. She will never again say to her two young sons "Don't be a little girl" when they start to cry. We both want our children to understand that the world must be fair to women and that they should help make it that way.

As we wait for the check, we look around and notice that we are the only women in the restaurant unaccompanied by a man. Out on elegant Paseo de la Reforma, we see that the vast majority of people going to and from work also are men. And we remember why we began talking in the first place. Because we are guests in Macholandia, a world owned and operated by men.

Cecilia Rodríguez, a Colombian journalist in Mexico City, writes about Latin affairs for U. S. publications, Marjorie Miller is The Los Angeles Times' Mexico City bureau chief.

PART III—READINGS FROM THE UNITED STATES

1. EARL SHORRIS, "SOMEONE FROM MEXICO"

In the first of three readings about the three major Latino groups in the United States, Earl Shorris examines the past history and present status of Mexican-Americans in "Zutano de Mexico" ("Someone from Mexico," from *Latinos: A Biography of the People*). As he does in discussing Puerto Ricans and Cuban Americans, Shorris focuses on the individual characteristics of the Mexican-Americans, the largest group of Latinos in the United States (around 13 million). As Shorris explains, this group of U. S. Latinos, which traces its ancestry from Mexico, has played a key role in the development of America from the sixteenth century to the present age.

After exploring the awakening of a people's self consciousness during World War II and afterwards, Shorris traces the rise and decline of the Chicano movement and its most noteworthy personalities. Shorris then delves into the uniqueness of the Mexican-American personality, explaining the concepts of *aguantar* and *respeto* and how these traditional modes of behavior fair in twentieth-century Anglo America. In analyzing Mexican-Americans (as well as Puerto Ricans and Cuban Americans), Shorris avoids stereotyping specific behavior through an approach which examines broad cultural trends. He also notes the strong ties of family, language, and a shared history that ultimately bind together the diverse Latino communities in America.

Zutano de Mexico

Mejicanos and Mexican-Americans differ from other Latinos by duration and number, as well as by character. Most Latinos in the United States, perhaps two-thirds or more, are of Mexican descent. Some are here temporarily, part of the labor force that fills the lowest paying, most onerous jobs; others have been here for generations. If one includes some of the early settlers of the Southwest who came from Spain via Mexico as Mexican, the Mexican-American community is moving toward its sixth century in what is now the United States. Unlike the Cubans, mainland Puerto Ricans, and other Latinos, most of whom arrived in the second half of the twentieth century, the Mexican-Americans live in the light of their own history in the United States.

Several scholars, among them Mario García and Rodolfo Alvarez have begun to break down this long history into distinct periods of development. Alvarez, writing in 1973, described four generations: "The 'Creation Generation,' characterized by economic subjugation and being the object of race and ethnic prejudice, appeared in 1848 when the Mexican-American people were created as a people by the signing of the Treaty of Guadalupe Hidalgo. By 1900 the majority of Mexican-Americans were members of the 'Migrant Generation' who left a lower-class status in Mexico to enter a lower-caste status in the United States. Around the time of World War II there developed another state of collective consciousness termed here the 'Mexican-American Generation.' This generation moved to the cities, experienced some upward mobility, and managed to establish their claims as bonafide citizens of the United States in the eyes of only one of the social psychologically relevant populations—themselves. Finally, in the late 1960s, a new consciousness began to make itself felt among the Mexican-Americans with the emergence of the 'Chicano Generation.'"

García adds a fifth generation, which he calls "post-chicano." He says of this current generation, "Mexican-American leadership on the whole has seemed more disposed to conform to the conservative temper of the times. Mexican-American leaders, besides pursuing a reduced agenda on the civil rights front, have allowed government and the mass media to define them as 'Hispanics' and thus obliterate or disguise the historically based effort by Mexican-Americans at self-definition.

"... To regain ... momentum this new political generation will need to discard the historical amnesia of the 1980s, so well revealed in Richard Rodriguez's classic statement of the decade, *Hunger of Memory,* and instead recapture a 'memory of history'—a history of uncompromising dedication and struggle for full equality with other Americans."

Events in Mexico at the beginning of the twentieth century created a special cohort of Mexican-Americans, less than a generation but more than an anomaly: the educated and often wealthy families who left the country during the Revolution of 1910. These exiles were much like the people who came from Cuba in the 1960s and the first wave of Nicaraguans who left after the overthrow of the Somoza regime in the 1980s; they quickly established themselves as an elite. Most of them planned to go back to Mexico as soon as political and economic conditions returned to normal, and indeed many of them did eventually reclaim lands and lives temporarily lost to the revolution that degenerated into a civil war. Those who stayed did not become immigrants until long after they arrived in the United States.

During the sixties it was proper for people who called themselves chicanos to think of the Mexican-American generation as docile assimilationist, utterly bourgeois in its goals and attitudes. In fact, as Mario García has demonstrated in two volumes of Mexican-American history, the parents of the chicanos were not all *vendidos*; although many did sell out, or attempt to sell out, others fought for change. There was a union movement, particularly among the mine workers in West Texas and New Mexico. In California there was a radical faction allied with the Communist party, if not controlled by it. An intellectual tradition was growing in New Mexico and Texas, and LULAC, the League of United Latin

From LATINOS: A Biography of the People by Earl Shorris. Copyright © 1992 by Earl Shorris. Reprinted by permission of W. W. Norton & Company, Inc.

American Citizens, although middle class to a fault, was fighting against segregation in schools, theaters, and swimming pools. It was a difficult time. The word "Mexican" was so connected with prejudice that the members of LULAC decided to call themselves Latins in an attempt to improve their status.

Consciousness of the United States as a deeply racist nation, one that used racism for purposes of economic exploitation, came during the generation of World War II veterans. Measured by the number of Medal of Honor winners who were Mexican-American and the rate at which Mexican-Americans suffered casualties, no other racial or ethnic group served with greater courage. According to Raúl Morín, who wrote *Among the Valiant*, 25 percent of the U.S. soldiers on the Bataan Death March were Mexican-Americans. Yet in June of 1943 in California, hundreds of Mejicanos and Mexican-Americans were beaten and stripped of their zoot suits by Anglo soldiers and sailors. The Los Angeles police provided no protection for the Latinos; instead of arresting the rioting soldiers and sailors, they arrested hundreds of their victims. According to some historians, it was only the intervention of the military police that stopped the Zoot Suit Riots from becoming a full-scale mutiny by the military. In Los Angeles, the Latinos found no allies in local government or in the press; when Eleanor Roosevelt blamed the riots on "longstanding discrimination against the Mexicans in the Southwest," the Los Angeles *Times* took her to task for her views.

The veterans came home angered and disillusioned by the riots, but there was worse news to come. In Three Rivers, Texas, a funeral parlor refused to bury Félix Longoria, a Mexican-American soldier who had been decorated for heroism in World War II. Rage over the Longoria case (he was finally buried in Arlington National Cemetery) led Dr. Hector García of Corpus Christi to found the American GI Forum. It was exactly what the vets had been looking for. Within a few months, there were a hundred chapters. As the name implies, its members wished to obliterate any distinction between themselves and the rest of society.

World War II, more than any other event, changed the character of the Mexican-American. A people that had won more Medals of Honor than any other racial or ethnic group during the war could not feel quite so humble at home. The private machismo of the man who suffered humiliations in public was not longer the only solace for the Mexican-American husband; a public expression of anger was possible.

War had also given Mexican-Americans the chance to serve as commissioned and noncommissioned officers. Men who had commanded Anglo troops in battle did not cringe before them in civilian life; the experience of command and observing others in command taught them that they did not have to resort to the role of overseer in order to have power. Sergeants and captains and buck privates turned into professional men and entrepreneurs; the vets no longer felt like intruders in a strange country. They were Americans, men who fought for their country. It was a melting-pot army, one in which Mexican-Americans had often been treated as white ethnics. Nearly half a million Latinos, most of them of Mexican descent, came home from the war with one idea in mind: They had been Americans; they could be Americans; they didn't want to be Mexican anymore.

Until the war, few Mejicanos or Mexican-Americans had gone beyond high school. Language problems, segregated schools, and economic pressures made it almost impossible for them to go to college. Furthermore, parents were reluctant to see their children, especially daughters, go far from home. Junior college or the local branch of a state university was all that was available even to the few students who could overcome the economic barriers. The GI Bill and the independence from family pressures learned in years away from home during the war suddenly made it possible for thousands of Mexican-Americans to earn college degrees. The burden of violent necessity had been lifted from an entire generation; World War II ended a hundred years of feudalism in the American Southwest.

If any one person embodied the change that came over the Mexican-American community after the war, it was a young veteran from El Paso, Texas, Raymond L. Telles, who had joined the army as a private and been discharged with the rank of major. His family had been involved in local politics, but no one had dared to run for office until they persuaded Raymond to take the chance. In 1948 he was elected county clerk. Nine years later he ran for mayor. There had not been a Mexican-American mayor of a major city in the Southwest in the twentieth century when Raymond Telles entered the Democratic primary.

The El Paso newspapers were split on his candidacy. The *Times* supported the establishment candidate in the Democratic primary, which was the only contest in Texas in 1957. The *Herald-Post*, edited by E. M. Pooley, sided with Telles. I knew Pooley slightly, having worked for him as a reporter during that period. He was the most unpleasant decent man I ever met. The city editor, a gentleman who wore a green eyeshade, was terrified of him. The only young reporter he ever showed any interest in was Rubén Salazar. Pooley was crotchety, miserable, opinionated, and on the decent side of almost every issue. He fought like a lion for the election of Raymond Telles. He defended him against charges of cronyism and communism. He lauded Telles and excoriated his opponent day after day, partly because he believed in Raymond L. Telles and partly, I think, because he hated the owner and the editor of the extremely conservative morning paper.

Telles had another important ally in the race. As part of his ticket, he had chosen Ted Bender, the popular television weatherman and the host of the town's only talk show on radio. Bender had a phenomenal memory for facts, which somehow convinced his audience that he was a man of great wisdom. Since the majority of the citizens were Latino, but the majority of the voters were Anglo, Bender's willingness to support Telles by running on the People's party ticket with him may have been the deciding factor.

Whatever combination of factors gave Telles the election, on April 1, 1957, he became the mayor of El Paso, Texas. It was a victory for the liberals, for LULAC, for the VFW and the unions. Raymond Telles, a tall, thin man, an officer and gentleman in his bearing and his language, had come home from the war and won self-respect for every Mexican-American in Texas.

At the same time, in the same town, another man named Tellez (the names were pronounced the same although spelled differently) had become the leading radio and television personality. Rudy Tellez[1] was also a veteran. Unlike the mayor, who went to business college, Rudy Tellez had a real bachelor's degree from Texas Western College (now the University of Texas at El Paso). Although he was fluent in Spanish, he spoke English with a network announcer's accent and precision. At KTSM he was the guy with show business connections, a mixture of Hollywood and New York, interested in politics, music, and theater, the most up-to-date man in town. And when we jumped into his Triumph sports car and went across the border to a tiny homestyle restaurant in Ciudad Juárez to have the *comida corrida*, he was as comfortable with the Mexican version of the blue pate special as any person in the room.

A third Mexican-American reached prominence at the same time: In the El Paso police department Arturo Islas[2] was promoted to lieutenant and then to captain. When he joined the department in 1942, he was only the seventh Mexican-American on the force. Thirty years later, long since retired with the rank of inspector, he remembered the difficulties of getting ahead in the department. He spoke of the other Latinos as men who were still uncomfortable going into a downtown restaurant to have a cup of coffee. They were men who were satisfied with being in the department; they didn't even take the examinations for promotion—not Islas. When he was passed over for sergeant in favor of an Anglo who scored lower than he did on the test, he complained. He didn't get anywhere, he said, until Ed Pooley "interceded with the powers that be" on his behalf.

Islas achieved near legendary stature as a policeman. He was known as the smartest detective, the toughest cop, the best diplomat with other law enforcement agencies. He had a certain lack of finesse, however, in dealing with superiors in his own department: When he felt he was ill-treated in some way, he said, he did not hesitate to advise the person who had wronged him to "kiss the Mexican side of my ass," even if that person was the chief of police.

Going into the 1960s, the Mexican-American generation seemed to have won its rightful place in El Paso, the traditional starting place for Mexicans in the United States. Rubén Salazar was a trouble maker, but a brilliant reporter. Ray Sánchez was the sports editor of the *Herald-Post*, Raymond Telles was the mayor of the town, Art Islas was the best known cop, Rudy Tellez was El Paso's favorite son, and Ed Pooley assured Mexican-Americans a public voice in the English-language media. The Anglos still had all the money, but the Telles election had proved that, despite the poll tax, Mexican-Americans would vote in larger numbers than anyone expected and that Anglos did not necessarily vote along straight ethnic lines.

---

1. Rudy and I worked together for several years. He and his wife, Yvette, and my wife and I were close friends. When Rudy and his family moved to San Francisco, we followed in a few months. Rudy and I had plans to go into business together, but we had little capital and less luck. He stayed in broadcasting, eventually becoming the producer of the "Tonight Show" on the NBC network.

---

2. He is the father of the novelist Arturo Islas, Jr.

The first year of the new decade gave even more hope to the generation of assimilationists: A Roman Catholic was elected president of the United States, and he owed his victory, in part, to the Mexican-American vote in Texas. The poll tax was dead. Passage of some sort of civil rights act was possible. Federally funded health care for the poor was promised. On the left, there was a different view: While there had been some outstanding Latino successes in towns like El Paso during the fifties, the systemic problems had not been overcome. The number of employed people in the city of El Paso doubled during the decade, but per capita income actually fell. In San Antonio, half of the Mejicanos and Mexican-Americans were living without indoor plumbing. Economic conditions in South Texas were worse.

In Los Angeles, Edward Roybal had been elected to the city council in 1949, the first Mexican-American to sit on the council since 1881. But Edmund G. Brown, Sr., the governor of California during most of the sixties, named only thirty Mexican-Americans among his first five thousand appointees, arguing that there were no qualified Mexicans in the state. Mexican-American children who could not speak English when they entered California schools were still put into classes for the mentally retarded. It was the same everywhere: The Mexican-American generation had made history, they had proved that change was possible, but they had not created a revolution. For most Mejicanos and Mexican-Americans in the United States in 1960 life was still miserable.

The chicano generation began in the late 1960s and lasted about six or eight years, dying slowly through the seventies. Nothing remains of it now but a handshake practiced by middle-aged men. Some people still call themselves chicanos, but the definition is vague and the word has lost its fire. Six months before he was killed, Rubén Salazar wrote a column for the Los Angeles *Times* in which he attempted to define the chicano concept for both Mexican-Americans and Anglos. This concept emerged early in the movement, and it had strong assimilationist overtones. It is of historical value to reprint the column here, for it was a bridge between the Mexican-American and chicano generations, a moderate position.

Salazar who was born in Chihuahua, should have known the original meaning of the word chicano.[3] If not, he could certainly have asked his father. Perhaps he did, and then chose not to use the answer in his column for fear of giving ammunition to the enemy. The column, reprinted below, has a few of the oversights common to daily journalism.

The history of the newspaper demanded that Rubén write with some discretion, for the Los Angeles *Times*, which had been overtly anti-Mexican since it began publishing in the nineteenth century, was just beginning to learn under Rubén's mentor, Ed Pooley, who railed against fancy writing and posted notes on the city room bulletin board about the sixth-grade reading level of newspaper readers.

A chicano is a Mexican-American with a non-Anglo image of himself.

He resents being told Columbus "discovered" America when the chicano's ancestors, the Mayans and the Aztecs, founded highly sophisticated civilizations centuries before Spain financed the Italian explorer's trip to the "New World."

Chicanos resent also Anglo pronouncements that chicanos are "culturally deprived" or that the fact that they speak Spanish is a "problem."

Chicanos will tell you that their culture predates that of the Pilgrims and that Spanish was spoken in America before English and so the "problem" is not theirs but the Anglos' who don't speak Spanish.

Having told you that, the chicano will then contend that Anglos are Spanish-oriented at the expense of Mexicans.

They will complain that when the governor dresses up as a Spanish nobleman for the Santa Barbara fiesta he's insulting Mexicans because the Spanish conquered and exploited the Mexicans.

It's as if the governor dressed like an English Redcoat for a Fourth of July parade, chicanos say.

When you think you know what chicanos are getting at, a Mexican-American will tell you that chicano is an insulting term and may even quote the Spanish Academy to prove that chicano derives from chicanery.

A chicano will scoff at this and say that such Mexican-Americans have been brainwashed

---

3. In Chihuahua, a chicano was a *marrano* or a small pig, according to Joaquín Avila, Sr., and others. The very poor and people who labored at the lowest level were known as chicanos. Although the word was derogatory, it was the mildest of insults. Nevertheless, many older people continue to be appalled at the use of the term to describe people of Mexican descent.

On the issue of capitalization, I have not used an initial capital letter, just as I would not use an initial capital for black, brown, gringo, or white.

by Anglos and that they're Tio Tacos (Uncle Toms). This type of Mexican-American, chicanos will argue, doesn't like the word chicano because it's abrasive to their Anglo-oriented minds.

These poor people are brown Anglos, chicanos will smirk.

What, then, is a chicano? Chicanos say that if you have to ask you'll never understand, much less become a chicano.

Actually, the word chicano is as difficult to define as "soul."

For those who like simplistic answers, chicano can be defined as short for Mexicano. For those who prefer complicated answers, it has been suggested that chicano may have come from the word Chihuahua—the name of a Mexican state bordering on the United States. Getting trickier, this version then contends that Mexicans who migrated to Texas call themselves chicanos because having crossed into the United States from Chihuahua they adopted the first three letters of that state, Chi, and then added cano, for the latter part of Texano.

Such explanations, however, tend to miss the whole point as to why Mexican-American activists call themselves chicanos.

Mexican-Americans, the second largest minority in the country and the largest in the Southwestern states (California, Texas, New Mexico and Colorado), have always had difficulty making up their minds what to call themselves.

In New Mexico they call themselves Spanish-Americans. In other parts of the Southwest they call themselves Americans of Mexican descent, people with Spanish surnames or Hispanos.

Why, ask some Mexican-Americans, can't we just call ourselves Americans?

Chicanos are trying to explain why not. Mexican-Americans, though indigenous to the Southwest, are on the lowest rung scholastically, economically, socially and politically. Chicanos feel cheated. They want to effect change. Now.

Mexican-Americans average eight years of schooling compared to the Negroes' ten years. Farm workers, most of whom are Mexican-Americans in the Southwest, are excluded from the National Labor Relations Act unlike other workers. Also, Mexican-Americans often have to compete for low-paying jobs with their Mexican brothers from across the border who are willing to work for even less. Mexican-Americans have to live with the stinging fact that the word Mexican is the synonym for inferior in many parts of the Southwest.

That is why Mexican-American activists flaunt the barrio word chicano—as an act of defiance and a badge of honor. Mexican-Americans, though large in numbers, are so politically impotent that in Los Angeles, where the country's largest single concentration of Spanish-speakers live, they have no one of their own on the City Council.[4] This in a city politically sophisticated enough to have three Negro councilmen.

Chicanos, then, are merely fighting to become "Americans." Yes, but with a chicano outlook.

The movement had no official beginning. It may have started in the mid-sixties with the Brown Berets or in 1967 with the publication of the epic poem *I Am Joaquín*, by the former professional boxer, Rodolfo "Corky" Gonzales. The chicanos showed their power for the first time in Los Angeles in March of 1968 when ten thousand students walked out of barrio high schools. The Brown Berets were cited by some public officials and journalists as the organizers of the walkout. In reality, the Brown Berets were a poor imitation of the Black Panthers, and like the Panthers, they were wildly romanticized in the newspapers. The leaders of both organizations exhibited the style of charming ferocity required of radicals in America, but their followers were platoons of children, many of them seeking to overcome some physical or emotional handicap by wearing the appropriate headgear and marching in line, if not in step.

No one noticed the reality of the Brown Berets. The myth of resistance, of an army of Mejicanos as politically pure as Zapatistas and as tough as Pancho Villa's Division del Norte, fed the spirit of Chicanismo. The Brown Berets were the dream marines of the movement, Mejicanos who scared the gringos. There were more walkouts.

Chicano students protested in Colorado, Texas, and Arizona. The complaints were always the same: poor facilities, racism, cultural bias, and a tracking system that prepared Latino students for

---

4. Edward Roybal was then serving in the U.S. House of Representatives.

the worst, lowest-paying jobs. Lewis Terman, the foolish psychologist from Stanford, had put the academic imprimatur on racism, supporting the idea that Mexicans could not compete intellectually with Anglos. As a result, schools all over the Southwest expected Mejicano and Mexican-American students to drop out. And they did. The dropout rate for Latinos was about 50 percent, which was an improvement over the early years of the twentieth century, when the dropout rate was about 90 percent in towns like El Paso: Of those who graduated from high school between 1898 and 1920, 812 were Anglos and 22 Latinos, even though more than 60 percent of the elementary school students during that period were of Mexican descent. San Antonio packed Latinos into poorly staffed, crumbling schools, according them half the space and less than half the facilities given to Anglo students. In 1968 there was no city or town in the United States in which Latino students were educated according to constitutional guarantees of equality of treatment under the law.

The Los Angeles walkout, which began as a demand to be educated as well as blacks and Anglos, turned into the linchpin for a national movement. It was the single largest, most concerted action in the brief history of Chicanismo. The United Farm Workers boycotts were the most broadly based actions and the Crystal City, Texas, overthrow of the Anglo power structure was the most successful, but nothing equaled the 1968 walkout as a demonstration of the will of the people. Political and student groups were formed, among them La Raza Unida party, the Mexican-American Youth Organization (MAYO), United Mexican-American Students (UMAS), and El Movimiento Estudiantil Chicano de Aztlán (MECHA). William (Willie) Velásquez, the son of a butcher in San Antonio, founded the Southwest Voter Registration and Education Project, and McGeorge Bundy, then president of the Ford Foundation, sent money to a small legal services organization with the proviso that it take on important cases in the style of the NAACP, which changed the Mexican American Legal Defense and Education Fund from a poverty law office into an effective civil rights organization.

On August 29, 1970, in the aftermath of an antiwar demonstration that had turned into a riot, Rubén Salazar was killed and Chicanismo lost its clearest voice. There were other marches, other riots, other writers, but the killing of Rubén was the beginning of the end of the movement. He did not become a martyr; his death became a different sym-

bol. The sheriff had threatened him, and the sheriff's deputies had killed him. No one was indicted in the killing; no one was reprimanded. The Los Angeles *Times* and a few of the radical weeklies of the sixties protested briefly, but there was no uprising by the media over the killing of one of their own. Within a few months the newspapers and television stations in Los Angeles returned to speaking for the police in any confrontation with chicanos. The voice of the resistance was gone.

In all the history of the Mexica[5] the pattern had been the same. A man rose to prominence and led the people in war. He was killed in ambush or in battle, and he was neither replaced nor remembered in anger. The Mexica believed in heroes but not in martyrs. Conquered cities did not rise again; destroyed temples were not rebuilt. The Náhua poet asked, "Is it true that we pass this way but once?"

For these ancient reasons, the killing of Rubén Salazar was a Mexican death. As in the past, some people survived, but the spirit of the civilization died. Of those who survived, some were used as slaves and servants by the conquerors; others in their worldly wisdom chose to become like the conquerors and prospered. Soon it was the 1980s and Ronald Reagan was elected president of the United States. His California cadre called out to the crowd, "Viva!" and the crowd answered, "Olé!" Never before had so many Mexican-Americans voted for a Republican presidential candidate.

2.

We must gently obey and endure the laws of our condition. We are subject to grow aged, to become weak, and to fall sick, in spite of all physic. It is the first lesson the Mexicans give their children. When they come out of their mothers' wombs, they thus salute them: My child, thou art come into the world to suffer; therefore suffer and hold thy peace.
Montaigne, "Of Experience"

How quickly the world learned about the Mexicans! In France, in the waning years of the sixteenth century, Montaigne admired that aspect of character which the older generation of Mejicanos and Mexican-Americans still say is most important in

---

5. The people commonly known as Aztecs referred to themselves as "Mexica" (pronounced "Mesheeka"), hence "Mexico."

their world-view. Answering the challenge to describe their character in a single word, they say, "*Aguantar.*" The verb means to bear, to endure, to stand, to tolerate, to put up with. The noun formed from it, *aguante*, means fortitude, patience, endurance, resistance to toil or fatigue. In the lexicon of the bullfight, *aguantar* means to stand firm. The signs of courage (defined as overcoming one's fear) in the bullring is to hold one's ground when the bull charges. "Aguantar la vara como venga" means to bear whatever comes, as the bull must bear the *vara* used by the picador.

Aguantar is thus not entirely Mexican; under certain circumstances it is Spanish as well. In the Mestizo character of Mexico, the fatalism of the Indians combined comfortably with the Spanish willingness to endure danger and suffering. Thus, *aguantar* came to mean enduring one's fate bravely and with a certain style. The Mexican *aguantar* differs from Faulkner's concept of what poor blacks in the South do—"and they endure"—in that the Mexicans do not mean merely to live long without dying, but to have fortitude, to consider endurance a virtue.

In Mexico, the concept of *aguantar* enabled the conquerors to make use of the poor, particularly the Indian poor, as cheap labor. The North Americans were quick to learn from the criollos.[6] Based on the Mejicano's willingness to endure, the Anglo decided that Mejicanos were docile, easily managed. *Aguantar*, the virtue, betrayed Mexican immigrants in labor negotiations, education, housing, every aspect of life in the United States. Because of the Mejicano's willingness to endure danger, intolerable working and living conditions, and so on, the Mejicanos became the safety valve for labor in the Southwest, low-paid casuals, relegated to the worst jobs, and hired and fired almost capriciously as a means of maintaining stable employment in the best jobs for Anglos.

Mejicanos still hold to the virtue of *aguantar*. Among Mexican-Americans only the old generation promotes the heroics of fatalism; younger people say the single word that best describes the character of the Mexican-American is *respeto*, which means respect, but also has overtones of deference and awe. *Respeto* is more than the tone of social relations; it is the relation of one person to another, child to parent, student to teacher, citizen to police officer, worker to boss, and neighbor to neighbor. Ideally, *respeto* does not operate in only one direction; ideally, *respeto* serves as a brake on the driving individualism of Anglo society and makes a person more familial, more communal in his orientation. In reality, *respeto* may combine with the notion of *aguantar* to produce passivity.

Latino educators find that the rule of *respeto* too often leaves Mejicano and Mexican-American students so passive they seem almost to be asleep. Emily Cole, a Latina who had recently become the principal of Jefferson High School in Houston, lamented that "Latino kids will allow an adult to talk down to them. Culturally, we don't defend ourselves. Kids just accept anything anybody tells them. They respect adults too much.

"The teachers like that. Some teachers[7] who are assigned to honors classes complain that the kids ask questions. And the teachers can't handle that."

Almost all of the children in Jefferson High School are Latinos. Recently, some Salvadoran refugee children have joined the Mexicans, Mejicanos, and Mexican-Americans. Ms. Cole, who prefers the role of realist to that of apologist, gave the painful statistics of Jefferson High: In the entering class, 650; in the tenth grade, 200; in the graduating class, 200. By her straightforward calculation, the dropout rate is almost 70 percent.

She also finds the idea of *aguantar* a danger to the children. They endure whatever happens to them. In many cases children are asked to drop out of school to work or to take care of other children at home, and they do so uncomplainingly. Neither the children nor their parents are willing to speak out in defense of themselves.

On the other hand, when the concept of *respeto* is absent, as in some of the very poor children now coming across the border in West Texas, there is nothing in the culture to replace it. Teachers in Socorro, a small town in the Lower Valley of eastern El Paso County, find the new immigrant children uncontrollable, different from the children they have come to know in decades of working there in the Lower Valley. The new immigrants are often children of homeless people or the squatters who live near the garbage dump in Ciudad Juárez. How their lack of *respeto* will affect their lives is uncertain. According to the teachers in Socorro schools, the children arrive in the United States with virtually no skills in Spanish, and they are not emotionally or intellectually capable of learning in English or in bilingual classes.

---

6. People of European descent.

7. The teachers in Jefferson High School were mainly Anglo, men and women who did not understand the Mejicano and Mexican-American culture sufficiently well to teach the children within the context of their own culture.

The origin of the concept of *aguantar* is very old. It is an Indian way of understanding how to live in the world. Claude Lévi-Strauss compared this "savage" way of thinking with modern Western thought and found the "savage mind" complex, brilliant, and very much the equal of the modern mind. For the Belgian anthropologist the difference came with writing and the accumulation of knowledge, which led to a linear mode of thinking, the modern replacement for the neolithic vision of time and the world as circular. Lévi-Strauss compared the two modes of thinking to a train and a clock. With homage to Rousseau, he wrote lovingly of the "youth of the world" and agreed that modern man is its "decrepitude."

The problem of *Aguantar* is that in a modern acquisitive society the character of the person who acquiesces to nature is out of step. Neolithic man has no greater wish than to be in harmony with nature, while modern man wishes to control nature. The irony of the Mexican tie to neolithic thinking is that both the Aztec and the Mayan societies were on the verge of modernity. Both had begun to accumulate knowledge, although they still believed, in the neolithic way, that everything could be explained through myth and religion.

When people bring fatalistic views with them to society intent upon controlling its own fate, the newcomers find accommodation extremely difficult. The aims of the new society make no sense to them: Nature has a built in sense of limits, which the mestizo world-view accepts, but the same world-view staggers before the failure of a civilization that often lacks any sense of limits. *Aguantar* and *respeto* are concepts perfectly suited to the view of the world as a circle, a view in which any break in the circle is catastrophic. In Aztec mythology, for example, the sun renews itself in fifty-two-year cycles; if the sun fails to renew itself and the circle is broken, the world will end.

Living according to the concepts of *aguantar* and *respeto*, one can get along perfectly well in a small, very stable society, in a village culture. To compete, to be acquisitive, to be selfish, the traits valued in a modern capitalist society, have no place in a village culture. It is a gentler but more formal place, one in which the rules of society, which accommodate themselves to the laws of nature, are observed more carefully than in a tumultuous modern urban setting.

Anglos and other Latinos encountering Mejicanos and Mexican-Americans who still hold on to the old values find them gentle, charming, passive, easy to manage, docile, and they are quick to take advantage of them. The Mejicanos who suffer from being used by modern Anglo society react in several ways: they adopt Anglo values, they sink into passivity, or they resort to machismo, with all of its attendant interpersonal and social problems. During the late sixties and early seventies the chicano movement attempted to find a middle ground in which one could retain the value of *respeto* while shedding the fatalism of *aguantar*, picking and choosing the best and most useful aspects of both cultures. The movement did not survive, but there can be no doubt that for many people it did shift the world-view toward *respeto*, but a healthy *respeto*, without the overtones of awe and deference, engendered by the unifying character of culture rather than the divisive power of class.

In those Mexican-Americans who have succeeded best in the United States the quality of *aguantar* seems largely to have disappeared. Robert Ortega, who heads CMA Construction, is the antithesis of the fatalistic villager who lived by the whim of nature, yet Ortega demonstrates the closeness to his family and community of *respeto*. The combination of the two sets of values produces some interesting contradictions in Ortega: Although he considers himself a Republican, he is a major funder of a radical community action group.

Vilma Martínez, who was general counsel of the Mexican American Legal Defense and Education Fund (MALDEF), grew up in a small town in Texas, where her high school counselors advised her not to waste her time preparing for college. *Aguantar* required that she accept the judgment of the school and prepare for the barefoot and pregnant life of a rural Mejicana, but she did not put up with what seemed to be her lot in life. Although her family was Mexican, culture did not determine her behavior. She chose her life. After graduating from law school, she worked at public interest law, becoming president and general counsel of MALDEF, then moving to a private firm, Munger, Tolles & Olson.

Although she is more gracious and far more informal than most members of prestigious law firms, even in Los Angeles where she practices, one does not become a regent of the University of California and a member of the board of directors of Anheuser Busch through fatalism; Vilma Martínez continues to choose her own path. The practice of law in the United States, particularly public interest law, requires character traits opposite to those of *aguantar*. A particularly individualistic world-view is required of a former public interest lawyer who defends a corporation against charges of discrimination against Mexican-Americans; although she was criticized for it by some of her former allies, Ms. Martínez took on such a case.

A highly trained lawyer or a successful businessman seems to have moved beyond the cultural determinism that wounds so many Mexican-Americans. Or is it a wound? Concha Saucedo, who heads the Instituto La Raza Familiar in San Francisco, argues in favor of cultural determinism. She sees refugees and many poor people for whom the old culture is the best and the only grip on life. "People who have made it here," she says, "have paid a high price. I see many who are suffering, who have had to turn off part of themselves. I see them here as patients."

Saucedo, a psychologist, said she named the clinic on the advice of *las viejas*, for the old women are very wise and very intellectual. She knew after talking with them that if she simply translated the English phrase and called it *salud mental*, no one would come to the mental health clinic. All of her work is based on the old culture. She keeps an altar in her office, and she wears jewelry of jade and silver.

Although she is small physically, her presence, in her office or across the table in a restaurant, is commanding. It is possible, her face says, that she knows something, which is required of psychologists who practice the healing system of the youth of the world. What she knows was learned partly in school and in studying with a well-known psychiatrist, but it was also learned partly in the old way. "I went with my father who was a *maestro*—we didn't use the word *curandero* then. I went with him when he treated people. In the last eight years I've spent time in the mountains of Oaxaca learning from a woman there. I don't talk much about that. We're usually asked not to."

Everything in the Instituto is rooted in Latino culture. Concha Saucedo's speech is laced with Spanish; the Virgin of Guadalupe appears in her office on the altar along with things found or given to her by patients: a curled glass tube meant to hold a flower, tiny decorated pots, a small feather, a painted card about peace. The altar is more like the contents of a medicine bundle on display than the altar of a Western church. She is Indian, descended form Yaquis, Coros, and Huicholes, and the holder of an advanced degree from UCLA. Her medicine is not much of this time. On the walls outside her office the brief biographies under the photographs of the members of the board of directors of the instituto tell their names, family names, nationalities, and "favorite pastimes," but give no information about profession or employment; in Mejicano culture a job does not define a person. Everything about the work of Concha Saucedo is rooted in Indian or mestizo culture, the culture of *aguantar*, but the *curandera* is also a psychologist from UCLA; she treats patients in the real world of California, not in the mountains of Oaxaca. "To be healthy," she said, "means to have power over your own life."

2. Alberto Alvaro Ríos, "The Iguana Killer"

Is there a border between the United States and Mexico? Politically speaking, the answer would be yes; but from the perspective of culture the reply would be in the negative. Language, customs, foods, ideas, and art have always freely passed in both directions along one of the most famous frontiers in the world. Indeed, the Tijuana/San Diego border is the busiest border crossing on earth. Capturing the uniqueness of the border and its effect both on Mexicans and Mexican-Americans is the contemporary short story writer Alberto Alvaro Ríos. He is the author of several works of poetry (such as *Whispering to Fool the Wind*, 1982) and also of fiction (*The Iguana Killer: Twelve Stories of the Heart*, 1984, from which this selection is taken). Ríos writes of his growing up:

I grew up on the border in regards to all kinds of metaphorical borders: in between countries, languages, cultures, decades. In essence, all of this adds up to using binoculars, using two lenses to bring something closer in which you see it better and understand it more.

In the story which follows, we hear Ríos' voice as he describes the young boy Sapito, who lives in Mexico (in Villahermosa, the capital city of Tabasco) but visits his *abuela* in Nogales, Arizona. Spanish, shared customs, and especially love bind Sapito to both sides of his dispersed family. The international border exists, but not as an obstacle; rather, it provides Sapito with a cultural artifact of *El norte*, a baseball bat put to another use in Sapito's pueblo.

THE IGUANA KILLER

Sapito had turned eight two weeks before and was at this time, living in Villahermosa, the capital city of Tabasco. He had earned his nickname because his eyes bulged to make him look like a frog, and besides, he was the best fly-catcher in all Villahermosa. This was when he was five. Now he was eight, but his eyes still bulged and no one called him anything but "Sapito."

Among their many duties, all the boys had to go down to the Río Grijalva every day and try to sell or trade off whatever homemade things were available and could be carried on these small men's backs. It was also the job of these boys to fish, capture snails, trick tortoises, and kill the iguanas.

Christmas had just passed, and it had been celebrated as usual, very religious with lots of candle smoke and very solemn church masses. There had been no festivities yet, no laughing, but today would be different. Today was the fifth of January, the day the children of Villahermosa wait for all year. Tomorrow would be the *Día de los Reyes Magos*, the Day of the Wise Kings, when presents of all sorts were brought by the Kings and given to friends. Sapito's grandmother, who lived in Nogales in the United States, had sent him two packages. He had seen them, wrapped in blue paper with bearded red clown faces. Sapito's grandmother always sent presents to his family, and she always seemed to know just what Sapito would want, even though they had never met.

That night, Sapito's mother put the packages under the bed where he slept. It was not a cushioned bed, but rather, a hammock, made with soft rattan leaves. Huts in Villahermosa were not rented to visitors by the number of rooms, but, instead, by the number of hooks in each place. On these hooks were hung the hammocks of a family. People in this town were born and nursed, then slept and died in these hanging beds. Sapito could remember his grandfather, and how they found him one afternoon after lunch. They had eaten mangoes together. Sapito dreamed about him now, about how his face

would turn colors when he told his stories, always too loud.

When Sapito woke up, he found the packages. He played up to his mother, the way she wanted, claiming that the *Reyes* had brought him all these gifts. *Look and look, and look here!* he shouted, but this was probably the last time he would do this, for Sapito was now eight, and he knew better, but did not tell. He opened the two packages from Nogales, finding a baseball and a baseball bat. Sapito held both gifts and smiled, though he wasn't clearly sure what the things were. Sapito had not been born in nor ever visited the United States, and he had no idea what baseball was. He was sure he recognized and admired the ball and knew what it was for. He could certainly use that. But he looked at the baseball bat and was puzzled for some seconds.

It was an iguana-killer. "*¡Mira, mamá! un palo para matar iguanas!*" It was beautiful, a dream. It was perfect. His grandmother always knew what he would like.

In Villahermosa, the jungle was not far from where Sapito lived. It started, in fact, at the end of his backyard. It was not dense there, but one could not walk far before a machete became a third hand, sharper, harder, more valuable than the other two in this other world that sometimes kept people.

This strong jungle life was great fun for a boy like Sapito, who especially enjoyed bringing coconuts out of the tangled vines for his mother. He would look for monkeys in the fat palm trees and throw rocks at them, one after the other. To get back, the monkeys would throw coconuts back at him, yelling terrible monkey-words. This was life before the iguana-killer.

Every day for a week after he had gotten the presents, Sapito would walk about half a mile east along the Río Grijalva with Chachi, his best friend.

"The Iguana Killer" is reprinted from The Iguana Killer by Alberto Rios, Copyright 1984 by Alberto Rios. Reprinted by permission of Confluence Press, Inc. at Lewis-Clark State College, in Lewiston, Idaho.

Then they would cut straight south into the hair of the jungle.

There is a correct way to hunt iguanas, and Sapito had been well-skilled even before the bat came. He and Chachi would look at all the trees until the telltale movement of an iguana was spotted. When one was found, Sapito would sit at the base of the tree, being as quiet as possible, with baseball bat held high and muscles stiff.

The female iguana would come out first. She moved her head around very quickly, almost jerking, in every direction. Sapito knew that she was not the one to kill. She kept the little iguanas in supply—his father had told him. After a few seconds, making sure everything was safe, she would return to the tree and send her husband out, telling him there was nothing to worry about.

The male iguana is always slower. He comes out and moves his head to one side and just stares, motionless, for several minutes. Now Sapito knew that he must take advantage, but very carefully. Iguanas can see in almost all directions at once. Unlike human eyes, both iguana eyes do not have to center in on the same thing. One eye can look forward, and one backward, like a clown, so that they can detect almost any movement. Sapito knew this and was always careful to check both eyes before striking. Squinting his own eyes which always puffed out even more when he was excited, he would not draw back his club. That would waste time. It was already kept high in the air all these minutes. When he was ready, he would send the bat straight down as hard and as fast as he could. Just like that. And if he had done all these things right, he would take his prize home by the tail to skin him for eating that night.

Iguanas were prepared like any other meat, fried, roasted, or boiled, and they tasted like tough chicken no matter which way they were done. In Tabasco, and especially in Villahermosa, iguanas were eaten by everybody all the time, even tourists, so hunting them was very popular. Iguana was an everyday supper, eaten without frowning at such a thing, eating lizard. It was not different from the other things eaten here, the turtle eggs, *cahuamas*, crocodile meat, river snails. And when iguanas were killed, nobody was supposed to feel sad. Everybody's father said so. Sapito did, though, sometimes. Iguanas had puffed eyes like his.

But, if Sapito failed to kill one of these iguanas, he would run away as fast as he could—being sad was the last thing he would think of. Iguanas look mean, they have bloodshot eyes, and people say that they spit blood. Sapito and his friends thought that, since no one they knew had ever been hurt by these monsters, they must not be so bad. This was what the boys thought in town, talking on a summer afternoon, drinking coconuts. But when he missed, Sapito figured that the real reason no one had ever been hurt was that no one ever hung around afterward to find out what happens. Whether iguanas were really dangerous or not, nobody could say for certain. Nobody's parents had ever heard of an iguana hurting anyone, either. The boys went home one day and asked. So, no one worried, sort of, and iguanas were even tamed and kept as pets by the old sailors in Villahermosa, along with the snakes. But only by the sailors.

The thought of missing a hit no longer bothered Sapito, who now began carrying his baseball bat everywhere. His friends were impressed more by this than by anything else, even candy in tin boxes, especially when he began killing four and five iguanas a day. No one could be that good. Soon, not only Chachi, but the rest of the boys began following Sapito around constantly just to watch the scourge of the iguanas in action.

By now, the bat was proven. Sapito was the champion iguana-provider, always holding his now-famous killer-bat. All his friends would come to copy it. They would come every day asking for measurements and questioning him as to its design. Chachi and the rest would then go into the jungle and gather fat, straight roots. With borrowed knives and machetes, they tried to whittle out their own iguana-killers, but failed. Sapito's was machine-made and perfect.

This went on for about a week, when Sapito had an idea that was to serve him well for a long time. He began renting out the killer-bat for a *centavo* a day. The boys said yes yes right away, and would go out and hunt at least two or three iguanas to make it worth the price, but really, too, so that they could use the bat as much as possible.

For the next few months, the grown-ups of Villahermosa hated Sapito and his bat because all they ate was iguana. But Sapito was proud. No one would make fun of his bulging eyes now.

Sapito was in Nogales in the United States visiting his grandmother for the first time, before going back to Tabasco, and Villahermosa. His family had come from Chiapas on the other side of the republic on a relative-visiting vacation. It was still winter, but no one in Sapito's family had expected it to be cold.

They knew about rain, and winter days, but it was always warm in the jungle, even for these things.

Sapito was sitting in front of the house on Sonoita Avenue, on the sidewalk. He was very impressed by many things in this town, especially the streetlights. Imagine lighting up the inside inside *and* the outside. It would be easy to catch animals at night here. But most of all, he was impressed by his rather large grandmother, whom he already loved very much. He had remembered to thank her for the iguana-killer and the ball. She had laughed and said, "*Por nada, hijo.*" As he sat and thought about this, he wrapped the two blankets he had brought outside with him tighter around his small body. Sapito could not understand or explain to himself that the weather was cold and that he had to feel it, everyone did, even him. This was almost an unknown experience to him since he had never been out of the tropics before. The sensation, the feeling of cold, then, was very strange, especially since he wasn't even wet. It was actually hurting him. His muscles felt as if he had held his bat up in the air for an hour waiting for an iguana. Of course, Sapito could have gone inside to get warm near the wood-burning stove, but he didn't like the smoke or the smell of the north. It was a different smell, not the jungle.

So Sapito sat there. Cold had never been important in his life before, and he wasn't going to let it start now. With blankets he could cover himself up and it would surely pass. Covered up for escape, he waited for warmness, pulling the blankets over his head. Sometimes he would put out his foot to see if it was okay yet, the way the lady iguana would come out first.

Then, right then in one fast second, Sapito seemed to feel, with his foot on the outside, a very quiet and strange moment, as if everything had slowed. He felt his eyes bulge when he scrunched up his face to hear better. Something scary caught hold of him, and he began to shiver harder. It was different from just being cold, which was scary enough. His heartbeat was pounding so much that he could feel it in his eyes.

He carefully moved one of the blankets from his face. Sapito saw the sky falling, just like the story his grandmother had told him the first day they had been there. He thought she was joking, or that she didn't realize he was already eight, and didn't believe in such things anymore.

Faster than hitting an iguana Sapito threw his blankets off, crying as he had not cried since he was five and they had nicknamed him and teased him. He ran to the kitchen and grabbed his mother's leg.

Crying and shivering, he begged, "*¡Mamá, por favor, perdóneme!*" He kept speaking fast, asking for forgiveness and promising never to do anything wrong in his life ever again. The sky was falling, but he had always prayed, really he had.

His mother looked at him and at first could not laugh. Quietly, she explained that it was *nieve*, snow, that was falling, not the sky. She told him not to be afraid, and that he could go out and play in it, touch it, yes.

Sapito still didn't know exactly what this *nieve* was, but now his mother was laughing and didn't seem worried. In Villahermosa, *nieve* was a good word, it meant ice cream. There was a *nieve* man. Certainly the outside wasn't ice cream, but the white didn't really look bad, he thought, not really. It seemed, in fact, to have great possibilities. Sapito went back outside, sitting again with his blankets, trying to understand. He touched it, and breathed even faster. Then, closing his eyes, which was not easy, he put a little in his mouth.

Sapito's family had been back in Villahermosa for a week now. Today was Sunday. It was the custom here that every Sunday afternoon, since there were no other amusements, the band would play on the *malecón*, an area something like a park by the river, where the boats were all loaded.

Each Sunday it was reserved for this band—that is, the group of citizens that joined together and called themselves a band. It was a favorite time for everyone, as the paddle boat lay resting on the river while its owner played the trumpet and sang loud songs. The instruments were all brass, except for the marimba, which was the only sad sounding instrument. Though it was hit with padded drumsticks, its song was quiet, hidden, always reserved for dusk. Sapito had thought about the marimba as his mother explained about snow. Her voice had its sound for the few minutes she spoke, and held him. Before the marimba, before dusk, however, the brass had full control.

As dusk came, it was time for the *verbenas*, when the girls, young and old, would come in and walk around the park in one direction and the boys would walk the opposite way, all as the marimba played its songs easily, almost by itself. On these Sundays no one was a man or a woman. They were all boys and girls, even the women who always wore black. This was when all the flirting and the smiling of smiles bigger than people's faces took

191

place. Sapito and Chachi and the rest of the smaller boys never paid attention to any of this, except sometimes to make fun of someone's older sister.

An old man, Don Tomasito, the baker, played the tuba. When he blew into the huge mouthpiece, his face would turn purple and his thousand wrinkles would disappear as his skin filled out. Sapito and his friends would choose by throwing fingers, and whoever had the odd number thrown out, matching no one else, was chosen to do the best job of the day. This had become a custom all their own. The chosen one would walk around in front of Don Tomasito as he played, and cut a lemon. Then slowly, very slowly, squeeze it, letting the juice fall to the ground. Don Tomasito's lips would follow.

On this first Sunday afternoon after he had returned, Sapito, after being chased by Señor Saturnino Cantón, who was normally the barber but on Sunday was the policeman, pulled out his prize. Sapito had been preparing his friends all day, and now they were yelling to see this new surprise. This was no iguana-killer, but Sapito hoped it would have the same effect.

Some of the people in Villahermosa used to have photographs of various things. One picture Sapito had particularly remembered. Some ladies of the town, who always made their own clothes, once had a picture taken together. They were a group of maybe ten ladies, in very big dresses and hats, some sitting and some standing. What Sapito recalled now was that they were all barefoot. They were all very serious and probably didn't think of it, but now, Sapito, after traveling to the north and seeing many pictures at his grandmother's house, thought their bare feet were very funny, even if shoes were hard to get and couldn't be made like dresses could. Sapito knew about such things now. He remembered that people in Nogales laughed at him when he was barefoot in the snow.

But now, Sapito had a photograph, too. This was his surprise. Well, what it was, really, was a Christmas card picturing a house with lots of snow around. He had gotten the picture from his grandmother and had taken great care in bringing it back home. He kept the surprise under his shirt wrapped in blue paper against his stomach, so it would stay flat. Here was a picture of the *nieve*, just like he had seen for himself, except there was a lot more of it in the picture. An awful lot more.

At the end of this Sunday, making a big deal with his small hands, he showed this prize to his friends, and told them that *nieve*, which means both snow and ice cream in the Spanish of those who have experienced the two, would fall from the sky in

Nogales. Any time at all. His bulging eyes widened to emphasize what he was saying, and he held his bat to be even more convincing.

No one believed him.

"Pues, miren, ¡aquí está!" He showed them the picture, and added now that it was a picture of his grandmother's house, where he had just visited.

When Chachi asked, as Sapito had hoped, if it came down in flavors, he decided that he had gone this far, so why not. *"Vainilla,"* he stated.

As the months went by, so did new stories, and strawberry and pistachio, and he was pretty sure that they believed him. After all, none of them had ever been up north. They didn't know the things Sapito knew. And besides, he still owned the iguana-killer.

Three months after the snow-picture stories had worn off, Señora Casimira, with the help of the town midwife, had a baby girl. The custom here was that mother and baby didn't have to do any work for forty days. No one ever complained. Mostly the little girls would help in the house, doing the errands that were not big enough to bother the boys or the big girls with. They'd throw water out front to quiet the dust. Neighbors would wash the dishes.

For the boys, usually because they could yell louder and didn't want to work with the girls, their job was to go and bring charcoal from the river, to bring bananas and coconuts, and whatever other food was needed. Every morning Sapito and his friends would stand outside the door of Señora Casimira's house, with luck before the girls came, and call in to her, asking if she needed anything. She would tell them yes or no, explaining what to bring if something was necessary.

Spring was here now, and today was Saturday. Sapito thought about this, being wise in the way of seasons now, as he looked down on the Casimira *choza*, the palm-thatched hut in which they lived. Señor Casimira was sure to be there today, he figured. There was no need to hang around, probably. Sapito had saved a little money from renting the killer-bat, and he suggested to his friends that they all go to Puerto Alvarado on the paddle boat. They were hitting him on the back and laughing yes! even before he had finished.

The Río Grijalva comes down from the Sierra Madre mountains, down through the state of Tabasco, through Villahermosa, emptying through

Puerto Alvarado several miles north into the Gulf of Mexico. The boys looked over at the Casimira *choza*, then backward at this great river, where the paddle boat was getting ready to make its first trip of the day to Puerto Alvarado. They ran after it, fast enough to leave behind their shadows.

Sapito and his friends had been in Alvarado for about an hour when they learned that a *cahuama*, a giant sea turtle, was nearby. They were on the rough beach, walking toward the north where the rocks become huge. Some palm trees nodded just behind the beach, followed by the jungle, as always. Sometimes Sapito thought it followed him, always moving closer.

Climbing the mossy rocks, Chachi was the one who spotted the *cahuama*. This was strange because the turtles rarely came so close to shore. In Villahermosa, and Puerto Alvarado, the money situation was such that anything the boys saw, like iguanas or the *cahuama*, they tried to capture. They always tried hard to get something for nothing, and here was their chance—not to mention the adventure involved. They all ran together with the understood intention of dividing up the catch.

They borrowed a rope from the men who were working farther up the shore near the palm trees. "*¡Buena suerte!*" one of the men called, and laughed. Sapito and Chachi jumped in a *cayuco*, a kayak built more like a canoe, which one of the fishermen had left near shore. They paddled out to the floating turtle, jumped out, and managed to get a rope tied around its neck right off. Usually, then, a person had to hop onto the back of the *cahuama* and let it take him down into the water for a little while. Its burst of strength usually went away before the rider drowned or let go. This was the best fun for the boys, and a fairly rare chance, so Sapito, who was closest, jumped on to ride this one. He put up one arm like a tough cowboy. This *cahuama* went nowhere.

The two boys climbed back into the *cayuco* and tried to pull the turtle, but it still wouldn't budge. It had saved its strength, and its strong flippers were more than a match for the two boys now. Everyone on shore swam over to help them after realizing that yells of how to do it better were doing no good. They all grabbed a part of the rope. With pure strength against strength, the six boys sweated, but finally outpulled the stubborn *cahuama*, dragging it onto the shore. It began flopping around on the sand until they managed to tip it onto its back. The turtle seemed to realize that struggling was a waste of its last fat-man energy, and started moving like a slow motion robot, fighting as before but, now, on

its back, the flippers and head moved like a movie going too slow.

The *cahuama* had seemed huge as the boys were pulling it, fighting so strong in the water, but it was only about three feet long when they finally took a breath and looked. Yet, they all agreed, this *cahuama* was very fat. It must have been a grandfather.

Chachi went to call one of the grown-ups to help. Each of the boys was sure that he could kill a *cahuama* and prepare it, but this was everybody's, and they wanted it cut right. The men were impressed as the boys explained. The boys were all nervous. Maybe not nervous—not really, just sometimes they were sad when they caught *cahuamas* because they had seen what happens. Like fish, or iguanas, but bigger, and bigger animals are different. Sad, but they couldn't tell anyone, especially not the other boys, or the men. Sapito looked at their catch.

These sailors, or men who used to be sailors, all carried short, heavy machetes, specially made for things taken from the sea. Chachi came back with a man who already had his in hand. The blade was straight because there was no way to shape metal, no anvil in Alvarado. The man looked at Sapito. "*Préstame tu palo,*" he said, looking at Sapito's iguana-killer. Sapito picked it up from where he had left it and handed it to the man, carefully. The fisherman beat the turtle on the head three times fast until it was either dead or unconscious. Then he handed the bat back to Sapito, who was sort of proud, and sort of not.

The man cut the *cahuama's* head off. Some people eat the head and its juice, but Sapito and his friends had been taught not to. No one said anything as it was tossed to the ground. The flippers continued their robot motion.

He cut the side of the turtle, where the underside skin meets the shell. He then pulled a knife out of his pocket, and continued where the machete had first cut, separating the body of the turtle from the shell. As he was cutting he told the boys about the freshwater sac that *cahuamas* have, and how, if they were ever stranded at sea, they could drink it. They had heard the story a hundred times, but nobody knew anybody who really did it. The boys were impatient. Then he separated the underpart from the inside meat, the prize. It looked a little redder than beef. The fins were then cut off—someone would use their leather sometime later.

The man cut the meat into small pieces. The boys took these pieces and washed them in salt water to make the meat last longer. Before cooking them, they would have to be washed again, this time in fresh water to get all the salt off. In the meantime, the salt water would keep the meat from spoiling. One time Sapito forgot, or really he was in too much of a hurry, and he took some *cahuama* home but forgot to tell his mother. It changed colors, and Sapito had to go get some more food, with everybody mad at him. The boys knew that each part of the *cahuama* was valuable, but all they were interested in now was what they could carry. This, of course, was the meat.

The man gave each of the boys some large pieces, and then kept most of it for himself. The boys were young, and could not argue with a grown-up. They were used to this. The fisherman began to throw the shell away.

"*No, por favor, dámelo,*" Sapito called to him. The man laughed and handed the shell to Sapito, who put his pieces of meat inside it and, with the rest of the boys, wandered back to the river to wait for the paddle boat. The shell was almost too big for him. The boys were all laughing and joking, proud of their accomplishment. They asked Sapito what he was going to do with the shell, but he said that he wasn't sure yet. This wasn't true. Of course, he was already making big, very big, plans for it.

They got back early in the afternoon, and everyone went home exhausted. Sapito, before going home, went into the jungle and gathered some green branches. He was not very tired yet—he had a new idea, so Sapito spent the rest of the afternoon polishing the shell with sand and the hairy part of some coconuts, which worked just like sandpaper.

When it was polished, he got four of the best branches and whittled them to perfection with his father's knife. Sapito tied these into a rectangle using some *mecate*, something in between rope and string, which his mother had given him. The shell

fit halfway down into the opening of the rectangle. It was perfect. Then, onto this frame, he tied two flat, curved branches across the bottom at opposite ends. It moved back and forth like a drunk man. He had made a good, strong crib. It worked, just right for a newborn baby girl.

Sapito had worked hard and fast with the strength of a guilty conscience. Señora Casimira just might have needed something, after all. It was certainly possible that her husband might have had to work today. All the boys had known these facts before they had left, but had looked only at the paddle boat—and it had waved back at them.

Sapito took the crib, hurrying to beat the jungle dusk. Dusk, at an exact moment, even on Sundays, owned the sky and the air in its own strange way. Just after sunset, for about half an hour, the sky blackened more than would be normal for the darkness of early night, and mosquitoes, like pieces of sand, would come up out of the thickest part of the jungle like tornadoes, coming down on the town to take what they could. People always spent this half hour indoors, Sundays, too, even with all the laughing, which stopped then. This was the signal for the marimba's music to take over.

Sapito reached the *choza* as the first buzzings were starting. He listened at the Casimiras' door, hearing the baby cry like all babies. The cradle would help. He put it down in front of the wooden door without making any noise, and knocked. Then, as fast as he could, faster than that even, he ran back over the hill, out of sight. He did not turn around. Señora Casimira would find out who had made it. And he would be famous again, thought Sapito, famous like the other times. He felt for the iguana-killer that had been dragging behind him, tied to his belt, and put it over his right shoulder. His face was not strong enough to keep away the smile that pulled his mouth, his fat eyes all the while puffing out.

3. JUAN DELGADO, THE GREEN WEB

Contemporary poet Juan Delgado has captured in his award-winning verse much of the consciousness of the Mexican-American community, reflecting many experiences that Latinos have shared growing up in America. Responding to the poetry of Delgado, who is a Professor of English at California State University, San Bernardino, Larry Kramer writes: "Juan Delgado's poems remind us that the great thing, the essential thing, the terrible thing about America is that it must be discovered over and over, and while we all want to be secure citizens, none of us truly are or ever can be." In the following poems (taken from *The Green Web*), we hear Juan Delgado picturing the lives of several Mexican-Americans who remember their past and their roots in Mexico while at the same time reflect on the consequences of living in a world that is at the same time Latino and Anglo.

MY MOTHER'S STORIES

Mother nailed
a cross of palm leaves,
its end yellowing, frayed.

At night Mother said if we noticed it, especially its arms
reaching down to the feet, we would see a woman dressed in
cotton, a whore loosening the ankle strap of her sandal. She
tapped her shoe against a wall and rubbed her sore foot. She
pointed to a street unlike ours where men stomped the ground,
dancing and blowing out fireballs. The feathers around their
heads and waists bounced and flared. The fire breathers danced
around their gas tanks, whirling their torches for the passing
cars. On the corner women with red ribbons woven into their
long braids peeled potatoes, cutting them into thin slices, then
fried them in ash-colored coffee cans. Their children blew into
small plastic bags, then filled them with hot chips and sold them.
A man who also left his town came to play lemon leaves, the way
one plays a blade of grass.

And a slow-paced greyhound sniffed
at the hunger around them.

Before that the cross was an Indian girl who hobbled, helped by
a wooden crutch. She waited for tourists, especially young
couples. Leaning on the crutch, she twisted her leg and held out
her hand for the walkers. Yet when the rain came, she threw the
crutch over her shoulder and ran, skipping over the pools in the
plaza. Her sandals slapped the wet cobbles.

"Please, one more, tell us one more."

Our bed's worn out springs drew us in the middle, huddled like
flour sacks. Mother read us the Bible and when we were bored
she made up stories. At school Sister Maria asked: "Where did
you hear that? Who told those evil lies? Child, I'll not hurt you if
you tell me now."

She was also a wife
who braved a smile
while she crossed a muddy river.
She held her skirt up,
wading through the currents
trying not to spill a pot of coffee beans
she had just bought at the market.

Selections on pp. 197-202: From GREEN WEB by Juan Delgado. Copyright 1994. Reprinted by permission of The University of Georgia Press.

Foam glistened on her thighs
and the river soiled her dress.

Mother told us the wife
found herself waiting for a train.
There was a war; a revolution started.
Her fellow soldaderas rested,
too tired to speak.
They wore their bandoliers loose,
their shawls tied around their waists,
dragging when they marched.
They leaned on cargo boxes
and on bundles of clothing;
only their hands seemed to move;
the rest was reposed.
As the wife stood,
her rifle was planted
in front of her legs,
both hands grasping it,
elbows slightly out,
the rifle steadying her wait,
her war.

CRAYONS

Coco, my youngest aunt, dropped her fan,
sat behind her father's store counter,
sifted through the rice pail, bored,
then studied my crayon drawings,
their smooth textures and warned me
not to stare at a pissing dog
because I would go blind—I jumped
from her lap, pretending to fly,
speaking of America, my other home.

Grown up, I returned to Mexico
and stood by my aunt's deathbed.
Her four daughters, half-dressed,
stared at me, the stranger.
I turned from their mother's face,
feeling sickened by the countless flies
living and breeding on the walls.

One girl rattled Coco's pain killers,
the others sprinkled the dirt floor.
Coco had them put on shoes,
warning of worms in the moist soil.
Coco said on the first summer we met
I could draw her face with my crayons;
leaves surrounded her face,
egg-shaped, a squiggle for a mouth,
long bangs and eyes, new buttons.

MAD

Dad didn't get picked.
I guess a foreman drove off
with a truck full of workers,
leaving Dad at the curb
waiting all day for the next truck.
Usually he's hired for the day
and too tired to dog everyone.
Now he pounds the table
because he's hungry
and Mom's earrings jump.
She heats tortillas over the flames
and balances a plate of eggs
dancing in the hot grease.
All the time
a beer bubbles in Dad's hand
while he eyes everyone.
"Shouldn't eat alone, not right,"
he says, "Hurry up."
And I begin grace
for the second time this night.
I glance at Mom who hides
her hands behind her apron,
moving them as if she's going
to roll her apron into a ball.
After he's finished, he drinks more.
I study the field next door.
Mom hates the field and the foxtails
that dig and hide in my socks.
Behind her clotheslines
she curses the field and the drifters
who come and start their campfires,
then wrap themselves in newspapers
before falling asleep.
I trace their shadows
and the leaping flames in the nights
when the glass fogs up.
I make up stories about them
with no pain or anger.
Then Dad pounds for another beer.
I move, thinking about our dog
when he circles his pole
and tightens his chain,
knotting it up.
How he tries to leap,
snapping at himself.

Mrs. Lucy Rivera

At dusk I fade behind my screen.
A crow picks at a bag, the empty
plastic settles like a fog.

Like my friend, the crow
who sits on a wire like a clothespin,
I squawk at the dying light.

I smear my lipstick, then finger
my bleeding lips, my mascara.
My penciled-in eyebrows are too perfect.

When the young wife sees my face,
she will go on as if nothing is wrong,
both of us pretending.

I listen to sound no one hears:
a stirring trash can, a leaping cat,
a car with one headlight like a bullet.

I peer through half-closed blinds,
studying the flickering porch lights;
moths flutter like kites without tails.

The people of my street believe
in sleep, in their laboring days.
I linger in my room, and sleep.

A Mexican Fire Breather

Where the weather is not water
a man sips from a glass jar,
not swallowing the gasoline,
holding in his breath
while holding up his lighter.

In the cloud burst of fire
there are no legions of angels
beyond the air of his lungs,
saints holding the flame of life
on their upturned palms.

In the cloud burst of fire
the man is neither a cross,
fixed while the earth spins,
nor an ancient altar,
raised and tainted with blood.

He is only a man
cleaning your windshield
while you wait at the light.
He peers in your car,
holding in his breath and fire.

4. César Chávez, "A Step to Freedom"

One of the most famous Mexican-Americans of the twentieth century is César Chávez (1927-1993), founder and leader of the National Farm Workers Association. Chávez was born in Arizona; his grandparents had arrived in that state after fleeing the turbulence of the Mexican Revolution. During the Great Depression, the young Chávez and his family lost their farm, and were forced to join the growing number of migrants living in labor camps in both Arizona and California.

As he was growing up, Chávez became increasingly aware of the unequal treatment of white Americans and people of color. In 1943, when he was fifteen, Chávez refused to recognize segregated seating at a Delano, California, movie house and was forced to leave. Nevertheless, like many Mexican-Americans and other Latinos, César Chávez joined the U. S. armed forces during World War II, serving with the Navy under combat conditions in the Pacific.

Yet, the greatest battles of Chávez's life would confront him after the war, when he became active in various organizations that sought to organize and defend the rights of marginalized peoples. One such group was the Community Service Organization (CSO). Chávez soon realized that farm workers were not being fully represented organized labor and thus founded in 1962 the Farm Workers Association in Delano, California. His principal target at first were the wine-grape growers, and Chávez's union later focused on the table-grape growers with the same goal: to improve benefits and working conditions of the migrant workers employed by these two important industries.

Chávez continued to fight for the rights of farm laborers to the end of his life, employing non-violence as a successful strategy to bring about social change. In the following autobiographical statement, taken from the opening pages of the *Autobiography of La Causa*, by James E. Levy, Chávez tells how he first had to "organize" his wife, Helen, before organizing the farm workers. Chávez's family at the time was in a comfortable financial position, and any union activity would endanger the household budget. Yet Helen soon saw the necessity of giving up a regular family pay check in order to free César to accomplish his goals.

CHAPTER 1
A STEP TO FREEDOM

CÉSAR CHÁVEZ RECALLS

It took me four years to think it through. I studied the problem, talked to many people, and thought about it constantly. And every time I analyzed it, I came right back to one basic thing. One set of strings had me so wrapped up I couldn't move. That was my financial security.

I realized that I couldn't do what I felt must be done without first giving up one of the best jobs I'd ever had.

As national director of CSO, the Community Service Organization, I lived in East Los Angeles and helped organize people in the barrios, our Mexican ghettos, all over California. The paycheck came regularly, about $150 a week that my family could count on week after week.

Yet security doesn't really come with a paycheck. You think you have security, but it's just momentary when you cash the check, I guess, or when you think of it. Actually it doesn't bring either security or peace of mind.

More than anything else, I wanted to help farm workers. I was a farm worker when I had joined CSO ten years before, and I thought the organization could help us. That's why I soon became a paid organizer on the staff. While CSO was doing some good for the poor in the communities, after a few years I began to realize that a farm workers' union was needed to end the exploitation of the workers in the fields, if we were to strike at the roots of their suffering and poverty.

I had done a lot of reading about farm labor unions, thought about them, and questioned every farm worker I could find who had been involved in a strike. It was a sad history of defeat after defeat, strikes smashed with violence, the government in league with the growers, police helping to bring in scabs.

But the more I studied the mistakes that were made in the past, the more I believed growers were not invincible. If we fought them right, we could beat them. I had learned a lot in the CSO about organizing the barrios and the poor. I had learned about taking on the authorities to get help for the community, and I had learned tactics to curb injustice. I felt a union could succeed.

When I talked about starting a union, however, all I heard was that it had been tried many times before—never successfully—and it couldn't be done. One of my friends remarked, "Man, this Chávez is really nuts!" I couldn't convince the CSO directors to try it. I was tempted to strike out alone.

Only my financial security had me tied up and kept me from moving. There was my wife, Helen, and I knew it would be asking a lot of her to give up what we had. Here I was already thirty-five, with my first steady job in one location, after years of constantly drifting from one place to another, first as a migrant hunting for work and then as a CSO organizer. We had about twelve hundred dollars in the bank that wouldn't last six months if I left my job. And, more importantly, there were our eight children, the oldest thirteen and the two youngest only four and two and a half.

Helen and I had discussed the problem from many angles. There were the risks, the odds against success, and the desperate needs we saw daily all around us. Helen, naturally, was very worried about our children. If I quit, who knows what would happen? Where would the money come from for food and clothes and housing? I could only point to my own childhood where, despite our struggles and bitter experiences, ours was a very close and happy family. I was sure my own children could endure.

The more we talked about it, the more I organized her. I saw the trap most people get themselves into—tying themselves to a job for security. It was easier for us and our family to try to escape poverty than to change the conditions that keep so many workers poor. But we inherited the poverty

From CÉSAR CHÁVEZ, AUTOBIOGRAPHY OF LA CAUSA by Jacques Levy. Copyright © 1966 by Jacques Levy. Reprinted by permission of the author.

from our fathers and our fathers from our grandfathers and our grandfathers from their fathers. We had to stop someplace!

Finally one day I said, "We can't organize farm workers like this. I could talk about how bad conditions are for them, how much I've done for them, and how much I'd like to do, and I can stay here and keep my job. Or we give up the paycheck, nobody tells us what to do, and we organize the way we want to do it."

"If we're afraid of that, then we might as well just forget it," I said. "You and I have got to liberate ourselves."

The ground already had been tilled, the seed planted. It wasn't hard to convince her.

"I'm willing to stick it out for ten years and really give it a trial," she said. "If it doesn't work, we can figure out something else."

So I resigned my job and set out to found a union. At first I was frightened. But by the time I had missed the fourth paycheck and found things were still going, that the moon was still there and the sky and the flowers, I began to laugh. I really began to feel free. It was one of my biggest triumphs in terms of finding myself and of being able to discipline myself.

After all, if you're outraged at conditions, then you can't possibly be free or happy until you devote all your time to changing them, and do nothing but that. The affluence in this country is our biggest trap, because we can't change anything if we want to hold on to a good job, a good way of life, and avoid sacrifice.

We began to do away with a lot of little things we thought we just had to have, things we really did not need. We began to get that commitment, that gut commitment—"all right, then, this sacrifice won't be for nothing. I made it for six months, nothing will stop me now." Then we began to build a community, we began to build what would become the Union.

Today I don't think our members are going to stop just at building a farm workers' union. In the course of that accomplishment other things are going to be revealed to them, not through me, but through the experience of living. I've heard them say, "We're not going to get paychecks. We're willing to put ourselves with our families on the line! Let's go!" You can't stop people like that. They can change the world.

The need of radical change is great and urgent, in the cities as well as in the fields, and if we don't succeed, violence will spread. Other movements will try to do it with violence.

But in seeking social change, I am positive nonviolence is the way, morally and tactically, especially in our society where those in power resort to clubs, tear gas, and guns. I have seen nonviolence work many times in many ways. When we organized California's vineyards, for example, it was the growers' violence, their manipulation of the police and the courts, that helped win support for our cause.

We can remain nonviolent because people outside the Movement by and large don't want violence. By remaining nonviolent in the face of violence, we win them to our side, and that's what makes the strength. And we organize that strength to fight for change.

My experiences in the Union had happened to me ten or fifteen times before in CSO. Every time I organized a little group on a smaller scale, the same thing happened. I organized from the ground up, helped people, got them together, and started fighting for what was needed. Pretty soon they were using their power effectively and trying to get things changed.

The Union is the same thing, just on a much bigger scale. What happens next may be even bigger. Out of each experience enough light is generated to illuminate another little stretch. Who knows where it will lead? And who can tell where it started?

5. Earl Shorris, "Someone from Puerto Rico"

In "Mengano de Puerto Rico," or "Someone from Puerto Rico," Earl Shorris brings into sharp relief the importance of a Latino group which originates from an island 100 miles by 35 miles. Puerto Ricans make up the second largest Latino community in America (2.5 million on the mainland; 3.5 million on Puerto Rico, one of the most densely populated pieces of land on earth). Shorris traces the recent history of the Puerto Rican-American connection from the Spanish American War (1898) through to the present and Puerto Rico's unique political status. While all Puerto Ricans are automatically American citizens, those still living on the island have no voting representatives in the U. S. Congress and pay no income tax (and thus the island carries the name of "commonwealth" instead of "state").

As he does with the Mexican-American culture, Shorris then explores what other Latinos and Puerto Ricans themselves have said about the "boricuas," both those on the island and those especially in the New York City area. Four particular aspects—"partying," "struggling," "conquered," and "self respect"—are examined in depth as they relate to Puerto Rican culture. Shorris ends his essay with a brilliant recreation of a hot, humid night in the Puerto Rican section (the "barrio") of New York City, providing us the sights, sounds, smells, and above all the dreams of the *puertorriqueños* away from the island.

Mengano de Puerto Rico

la tierra prometida
eres
tú[1]

Clemente Soto Vélez

1.

Life in New York City is full of famous woes. Everyone in the city is afflicted with dreaming and gossip: Nothing private endures; the truth has no purchase on what is known; everything is made to fit the expectations of the market. No more cruel or democratic place exists or was ever imagined.

The tragedy of the Puerto Ricans began the moment they chose New York. It condemned them to live as the objects of invention even as it set them to furious dreaming. They ceased to be who they were. They became words and music. In Puerto Rico they had been conquered by force of arms and politics; in the new city they fell victim to disappointment and the *Daily News*.

One of the first books about being Puerto Rican in New York was *Island in the City* by Dan Wakefield, written in 1957. Wakefield used Spanish only three times in the book, and twice he was in error—"buenos noches" instead of *buenas noches* and "tu sabe" instead of *tú sabes*. Those mistakes would never have been tolerated in French or German, but Spanish was so foreign to the well-bred and well-educated in New York in 1957 that neither he nor his copy editor bothered to find out the gender of the night or the familiarity of the verb.

If Wakefield was liberal, distant, and kind, Stephen Sondheim and Leonard Bernstein were liberal, close, and unkind. The characters in *West Side Story* were based on Romeo and Juliet, but Sond-heim and Bernstein had taken them down the social scale from minor nobility to street killers. The musical was about immigrants of a decidedly lower cultural and moral level than the immigrants and immigrants' children who sat in the audience. Writers like Piri Thomas drove the point home in autobiographies of crime, drugs, and poverty. In the media capital of the world, the Puerto Ricans got plenty of coverage, and it was all bad.

The capstone was Oscar Lewis's enormously successful book on Puerto Ricans and the culture of poverty, *La Vida*. It was not a novel of righteous anger or an autobiography of painful experience in the classic Christian literary tradition, with its loving sense of the nobility of the poor. Lewis produced a book of explicit sexual detail—enough so that it would become a best-seller—and ubiquitous amorality. There was no sense of the possibility of redemption through suffering, as in Dostoyevsky's novels. His Puerto Rican men were lazy, stupid louts who lived off women or welfare, beat their wives and girlfriends, and then left them penniless and pregnant. His Puerto Rican women were whores, without exception. There was no sense of a human soul in the characters as presented by the omnipotent editor. Lewis called his work anthropology, science. The intellectual world adored the book, for it confirmed everything they thought they saw on the Upper West Side of New York. The women were hot, and the men were bums. No matter what Lewis had set out to do, he had ended up with a racist's dream, the truth and value of which were confirmed by Michael Harrington, the *New York Times*, *Newsweek*, *The New Yorker*, and the *National Book Award*.[2]

No defense of Puerto Ricans had a similar effect. A stereotype was created and internalized in a single generation. The grace of island life could not

---

1. *you*
   are
   the promised land

---

2. Lewis, an Anglo anthropologist with an interest in things Latin American, also produced several books about Mexicans living in poverty. The Mexicans did not fare much better than the Puerto Ricans.

From LATINOS: A Biography of the People by Earl Shorris. Copyright © 1992 by Earl Shorris. Reprinted by permission of W.W. Norton & Company, Inc.

survive in the brusque middle European culture of New York—the Puerto Ricans had to change or be physically destroyed by life in the city. They chose not to die or rather to die slowly, to be defined from without, stereotyped, defeated in their persons, enduring yet another conquest. This time, however, it was to be the last wounding of a battered bastard culture; this time it was to be the end.

Oscar Lewis would picture Puerto Ricans dying in small, hot rooms, on beds with no sheets, sweating, lubricious, third time fourth time fucking while the children waited in grandma's house, unattended by the old whore. And as if to be sure they are dead, to kill them forever, Linda Chavez, former executive director of the U.S. Commission on Civil Rights in the Reagan administration, a woman who claims to be of Spanish and Irish descent, wrote a book[3] in which, she told me, she said that "Hispanics are the same as any other ethnic group statistically, if we remove the Puerto Ricans from the category."

In fact, death is hunting the Nuyoricans on winter mornings when it is still dark and the Dominican who just bought the bodega on the corner has refused further credit. Death goes shivering into the stone cold of the subway, chasing the man who worked until three A.M. and must now begin again, riding the subway, then the train to New Jersey, two hours to work, then hours on the job, two hours to home, and then for as long as he can keep his eyes open working again in his cousin's uncle's shop.

Whites do not open the door to dark-skinned people for any reason other than to use them. New York is a business town, a plantation; the Puerto Ricans came to work—but not to live. New York killed them; it took their health and their hopes; it locked them up in dark rooms; it gave them to the landlords for a gift, a sacrifice. Even worse, it told them who they were and made it impossible for them not to accept that external definition. The Puerto Ricans became objects, people who were not the center or the beginning of anything. In such circumstances the present time and place were unbearable. There was no comfort for them but the past. Nostalgia became the dominant factor in the Puerto Rican character; the island achieved mythical status, became the Golden Age of King Muñoz Marín and the Knights of Operation Bootstrap.

---

3. It is a common practice among Latinos from New Mexico, like Ms. Chavez, to describe themselves as Hispanos, people with no Native American ancestors.

2.

They get one pat on the back here, and when they go outside they get ten slaps in the face.
  Antonia Rodriguez, Principal,
  Bilingual Bicultural Art School, District 4
  New York City

By the end of the 1980s statistical proof of the extraordinary pain of life for mainland Puerto Ricans became widely available: ASPIRA, a Puerto Rican social and political organization, announced that the poorest people in New York City were Puerto Rican single parent families—in 1988, they lived on an average of $205 a week. Oscar Lewis had been correct in one respect, the Puerto Ricans were poor. Even Linda Chavez had to be conceded her point: If Puerto Ricans were dropped out of the statistical sample, the profile of Latinos would look very different. Perhaps there was a culture that was no culture but poverty; perhaps the Puerto Ricans were not anybody, just fulano the poor, nothing more, nothing. I thought of Julia Arana. If anyone was condemned to the amoral life of the culture of poverty, it was Julia.

Julia lived on First Avenue and 114th Street in New York City. It is a block populated by a few remaining Italians (one of whom owns the building in which Julia and her five children live), the dregs of the Marielitos, and a mixture of Puerto Ricans, Dominicans, and perhaps a Mexican or two. Julia's tenement apartment faces a huge complex of gray housing projects. There is a small altar in front of the projects in the middle of the block. It was built by the mother of a boy who was shot to death in the street there just below Julia's third floor window. There are often shots fired in the night on 114th and First Avenue. Julia says that whenever she and the girls lie down together to sleep in the big bed beside the window they expect the sound of gunfire. When she hears the shots, she tells the girls not to stand up, to lie on the bed and keep their heads down, because a wild shot could come in through the window.[4] It is not paranoia. She watches the news on television; it has happened.

I first met Julia at a Christmas party in Upper Manhattan. She was not a member of the group that gave the party. I don't know how she got there, not that she was unwelcome. She was good humored,

---

4. In the space of a few weeks in 1990 six children in New York City were killed or gravely wounded by stray bullets.

dressed like what used to be called a tomboy, in bluejeans and tee-shirt and a puffy, downfilled jacket. She didn't wear lipstick or perfume. I remember thinking when she sat down next to me that her face was so open I could read her dreams.

She had a tough guy's way of talking, full of gravel and street sounds born in Brooklyn. I was surprised when she said she had five children, for there was no sign of motherliness about her. She was small and slightly muscular, like a gymnast, and her conversation had a sports fan's enthusiasms. "You think that's a good school, you should see the school where my daughter goes. No, she don't go to bilingual. You got to speak English if you want to do good. I know the principal real good, because I'm helping out there. I'll get you an interview with her. When d'you want to go?"

Then we shook hands. She said her name was Julia Arana. She wrote it for me on a page of my notebook: Arana, it means a trick or a swindle, Mrs. Trick.

After that, I saw her often: somehow she was always around when there was a major function in the school district in which I had arranged to observe bilingual classes for the year. We always had a moment to talk. We became pals. Julia was forever sending me somewhere, explaining something, my semi-official and for a while my official research assistant. She introduced me to the principal of the school attended by two of her daughters. I introduced her to the head of bilingual education for the district: "This is my friend, Julia Arana." She smiled. She liked to hear her name said with an English j. I said it that way.

One day she said, "Aren't you gonna interview me?"

We set a time. I told here I would ask my wife to join us. On the appointed day it was very cold. The sun goes somewhere south of Brooklyn in winter, too far from the barrio to warm the streets. No one was outside on First Avenue that afternoon. The street belonged to the wind.

Julia lives in one of the ancient tenements that line the east side of the avenue. A few of these brick buildings have been abandoned, boarded up, and left for dead. No one knows who climbs in and out of the windows and doorways behind the plywood or metal sheets. Julia says they make and sell rock cocaine in one of the buildings.

The mailboxes have been broken open in Julia's building, but the buzzer system still works. A boy carrying a brown paper bag rushed past us, hurrying up the steps, taking them two at a time, not even bothering to touch the old iron banisters. We

followed him, walking two generations slower. At apartment F on the third floor Julia greeted us. She wore the usual shortsleeved knit shirt. This one had a collar and three open buttons at the throat. I thought I detected the color of cosmetics on her mouth, but it may have been the flush of excitement.

"Where are the cameras?" she asked.

I reminded her that I wrote books. Had she ever seen me with cameras? Had we ever talked about cameras? She shook her head. She said nothing, but I saw the sigh of disappointment pass through her body. Behind her on the table in the kitchen area she had laid out cold cuts and meatballs and white bread and mustard. There was enough for the cameramen, too.

She took our coats, and in a room the width of a hallway we sat down on a couch covered with a brown blanket. I had failed her, I knew, but I did not know how. How had she made up the dream of the cameras? How? I knew why, but I did not know how.

She sat on a low chair, a child's chair, opposite us. The children gathered around. There was a homemade crèche to her left, a schoolchild's work, and to her right, on a battered metal cart, a television set and a videotape machine. It was comfortable in the apartment, but there were not enough places for Julia and her guests and all five children to sit.

The early years of Julia's life were not so different from those of any poor immigrant. Her parents came from Puerto Rico to New York. Her father was sickly, asthmatic at first and then suffering from heart disease. He worked as a carpenter when they first settled in Brooklyn, but he always liked to bake at home. Julia remembers him putting pastries on the window to cool. She filched them from the window sill, as children do in fairy tales of domestic life.

When he became ill and could not work at carpentry, life became difficult for his family. When he died, it became still more difficult. Her mother made cakes or sewed or worked as an aide at the school to add to their public assistance checks. They moved from the house of good memories in Brooklyn to the barrio (Spanish Harlem) and then to the South Bronx. Julia had two brothers who helped with the bills. The Aranas did not starve, but they did not have much. Her mother was forty-one when Julia was born. She was a very traditional woman, Julia said, one who tried to install traditional values in her children.

At sixteen, when she was a student at Benjamin Franklin High School, which was one of the worst, most violent high schools in New York City, Julia stopped eating in the school lunchroom. She got a job in a Greek restaurant during her school lunch hour. Sometimes she worked there after school too.

It was 1970, near the end of the Vietnam War. Julia met a young marine and got pregnant. She went down to South Carolina to marry the Marine, who said he had permission from his commanding officer, but when she got there the commanding officer refused to allow them to be married. She had three children with the marine. They lived together until he beat her up, and she took her children and left. He never helped her much after that, although he did stay in touch with the children.

Julia lived briefly with her putative mother-in-law, but they did not get along. The mother-in-law put Julia and her children out into the street. Those were bad years. There were times when they did not have enough to eat, Julia said. "I thought of selling my body to get food for my children. I knew other women who did it, but I remembered how my mother brought me up, and I got through it some way without doing that."

"I didn't use no drugs. I mean I tried a little when I was young, but I didn't do it, heroin. A girl I knew, she was beautiful as a model; she got into heroin, and she was so thin, like a skeleton. I don't know why I didn't, it was the tradition from my mother."

She moved to Manhattan, lived with a Dominican, and had two more children. When he beat her up, she threw him out. The worst years followed. With five children, she moved from Queens to Manhattan, from apartment to apartment, always late with the rent, often with not enough to eat. She had a job and lost a job when she stayed home with her sick child. As the years went by, she became closer and closer to the children.

The illnesses of the children have been a terrible burden for Julia. Her second child was born with a defective heart and mismatched legs. The girl's legs were broken and shortened to make them the same size. Her heart was repaired in a very difficult operation. Then the girl had a series of convulsions, for which she was given heavy doses of phenobarbital. Now, the convulsions have passed, but she has problems with both her muscular and nervous systems.

At one point, four of Julia's five children were ill. She knows doctors, hospitals. She can recommend a heart surgeon or an orthopedist. The doctors have become her friends. The heart surgeon is interested in her children. The family that takes on the girls every summer as part of the Fresh Air Fund has become attached to her.

Julia doesn't go out often now. She saw a Cuban man for a while, but after a few dates, she said, he wanted to move in to her house and take over, bringing his own family with him. She thinks about going out, "I get all dressed," she said, "and I even go downstairs, but when I get down there, I think about my children, and I come back up and put on my jeans and we eat some junk food and watch TV. We make a party, put out the lights, and I get some popcorn, and we watch TV like it was our own movie."

There is tragedy everywhere in her family. Her brother's child fell from a fifth floor window. When the baby's mother reached the yard where he had fallen, she picked him up, and by lifting him in her arms she caused the bones of his broken neck to sever his spinal cord and killed him. After that, two of her brother's small children were hit by cars in the street. Julia's brother left his wife then, taking the remaining children with him.

Julia's daughters by her first man have been going to New York Prep, which is one of the most innovative schools in the city. Her oldest daughter wants to be a doctor or, if not a doctor, a writer. She and a friend write plays together. Agustina, the one who had heart surgery and the operation on her legs, said she likes to write too; she always gets check plus on the stories she shows to her teacher. Julia's son, Luis, who is a gentle child and close to his mother, wants to join the marines when he finishes school. He would like to be an architect—— drawing is his talent—but he goes to a technical school, where they teach him the printing trade.

The liveliest of the children is the third daughter, the first child by the Dominican. She is pretty and plump and given to misbehaving. It is clear that she's her mother's pet, for of all the children, she is the best dressed and combed, fixed up like a prize. A chocolate-skinned child, whose hair falls in thick curls, she prances and pouts and shows off her dress, which is not of winter afternoons in tenement rooms but of sunny store windows where dream-girls in organdy make a fuss.

When the children go to school, Julia goes to beauty operator's college. Half the cost of the course is paid by a federal grant, the other half by a bank loan guaranteed by the government. "They treated me very good when I applied," Julia said, "but now they got my money, they slam the door in my face when I ask a question. I didn't go all last week, I might not go back the way they treat me."

And then she pronounces her motto, the one consistent rule in her life: "I don't take nothing from nobody."

Julia was born Puerto Rican, but that was a long time ago. She is Nuyorican now, scrappy, streetwise, tough, and crazy with dreams. "Things are getting better. I don't want to hurt it by saying so, but things are going good lately." The rent is paid. Her mother helps. The children usually eat at *Abuela's*[5] house. The telephone is in *Abuela's* house. Puerto Rico is in *Abuela's* house. Hope and help are in family. Julia's brother has moved to Florida where he has a little carpentry business. "It's going good. He has two part-time helpers. I'm going down to see him right after the first of the year. I got the money already for the ticket. Maybe I'll move to Florida with my brother. Not Miami, Orlando. Orlando is where it's at."

Maybe she'll take the children with her when she goes to visit her brother to see about moving. If they miss a few days of school, it will be all right. She tells the children they can take a day off from school now and then to see a movie. "Unless they take a day off sometimes, they'll just be sleepy in class."

Julia was raised a Roman Catholic, but she went to the Pentecostal Church for a while. "I went to a meeting one day and they were collecting for a sister who didn't have nothing to eat. I was surprised when they gave the money to me—thirty-one dollars. I was really happy. We needed that money for food." She doesn't go to the Pentecostal Church anymore, although she still sees the brothers and sisters on the street. She has returned to the Catholic Church.

At the end of the afternoon, Julia sent Luis to the refrigerator to get "the special thing." It came in a brown paper bag. "Here, it's for you," Julia said, "a New Year's gift."

I protested but Sylvia took the wine. She examined it and praised the maker. It was a kind we liked very much, she said. And when Julia offered some of the *albondigas* she and the girls had made, saying there was too much, we should take a few of the meatballs home, Sylvia accepted those, too, all with grace and gratitude.

After many *abrazos*,[6] Sylvia and I left. Luis walked to Second Avenue with us. He had not spoken much all afternoon, but on the brief walk west and north to 116th Street, he had a lot to say. He worried about his mother, his sisters, the way she

never let the girls out of the house. He worried about the gunfire in streets. Would they be safe after he left home to join the marines? He had a list of worries, a litany. Luis was seventeen, his mother was thirty-three. When he becomes a marine, he said, he would send money home.

The Florida trip did not work out. Luis did join the marines. Julia quit the beauty operator's school, which kept her money. There was a scene. She said again, "I don't take nothing from nobody." Now Julia is gone. I don't know where, I haven't seen her for a year. No one answers the phone at her mother's house. There is a new principal at P.S. 206. All the connections are gone.

I should have expected that. Julia does not stay with anyone or anything for long. Nothing lasts for her but family—and culture.

For a long time I did not know how to think about Julia. To say that here is the culture of poverty is to misunderstand completely the nostalgia of Puerto Ricans on the mainland. Their longing for the golden age of island life connects them not only to language, music, food, and custom, but to place. The Puerto Rican golden age is not a dream; it is a tree, a hill, a house open to the breeze, a culture reflected in nature, art, and artifact. A mountain is not poverty. Oscar Lewis missed the point: His Puerto Ricans have no memory; his book did not contain a tree.

At night, in the near darkness of First Avenue, Julia Arana and her girls lie together on the big bed beside the only window in the herniated corridor that is their flat. And they are all rich and safe together. Julia did not abort them when she was pregnant; she did not avoid their births when she lay with their fathers. Family is wealth. It does not disappear in the bodega or the Laundromat. Every morning it is new again. Julia is never alone, never bored. She is five times fulfilled: teacher, mother, sister, nurse. She entertains and is entertained. She teaches the value of the moment and the truth that the moment is not all. She loves and is loved.

Julia does not give her blessing formally, as the older generation did; there is no hand for her children to kiss in thanks for the blessing, but the sense of *bendición* binds mother and children. It is love's orthodoxy, the nucleus of culture. Hope is not out of the question.

---

5. Grandmother
6. Embraces.

Among Latinos, the sad distinction of Puerto Ricans is that so many of them live in New York City, which is very far from paradise and no longer close to possibility. In New York City, there is no social or economic peace; there are no plateaus, no places to rest. It is never now in New York City: tomorrow and its anxiety control the day and make an incessant and irregular noise in the night. In such a city, the gentleness of Puerto Ricans and their overdeveloped sense of loyalty is less successful every year. There are no *dichos*[7] to explain the murderous social and economic competition.

A Puerto Rican woman, a friend of many years, said she thought the failure of Puerto Ricans in New York City was due to the lack of a Puerto Rican criminal organization: "We don't sell drugs, we use them. The Italians, the Jews, the Irish, the Cubans, and now the Dominicans each established effective, highly organized criminal operations. The Puerto Ricans have not. That's been our problem. Crime gets you into this society. It gets you the money to lend to your own people at exorbitant rates, but that enables them to start small businesses. It gets you into legitimate businesses, lets you hire lawyers and accountants, and it gives you political clout. We have none."

She is a woman of accomplishment and great self-awareness; her comment on life in American cities is a bitter one, an inner-city, bottom-up perspective, but it is not to be dismissed. It reflects much of the frustration and envy of the Puerto Rican community in New York and the sense of being a minority among minorities, different somehow, without much luck. "*Bendito*," the Puerto Ricans say, but with an ironic overtone, for there are few Puerto Ricans who believe they are blessed. Life has been too difficult; the winters have been too cold.

The other side of the criminal theory is a curious, inside out version of conservative social theory: If the other immigrants succeeded, it must be because they are bad; therefore, the Puerto Ricans failed because they are good. Underlying the theory is the lack of aggressiveness of many Puerto Ricans—the fatalism that psychologists sometimes call depression—of the generation of people who came in the first wave of migration at the end of World War II.

Many Puerto Ricans say now of themselves, "We just get the worst ones here, for the welfare.[8] On the island, it's not so poor. The Dominican Republic is poor, not Puerto Rico." The distinction such people draw between rich and poor is elemental and accurate: Running water, electricity, and television are the signs of development. Many who leave the Dominican Republic for Puerto Rico, where they mix in with the rest of the population on the way north to New York, come from towns where water and electricity are uncertain. They risk a dangerous ocean crossing to Puerto Rico, but it is worth the risk to them, for the life of the poor in the Dominican Republic is dreadful. During the great wave of northward migration from Puerto Rico it simply was not so; people were poor, but life was not unbearable.

The immigrant histories differ in tone from those of other groups. Puerto Rico is a U.S. commonwealth. It was, and remains, at a lower level of development than the rest of the country, but it could not be described accurately as an underdeveloped country. One cannot make statistics of the dreams of immigrants, but many of their person histories follow a pattern. When Domingo Figueroa left Santurce for New York, he was the owner of eight houses and a yard-goods store. Why did he leave the solidity of that life for unknown New York? His children charge him with ambition: "When a man has something, he always wants more."

He came alone, leaving his family in Santurce. His wife ran the store; his children grew up. But life in New York did not produce more for Domingo Figueroa. Instead of riches, he found a grim job, and out of the job came an industrial accident that ruined him. Cleaning solution splashed into his eyes. He went to a doctor, who apparently did not wash his eyes with the proper antidote. He went to more doctors. The illness devoured the houses and then the store. The doctors removed one of his eyes, then the other. At the age of ninety-four, without eyes, he waited out his time in a government hospital, visited by his children and grandchildren. They said he was still a strong man, one who did not let his blindness deter him from dancing whenever he heard music.

Edward Rivera, the novelist, writes of such families, men who are never late to work, but who eventually suffer betrayal by their bosses and their bodies. Rivera's picture of Puerto Rican life in New York City is not sensational, but it is perhaps the

---

7. Sayings, proverbs.

8. The impression is not correct. Puerto Ricans who moved to the mainland during the 1980s and early 1990s were better educated and of higher economic status then ever before.

most accurate picture available, far more reliable than the work of Piri Thomas or Oscar Lewis. Nicholasa Mohr's novels produce the same picture: people with working-class or lower-middle class values whose hopes are frustrated by city life. Puerto Ricans in New York City have suffered from the diseases of stress and loyalty. Heart disease, strokes, accidents, ulcers, and cancer take away their health, their livelihood, and eventually their lives, and through it all they remain loyal to the employers who betray them.

The story of the layoff of a longtime, loyal employee that Rivera tells in *While Someone Else Is Eating* is so common to Puerto Ricans in New York that were it not for the wealth of detail in his writing the life of the man he calls Segundo would be a commonplace. It happens again and again: Puerto Ricans work in marginal businesses; they have no unions, no benefits, nothing but the weekly paycheck, from which social security may or may not have been deducted and paid; the employers milk the business, transferring every cent out of the little corporation into their private accounts; when the marginal business goes broke after a few or even many years or when the owners decide to liquidate the business and retire, the loyal Puerto Rican employee, fulano, is left with nothing, literally and figuratively out in the cold.

Lacking money, medical insurance, and hope, the Puerto Rican man settles into patriarchy and machismo; he plays dominoes and sings songs, and sometimes he drinks. If the break in his life plan comes early enough, the affront to his manhood of betrayal and broken dreams will excite his machismo, and he will become an abusive husband before his wife throws him out.

In the 1970s the Puerto Rican community—relieved of the pressure of the Cubans, who came to the barrio, established businesses, made some money, and moved out—was enjoying a renaissance. The stranglehold of the old ethnics on the school system had finally been broken, and Puerto Rican teachers, many of them bilingual, were moving into teaching and supervisory positions. Nuyoricans were graduating from two- and four-year colleges and professional schools. The stores and shops in the barrio were owned by people who lived in the barrio. La Marketa (or Marqueta) was thriving on Park Avenue under the railroad tracks; many of the stalls had been rented to Puerto Ricans. Barriers seemed to be braking down everywhere in the good feeling carried over from the sixties; Puerto Ricans were marrying into the immigrant strivers groups of the city. The most famous

marriage was that of Herman and Irma Badillo, a Puerto Rican who was elected to the U.S. House of Representatives and a scrappy New York Jew. In Spanish Harlem, the superintendent of School District 4, Anthony Alvarado, was creating a successful experiment. Awilda Orta, the principal of Intermediate School 99, informally known as Jailhouse 99, had taken over one of the sloughs of the city's educational system and turned it into a place where teachers taught and students were anxious to learn.

The single greatest sign of health in the community was the establishment of the Museo del Barrio in a storefront on Third Avenue. One exhibition consisted of a series of installations depicting the life in the barrio. In the centerpiece a conical orange nose adorned the grotesquely predatory face of the Statue of Liberty. A battered suitcase lay at her feet. Dollars emerged from her dress. In one hand she carried a large electric light bulb and with the other she offered brochures in Spanish and English explaining the food-stamp program. In the rooms around her, human brains were sold on the cheap, defaced political posters and advertisements for salsa concerts crowded the walls; a shrouded body, that of a recent murder victim, lay on the floor of a dark corridor; a Caribbean forest held altars and *cemies*, the stone gods of the Tainos. A window looked in upon a narrow bed and a crucifix in a dimly lit room. The exhibition was a series of confrontations: Arrive at the moment of being able to look at yourself, laugh, and go on, the artists urged.

Since no one came to the barrio to review the show, the artists looked to the community to learn how their work was received. In the office of the storefront, on a three-legged desk, they put out a guest book. A group of them gathered around to read the comment left by an old woman who laboriously wrote out a single sentence: "It lacks only the smell of rice and beans and the *pillo* (literally, "The mischief," but in the barrio an illegal tap on the wires of the hated Consolidated Edison)."

The series of installations in the storefront museum and the old woman's comment about them pointed to the strangling connection of the Puerto Ricans to governmental and quasi-governmental institutions. If the exhibits or the *pillo* left any doubt about the nature of the relationship, José Antonio Vásquez, a young photographer, clarified it. "The young people call the Welfare the Gestapo, because they're like the Nazis in the movies; they don't even look up at you, they just say, 'Papers, let me see your papers.'"

As the recession and the Reagan administration—combined with the arrival of the aggressive

Dominican population—drove the Puerto Rican community backwards by every social and economic measure, the truth of what the artists and the old woman thought was borne out: Like no other newcomers in the history of New York City, the Puerto Ricans were at the mercy of their government. And it was more than economic dependence that weighed on them: They were psychological prisoners of the state.

3.

One cannot observe Puerto Rican life close up without reaching the conclusion that every form of tutelage is morally degrading. As long as sovereignty does not reside in us, there will be genuflections and degradations before those in whom it does reside. This is the political illness of colonial Puerto Rico, and its only cure is a dose of unadulterated sovereignty.
Luis Muñoz Marín

When I asked Puerto Ricans to define their essence in a word, the answer that came most often from ordinary people was, "partying." Two other answers amplified that notion and further separated Puerto Ricans from other Latinos, "struggling" and "conquered." The notion of a people who are interested in partying (if that is a word) conforms with the opinion other Latinos hold of Puerto Ricans. There is nothing pejorative in that view, as there is in the idea that Puerto Ricans come to the mainland for no other purpose than to get welfare checks; it describes a happy-go-lucky attitude toward life, one that can be enormously attractive, although difficult to live with or to do business with.

Unfortunately, in this instance partying probably has more to do with despair than happiness: "happy-go-lucky" isn't so much rooted in love of the present as fear of the future. The partying mentality is often exhibited by troops expecting to go into battle or men in very dangerous jobs. To say that two-and-a-half million Puerto Ricans on the mainland have the same worldview as men about to go into combat implies a tragic essence. It can be heard in the comment of William López, a young Puerto Rican corporate executive: "I'm worried. Things are just going too good. Everything's falling into place. It's just too good. I'm really starting to worry." The sense of impending disaster so affected

a Puerto Rican investor that he took to buying gold, expecting a recession. When I reminded him that buying gold is considered good protection against inflation rather than recession, he said I didn't understand how bad things could get: "You can always barter gold, get food with it, if you need it." When I asked what kind of terrible disaster could cause gold to be useful that way, he said, "You'll see."

Struggle in the Puerto Rican world is not a struggle to succeed in business or other practical aspects of life; it is an Aristotelian struggle against fate, the classic situation of the tragic hero in literature. When the murderous cuts in social programs were instituted by the Reagan administration, many people in the Puerto Rican community shrugged—it was to be expected—but one man I know of jumped out the window of his fifth floor apartment when he could no longer pay the rent; not everyone from Puerto Rico is happy-go-lucky.

"Conquest" describes the Puerto Rican character for fewer people, and it may be that they mean to speak of a cause rather than an effect, but that is not what they say. "Conquered," is the answer to the question about essence not about history. Few nations, if any, in human history have not been conquered at one time or another, but to be conquered and to have been conquered are entirely different situations. Puerto Ricans consider themselves conquered now—not occupied, not defeated, but conquered. Occupied nations live in the expectation of overthrowing the enemies on their land, defeated nations hope to fight again, but those who are conquered have neither the wherewithal nor the will to overcome their situation; they live in hope that some external force will free them—gods, spirits, Russians, the lottery, or death. A conquered people cannot be other than fatalistic.

"Struggle" seems, at first, to describe the opposite of conquered, but that interpretation does not hold up to scrutiny; "struggle" in the context of the Puerto Rican character means the struggle to survive, the attempt to overcome one's fate. Without the aspect of struggle, the Puerto Rican character would be dolorous rather than tragic, the partying an expression of despair rather than a rage against the past. Without partying, the Puerto Ricans would not be wounded, they would be dead.

Almost all serious thinking about Puerto Rico and Puerto Ricans devolves from the ideas of Luis Muñoz Marín. Muñoz was not only the political leader of the island from 1940 through 1968, as senator, governor, and power behind the governor, he was the discoverer of the dangerous effect of colonialism on the character of the people. Like José Martí, he spent his youth in New York City where he first made his reputation as a writer. Muñoz Marín, the son of the man who won Puerto Rico's independence from Spain, was a poet and a good one. He was known affectionately in Puerto Rico as The Bard, El Vate.

When El Vate chose to enter politics in Puerto Rico, he encountered an island in poverty. It was one of the poorest places in Latin America, exploited by agricultural interests and despised by the country that controlled it. Puerto Rico was divided by race and class. Blacks were excluded from clubs and even political parties. The poor *jíbaros* who lived up in the hills were under-nourished, illiterate, often unemployed, not even part of the sugar economy. Muñoz made them his special concern. In his famous political campaign as head of a new party, he went up into the hills to meet the voters. ¡*Alda arriba*! was the description of his campaign as well as his slogan. He went up the hill to the voters, and he intended to bring Puerto Rico up the hill to development and prosperity.

He was elected governor in 1948, and by the time his party was voted out of office, twenty years later he had transformed the island from the poorest to the richest place in Latin America. He had used a mix of socialism and capitalism to increase per capita income from $118 in 1940 to $1,200 in 1970. He used public funds to build the cement plants to create the roads for the infrastructure necessary to industrialization, and then he used the tax advantages of Operation Bootstrap to bring industry to the island. The irony of his success did not escape El Vate, however. It had been his hope to maintain the character of the *jíbaro* in an industrial society, and in that he had failed; by 1968 the man who had developed the island's economy was campaigning for serenity. He said the noise level was too high in the cities, literally beyond the point at which it was said to cause pain to human beings; he fought to bring back the tranquil culture of the *jíbaro*, and his Popular Democratic party was defeated.

The psychologist and director of the Roberto Clemente Family Guidance Center on the Loisaida of New York, Jaime E. Inclán, finds Muñoz at the very center of the Puerto Rican character. He agrees with Muñoz that the chief issue in the Puerto Rican character is the problem of self-esteem, which Muñoz called by its more meaningful name—self-respect—and that the Spanish and U.S. conquests weigh heavily in Puerto Ricans' judgment of themselves. Inclán goes beyond the question of colonialism to the role of Muñoz Marín himself in Puerto

Rican psychology. He reasons that the first generation Puerto Ricans came to the mainland full of the dreams of success taught by Muñoz. El Vate had created an atmosphere in which anything seemed possible for Puerto Rico and Puerto Ricans. When the first wave of migrants, which Inclán calls the "beachhead generation," came to the mainland, Puerto Rico was in the bloom of development.

They found no such opportunity in New York City. Within a few years they became known as "the Puerto Rican problem." Landlords gouged them, employers took advantage of them, nothing worked for them, and they sank into a mire of self-doubt; the job of succeeding in New York was given to their children. Of these first two generations Inclán writes: "Puerto Ricans were able to survive marginally and to channel towards the self the blame and the anger that took the place of the shock. Muñoz Marín's rhetoric could not reach New York. The delusion of the man and the Island could persist, frozen like the myth of the return in memory and hope. Immediate reality was harsh and stagnant: wages low, racism rampant, winter months returned. It was not the time for 'our place in the sun.' Muñoz Marín retired from island politics in 1968 and exiled himself to Europe until his death in the summer of 1980. Ironically, second generation Puerto Ricans who hardly knew Muñoz the man, but who were expected by their parents to live his dreams, had the job, unbeknownst to them, of mourning him."

He goes on, "The low self-esteem and self-blame of the current second generation of Puerto Ricans is alarming to other Hispanics, who caricature Puerto Ricans as the only Latins who condemn themselves, reject their own peoples and products as inferior, and 'prefer' to work for others rather than for themselves—as demonstrated by the lowest percentage of businesses owned by themselves. One can only speculate that the over four hundred years of colonialism, as well as the attacks on nationalist sentiments by the left and right during the last fifteen years, must have significantly contributed to this depressive dynamism of collective and personal self."

The crisis, in his view, occurs in the third generation of Puerto Ricans, "who symbolically can be said to (have been) born in the summer of 1980, with the death of Muñoz Marín." As a prescription for the third generation, Inclán calls for "the rechanneling on to external objects of an anger that is addressed to the self." To do this he sees a need for the anger to be legitimized by political leaders in the community, but not, he argues, following "the patriarchal models of centralized control of power á la Muñoz Marín."

On a humid summer night in the New York City barrio the streets smell like a slaughterhouse. The customers in El Caribeño are mixed Puerto Rican and Dominican, but the owner and all the waitresses are Dominicans. The dishes on the menu are Dominican or vaguely Spanish, but there is a sign on the refrigerator advising that they have mavi, a Puerto Rican drink made of tree sap. Although it is not on the menu, the mofongo is magnificent, fresh and rich with little pieces of pork. At the next table a Dominican woman is dousing her tostones with catsup instead of dipping the fried plantains in garlic sauce. Two Puerto Ricans watch the act of culinary sacrilege with a mixture of pity and disgust. The jukebox plays only merengues. High above the door to the kitchen, next to the shelf on which the television set rests, is a statue of Santa Barbara and a votive candle to honor the great goddess of Santería. The manager of the restaurant comes in late, after the summer rain has passed and the water in the streets has turned to steam. He is light-skinned, dressed in guayabera,[9] a slim man with a fierce Spanish nose and Caribbean laughter. The dark-skinned waitresses attend him. He crackles with efficiency, importance. Everyone notices the owner.

Outside, on the next corner, under the awning of the bodega, four men play dominoes, holding the board on their knees, keeping it twice as steady as a four-legged table. The men are young, in their thirties; it is a surprise to see such young men playing dominoes on a weekend night. They drink beer, concentrate, clack, clack, clack, clack-clack, clack. Game. Curse. Chat. English. The losers turn the dominoes over the moment the score is counted. They stir the pieces. Each man picks seven and puts them in the small wooden stand in front of him. Double six, clack, clack, clack—Faster than bridge or poker or gin rummy, every man counts every number on the board, estimating the points in each hand, the lead players speaking to each through the choice of plays—clack, clack-clack, clack. The sign above the bodega is yellow; the streets stink and shine. The youngest man wears white sneakers and shows a stylish haircut, short on top and long at the neck. Clack, clack. Game. Curse. English chatter. Turn and mix. Double six. Clack, clack. Drink. Clack.

Two blocks away, next to the funeral home, down the street from the Pentecostal church, the neighborhood social club has opened for the night. Couples drift in. They are middle-aged and older. One man wears a cap to hide his baldness; another man shows his full head of white hair. The women have thickened. Two couples meet for the first time, introduced by the woman in the pants suit who serves dollar beers and talks to the customers in her thick voice. The couples ask the Puerto Rican question of each other: Where are you from?

"The capital."

"Oh, the capital! Santo Domingo!"

"I'm Puerto Rican. Born in the capital. And you?"

"Camagüey."

"Ay, Camagüey!"

They sit down together, order beer, and talk loudly. The man with the white hair dances the merengue with a woman who is surely his wife; their little steps are as practiced as budgets or breakfasts.

The social club is one room in a basement with a homemade bar at the near end facing a television set and a fan across the room twenty-five feet away. There are two toilets, each with the same hand-printed sign: "No más una persona en baño. No more than one person in the bathroom." In the Spanish version of each sign someone has made a carat and written in the article "el" before "baño." The English remains uncorrected.

Every social club has the same purpose: partying. In this club, all the preparations have been made for every possible kind of party. The ceiling and the walls are hung with crepe paper decorations, ribbons, and signs: hearts for Valentine's Day, jack-o'-lanterns for Halloween, posters for Puerto Rican cultural celebrations, and suspended from the low ceiling dozens of ribbons bearing the words, "HAPPY BIRTHDAY." Partying and Puerto Rico, homesickness and the moment, the limits of the world in which there is no tomorrow.

Outside on the streets, the people have begun to come out after the rain. Unadorned women and their children gather in front of the Pentecostal church; something is going on in the funeral home. Near the corner, in a doorway, a young man dressed in dark clothing and gold jewelry beckons. An abandoned building has been closed with metal shutters and padlocked. Two doors down a boy puts a radio on a milk crate beside the stoop, flicks

---

9. A loose-fitting shirt, usually white, worn outside the trousers.

the switch, and lets salsa blare. The slaughterhouse stench of the streets grows with the heat that comes back at the end of the rain. Two men in their early twenties hurry home to their fifth floor walkup apartment. They are first cousins, Puerto Ricans, but not from the city. The barrio frightens them. They avoid walking down deserted streets; they stay out near the curb, in the light, away from the doorways. They are young, middle-class men with middle-class ambitions, still subtle, still flexible, without the Nuyorican bluntness; they will live in the barrio until the first day on which they can afford to leave.

6. Ed Vega, "The Angel Juan Moncho"

Puerto Rican fiction writer Ed Vega specializes in bringing to life for his readers the area of East Harlem ("El Barrio"), the district of New York City in which the author himself lives. He layers his writing not only with his Puerto Rican heritage but also with his varied professional life which includes careers as a university professor, hockey player, social worker, husband and father.

"The Angel Juan Moncho" (taken from *Mendoza's Dreams*, 1987) is a half comical, half serious look at contemporary Puerto Rican life outside the island. Paulino Camacho, a butcher by trade, finds that he has spent all of his Christmas money on drink and can't face the fact that he will be unable to buy presents for his family. Enter Juan Moncho, his guardian angel, who helps his Puerto-Rican brother find a solution to his dilemma. Along the way, we hear Ed Vega addressing some of the same issues of Puerto Rican identity and culture examined earlier by Earl Shorris in "Mengano de Puerto Rico."

THE ANGEL JUAN MONCHO

One day late last fall when the days were growing shorter and colder and I was preparing to lock myself up for winter to catch up on a backlog of dreams, some of the people came to me and said, "Mendoza, you're too serious when you tell our dreams. Although what you write about us is true, there are times when we would prefer hearing something humorous." I nodded and explained that the recounting of dreams was a serious matter and that there were inherent difficulties in turning dreams into comedy. They replied that words were words and since I was supposed to be the expert, it was my responsibility to produce some humor from dreams. Arguments were useless once the people have made up their minds, so I asked what they had in mind. They said Christmas was approaching and tradition dictated they listen to the story of the Three Kings and the Infant Jesus, which was a very spiritually uplifting story except that a few months later they had to make promises which they never kept anyway, which made them feel very badly. Patiently, I explained to them that the story of Jesus was part of the yearly cycle of death and rebirth. "It's a metaphor of the seasons, part of ancient myth and therefore extremely important to the collective psyche," I said. They said that I certainly talked beautifully but that they weren't interested in philosophy.

Instead, they wished me to recount a miracle. I said the birth of the Child Jesus was a miracle and that the resurrection was most certainly a prime example of the same. They agreed but said they wanted to hear about a modern Christmas miracle, but one which would not frighten them like most miracles tended to do. I attempted to explain that germane to the idea of a miracle was the awe which the miracle inspired. They said that awe or not most miracles frightened them. I was silent, hoping they would recognize the futility of their quest and allow me to return to the recording of their dreams.

But they remained and insisted that the least I could do was explain what had taken place last year with Paulino Camacho, the butcher. How was it, they said, that after spending all his money drinking, Camacho was able to place such beautiful gifts under the Christmas tree for his wife and children? Gifts like no one in the neighborhood had ever seen? Like beautiful electric trains, expensive bicycles, fire engines and trucks with real rubber wheels and hoses; and, oh yeah, white dolls that seemed more alive than any white person they had ever seen, and doll houses with better furniture than the furniture in their own apartments, stuffed toys bigger than the children themselves, and clothes like they had never worn, and mind you, we're not jealous, they said, but to see his wife, Marta, in that mink coat Camacho gave her for Christmas just to go to the laundromat or the supermarket when it was 80 degrees was a little bit too much for any human being to have to endure. And how did that happen? They wanted to know.

I said I had no idea but that whatever had happened it certainly had the makings of miraculous intervention. "Well, there you have it," they said. I asked them if upon finding out that Camacho had been able to accomplish this seemingly impossible feat, which had all the makings of a miracle, they hadn't been frightened. They said they had not, but that plenty of people had been angry with Camacho and some even began whispering that perhaps he wasn't really a butcher but spent his spare time dealing in drugs. I said I didn't know anything about that but that I seriously doubted it. "Well then, how do you explain Camacho's good fortune?" they said, growing annoyed.

I again said I could not explain it, certainly not rationally, but that I thought perhaps an angel may have had a part in the matter. They then wanted to know if this angel I was talking about would frighten them. I said that angels were not generally intended to frighten people. They disagreed and were more annoyed than ever, insisting that angels, for the most part, came down to take people away and that the only reason they were dressed in white was so that people would be fooled and accompany the angel wherever it was he wanted to take them. "It's like doctors," they said. "As soon as you see them dressed in white, you think you're going to be

From MENDOZA'S DREAMS by Edgardo Vega Yunqué. Reprinted by permission of the author.

all right and then before you know it they're sticking needles into you and cutting you open and who knows what else and that's the way angels are." I told them I disagreed, that angels were inoffensive, ethereal beings and that I couldn't guarantee that Camacho's story would be as humorous as they wanted. They said that just as long as the angel wasn't frightening and they could at least smile a few times I could do whatever I wanted, as long as I finally explained how Camacho had gotten away with what he did. I said I'd do my very best.

So, I began by saying that it was the night before Christmas and all through El Barrio everybody was stirring, including Camacho. Especially Camacho and most certainly Camacho. Because, I mean, Christmas only comes once a year and what the hell: *Felicidades y Japi Nu Yíal*. Right? You see, you have to understand something about Camacho. Camacho enjoyed drinking. Not to excess but in the tradition of comradery, which dictates that whenever and wherever men gather bottle and glasses be on hand. So on this most festive of nights, Camacho was sitting at the long brown bar of *La Estrella de Borinquen*, on Lexington Avenue up the street from the subway station, and things were heating up. He was what we call *picao*. Somewhere between feeling mellow and passing out.

If you had seen Camacho you would've loved him immediately. He'd remind you of your father, all chubby and brown, sporting his big moustache and looking out into the world through those serious, sad eyes which used to make you shake when you were a child and made you say, penitently, "*Sí, papi*," and "*No, papi*." So, there was Camacho hitting on a bottle of Bud and saying things like: "Dis Bod for jew," and laughing and every once in a while one of his *panitas* would buy him a shot of Bacardi and down the hatch it went. And Camacho would feel so grateful for his friend's generosity that he'd slap a ten or twenty dollar bill on the bar and buy everyone a drink. No doubt about it. It was absolutely the best of nights, this *Nochebuena*. The jukebox was playing *salsa* and *aguinaldos* and one time when the disco version of "I'm Dreaming of a White Christmas" came on, Camacho got silly and danced, his belly hanging out and sweat rolling off his face.

About nine o'clock, as if everyone were hooked into the same circuit, men started making excuses about having to get home and be with their families. Snow was falling quite heavily and the streets gleamed brightly. Words went back and forth and in each one there was the aroma of *pernil*, *arroz con gandules*, *pasteles*, *salmoreja de jueyes*, *empanadas*, *alcapurrias*, *morcillas*, *mofongo*, *arroz con dulce*, *majarete*, *tembleque*, *almendras*, *nueces*, *turrón de alicante*, *turrón de jijona de mazapán* and to top it all off *coquito*. *Ay, madre santísima*. You couldn't believe how tongues were watering as men wished each other *Felicidades*.

Camacho snapped to. Oh, man, he thought. I've done it this time. He looked into his pockets and extracted three crumpled up dollar bills and some change. His stomach turned over a few times and he felt as if his legs would buckle and he'd fall over in a faint. All at once the Christmas decorations on the bar window became blurred and Camacho's eyes rolled up into his head. Holding on to the bar with both hands, he tried to steady himself. A feeling of complete desolation and regret hit him, tears came into his eyes, and then a long sobbing sound, which to the remaining patrons of the bar sounded like the flushing of the toilet, escaped from his chest.

One of Camacho's buddies, Epifanio Marrero, whom everyone knew as Ponce, came over and put his arm around Camacho's shoulder. Ponce was a worthless drunk, a piece of human driftwood, but the best guitar player in all of El Barrio. He lived for his art and if anyone had ever suggested that he take money for his music he would have been insulted.

"What's the matter, Camacho?" he said, tipping back a bottle of beer. "Don't cry. If it's a woman, forget her. If it's money, we'll rob a bank. Cheer up! It's *Nochebuena*, man!"

All Camacho could do was shake his head and another agonizing sob escaped from his chest. Why had he been so careless? The children were expecting so much this year. He had meant to get them all something earlier in the week but he'd never had a free moment at the butcher shop to get away and buy the presents. He should've let Marta buy the gifts but she always complained that whatever she bought for them they were never satisfied. The kids would just say Santa Claus was cheap. But that wasn't it. It was all his fault and, rather then being a man and doing his best, he had squandered all his money on drink.

"What am I going to do?" he said holding his head in both hands.

"You're drunk," said Ponce peering into Camacho's face.

"Yes, I know," said Camacho. "Leave me alone, Ponce. I'm no good. No good at all. I feel like dying."

"Well, in that case, let me have the rest of your beer and I'll sing at your funeral. What would you like me to sing? A *bolero*? Maybe a *guaracha!* I know, I know. You're from the mountains, right? Good, good. *Un seis chorreao.*" And having said this, Ponce kicked off his shoes, removed his socks, rolled up his pants to the calves and began singing a *seis*, introducing the song with that high pitched nasal *lelo-lai-lelo-lai* of the *jíbaros*. For Camacho all it did was give him a headache and make him feel as if his friend were mocking him.

"This is no laughing matter, Ponce," said Camacho regaining some of his composure.

"No, of course not, *compadre*," Ponce replied. "When it comes to my music I'm very serious. It's a pity that just this morning I had to hock my guitar."

"I'm in trouble," said Camacho.

"We all are, my friend. Plenty of trouble. Each day I'm faced with the same question. Should I go on living or should I step out in front of the Lexington Avenue Express and get it over with."

"Do you think that's what I ought to do?"

"Are you crazy? What kind of a man are you? What will people say, 'Camacho? He was a coward,' That's what they will say."

"Well, maybe they won't. You can be my witness. You will tell them I was very drunk and fell on the tracks."

Ponce held up his hand and shook his head violently.

"No, I will not be a part to deceiving people. I will not join you in this scheme to make them believe that you died accidentally. How would I face Chu Chu Barbosa down at Florindo's bar. He takes his job seriously. Suppose it is he that is driving the train and you jump out in front of it. Am I supposed to make him believe it as an accident? No way. *De ninguna manera.*"

"But he drives on the D Line, not the Lexington."

"It doesn't matter. He will ask questions. No, I won't do it. It is nothing but cowardice to kill yourself. Whatever it is, it will pass, it always does."

"You're no help," said Camacho, and stumbled forward out of the bar and into the snow, his jacket open. "No help at all," he yelled as he skidded on the sidewalk.

The snow was coming down harder, the wind blowing in wild gusts that made the snow drift up against cars and buildings. Camacho staggered forward, oblivious to the cold and snow. Which way was home? Yes, First Avenue. He must walk towards Third. No matter what happened he had to get home. What time was it? Ten o'clock. Should he pray? Maybe if he prayed hard enough a miracle would take place. What was he talking about? He didn't believe in any of that stuff. That was for old women. What did he care if Paco Miranda had seen a vision of the Virgin holding up a piece of cardboard with a number and then played it and hit for almost $600. Or stupid Gloria Franco, ugly as sin, praying every single day at Saint Cecilia's for 20 years to get married, and having that rich Cuban with the two restaurants up in Washington Heights courting her like she was a princess and then marrying her and buying her a damn condominium downtown. Everybody said that was a miracle. Maybe he should pray.

Rather than going down the subway stairs and perhaps as a deterrent against his original plan to do away with himself, he began walking towards what he thought was First Avenue, where he had grown up, but not where he now lived. He also walked west rather than east. He crossed Park Avenue and then Madison. Halfway down the block between Madison and Fifth Avenue, near an empty lot next to an abandoned building, Paulino Camacho slipped and fell banging his head against an iron railing and passing out in a deep snow drift. The street was deserted and no one saw him.

No one that is, except Juan Ramón Burgos, scanning the city of New York, at the Puerto Rican Department of the OFFICE FOR THE PROTECTION AND SALVAGE OF WAYWARD MORTALS. Dressed in his blue velvet V-neck robe, his beautiful wings tucked safely in a nonflying position, he was sitting at his monitor when he caught a brief glance of Camacho slipping and falling. Damn, he thought, another drunk. He'd come back to him later. He went on further south where in the Lower East Side a woman was threatening a man with a broken beer bottle and further on in Brooklyn someone was about to pass out on his bed with a lighted cigarette. What the hell were they doing down there! Christ Almighty they were worse than ever this year.

He pushed a couple of buttons and made the woman throw down the bottle in disgust and walk away. He then pushed another button and the man with the cigarette suddenly sat up and started screaming for his wife to hurry up and come to bed. Finally, he came back to Camacho but couldn't find him in the snow. He tried a closeup but still couldn't locate him. The scanner showed that he was there but he couldn't see him and therefore couldn't help him. He pushed a button and Camacho's data showed up on the screen.

Son of a bitch! He'd have to go down there.

He picked up the phone and dialed his supervisor's number. The phone rang a few times before he got an answer. He then explained that it was imperative that he go down.

"It's an emergency, Tillary," he said.

"Emergency? What kind of emergency?" his supervisor said.

"I got a drunk that fell into a snow drift in Manhattan. It's really coming down hard. There's a blizzard down there. What the hell are those people in weather doing! Tell them I don't appreciate their humor."

"I have nothing to do with the weather department," Tillary said.

"Well, I gotta go down and help this guy out."

"Maybe he got up?"

"Tillary, the scanner goes right to the spot. The board's lit up. It's an emergency. Take my word. He's there all right. I just can't see him."

"Can't you just scrape the snow away?"

"Scanners can't do that, Tillary. The Old Man's inventing all this electronic stuff but somehow he hasn't figured this one out yet."

"Have you tried everything?"

"Everything, Tillary: Bad dreams, sirens. Nothing. If every red light on my board's lit up, he's in trouble. It's all in the regulations. I have to go down."

"I can't let you go. There's nobody to run the scanner in your department."

His supervisor's response made Burgos angrier than he'd ever been in all the time he had been in heaven. It made him reflect again on why he had ever volunteered for this kind of duty. It was all guilt about the way he had lived down on earth and how just before he had died he had promised to reform. He died anyway and rather than going down he went up. Big deal! Boring and thankless work. Day and night rescuing idiots from their stupid mistakes.

"Give me a break, Tillary," he said. "This guy's gonna die. He'll freeze to death."

"Maybe I can put in a call to the Old Man and He can talk to him. He'll repent, die and you got somebody you can train."

"Tillary, this guy's got five kids to support. We're not talking about some worthless drunk. He's a hard worker, loves his wife and worships those five kids. He just screwed up, period."

"Worships?" Tillary said.

"Cut out the doctrinal stuff, okay? You know what I mean."

"Is he worth saving?"

"Goddamit, Tillary! What in the hell . . ."

"Careful, Burgos."

"Sorry, Tillary. I know. I know. Language. Regulations and all that. Okay, okay. Yeah, he's worth saving. He just screwed up and spent all his money drinking and now he can't buy anything to put under the Christmas tree. He's really a good guy. Just got carried away. Can't you get Blaisdell from the Wasp Department to help out? God, they're . . . Sorry. I mean, they're overstaffed over there."

"I'm sure you can understand that," Tillary said. "There are a lot more wasps than there are Puerto Ricans."

"Sure, I'm not gonna deny that. You don't even have anybody covering Puerto Ricans in Boston or Philly."

"They're covered. We got them split up. The Polish department's got some and the Irish, the rest. We're doing our best."

"But a 1 to 3 ratio, Tillary? One damned . . . oops . . . one angel to watch every three wasps and I gotta bust my hump watching all the Puerto Ricans in New York City to make sure they survive all this holy day crap . . ."

"Burgos!"

"Okay, okay. So it's the Kid's birthday and the Old Man's not gonna like it if I talk that way. But have a heart. I did the computations, and even if I'm at my best, I'm gonna lose at least a hundred people before the New Year comes in. People leaving kids alone and the building going up in flames, arguments that turn into murder, overdoses, people falling into subway tracks. A hundred souls and the way they're carrying on not one of them's got a chance to make it up here. It isn't easy, Tillary. Get me one of the guys from the Wasp Department. Some sociology professor that would enjoy slumming."

"They don't understand Spanish. It's in the regulations. The guy that runs the scanner has to speak Spanish. Your people got the thing passed last year as part of that affirmative action package."

Burgos thought for a moment.

"What about Sinclair?" he said. "He was a Peace Corps volunteer in South America. Some guerrillas blew him up."

"Speaks Quechua."

"Yes . . . sorry. What about Garrison? I've spoken Spanish with him. He was with the Lincoln Brigade. Got killed outside of Madrid back in the thirties."

"Burgos, you're jeopardizing the welfare of an entire community. The man is not well. Still carries on conversations with Hemingway, even though we have no communication channels with those people below."

"He'll have to do. Just send him down and I'll explain the whole scanning procedure to him. I'll have to take my chances."

"Okay, he'll be at your shop in five minutes."

"Five minutes? He's gotta be here now, I'm leaving."

"I'll do my best."

"Thanks, Tillary. Just keep me posted on who else is down in New York in case I need help. Log me off in five minutes."

A few moments later a pale young man entered the glass enclosed quarters where the giant Puerto Rican scanner was located and greeted Burgos in Spanish. Burgos explained everything very quickly, patted him on the back and thanked him.

"Just make sure that on each ten minute round you scan The Bronx, Manhattan and Brooklyn first. Don't worry too much about Staten Island. We don't have too many there. In Queens most of the people are pretty middle class. Once in a while there's the makings of a traffic accident or a faulty wire on a Christmas decoration, but nothing major. Just keep your eye on the upper and lower ends of Manhattan, the South Bronx and the four different locations in Brooklyn marked in blue. All right?"

The young man saluted and Burgos went off running into the decompressing chamber. He pushed several buttons for dress and stepped into the converter. Within seconds his blue robe and wings were off and he was dressed in the same clothes he'd worn that fateful night ten years before when, after celebrating his third round knockout of Bobby Russo in his fifth pro fight as a lightweight, he'd gone drinking and stepped out in front of a car going 80 miles an hour on the Grand Concourse and that was the end of Juan Moncho, as his mother had called him. He looked in the mirror and felt ashamed of the raggedy clothes, torn by the scraping metal, but he felt the blood pumping in his body and a fraction of a second later he was standing on the corner of Madison Avenue and 111th Street.

The snowfall was now a blizzard, obscuring objects no more than a foot away. Looking down through the snow at his locator he finally found the spot where Camacho had fallen and began shoveling away the snow with his bare hands. After a few minutes he found Camacho's chest. His heart was still beating but he was already stiff. He got him out of the snow and slung him over his shoulder. As he walked he called his own number at the Department and Garrison answered.

"*Teniente Garrison a sus órdenes,*" Garrison said.

"Garrison, this is Burgos. Screen up the file on Paulino Camacho, butcher."

"I'm afraid I would need a direct communication from control in order to do that."

"Garrison, knock off the shit. This is life and death."

"Regulations are regulations and I really don't feel I should jeopardize this operation by bending the rules."

"Garrison, screen up the fucking file or I'm gonna spread it around that you got shot in the back outside Madrid because you were scared shit and were running from the fascists, dammit. Screen up that information."

"Yes sir," Garrison said.

"Thank you."

"Here it is. Camacho, Paulino. Occupation, butcher. Age 38. Born, Cacimar, Puerto Rico. Married. Wife, Marta. Five children. Address, 405 East 6th Street, Apt. 4. Last Mass attended 4/17/77."

"Jesus Christ. He's all the way down there? I thought he lived in El Barrio. Thanks. I'll see you later."

As he walked he applied heat to Camacho's body with the hand resuscitator. By the time they were back on Lexington Avenue, Camacho was moaning. The angel Juan Moncho looked for a cab but there was no traffic at all on the street. They would have to take the subway. As they reached the subway stairs Camacho came to and began struggling.

"Let me down, Ponce," he said. "I can make it down the stairs by myself. What the hell are you doing, anyway? You're right, I would be a coward to kill myself. Are you gonna throw me in front of a train, you idiot? Let me down."

The angel Juan Moncho propped Camacho up against the wall and Camacho all of a sudden opened his eyes and peered into Burgos' face.

"Hey, you're not Ponce," he said. "Who the hell are you and where were you taking me? You were trying to mug me and then throw me in front of a train, right? You're a junkie."

"Just take it easy."

"Bullshit, you little bastard," said Camacho, and took a wild swing at the angel Juan Moncho.

Juan Moncho slipped the punch easily and pushed Camacho up against the wall.

"Hey, I told you to take it easy, Ace. You're in a lot of trouble and all I was doing was trying to help you. You fell in the snow and I'm trying to get you home."

The liquor having worn off somewhat, it once again dawned on Camacho what he was facing when he arrived home. He burst out crying and began pounding the wall near the token booth.

"I can't go home," he bawled. "My kids. I got nothing to put under the tree. I don't care what Ponce said, I'm gonna jump in front of the train."

And off he went crawling under the turnstile with the angel Juan Moncho behind him after slipping two dollars into the booth's window. He grabbed Camacho and pushed him down on a bench with the specific instructions that if he got up he'd feel a lot worse then if the train had run over him.

"Hey, I don't wanna hurt you, but if I have to I'm gonna knock you into next year if you keep it up. Now get hold of yourself and stop behaving like an asshole. Okay?"

"Okay, okay. Boy, you're pretty strong for a little guy. What's your name?"

"Juan Moncho," said the angel.

Camacho peered into the angel's face and then at his clothes.

"You look familiar as hell. Like you was in the newspaper or something. Ain't you cold in those summer clothes?"

"I'm fine. Don't worry about it."

"Hey, I'm in trouble, man."

"I know all about it. Here comes the train."

They got on the Lexington Avenue local, changed at 86th Street and got on the Express train, and all along Juan Moncho reassured Camacho that everything was going to be all right.

"How? Man, I spent all my money and those kids are gonna be disappointed as hell in the morning."

"Don't worry about it," Juan Moncho said. "We'll pick something up on the way there. There's gotta be a toy store or two down in the Village."

"Everything's closed right now, man. I really blew it."

"We'll find a way. Just leave it to me."

"What you gonna do, break into a toy store?"

"Just don't worry."

At that point, as the train was leaving 59th Street, Juan Moncho got a call from Tillary. He closed his eyes and concentrated on silent receiving and sending.

"Yeah, Tillary?"

"How's it going with the job?"

"Pretty good. We're going down to the Village and see if we can transmit some stuff to his Christ-mas tree. Another hour or so of work and I'll be back up there. How's Garrison doing?"

"No complaints yet. He hasn't called in any emergencies, but I had to send O'Brien from the Irish Department to show him how to operate the console. There was some party up in the Bronx and a bunch of people crashed it and all hell broke loose. Guns, knives, the whole works. O'Brien patched the cops and they just happened to show up in time to put a stop to the whole thing."

"Good, good. Well, I'll see you later. Thanks for calling."

Juan Moncho was about to click off when all at once Tillary was talking very fast and giving him orders.

"Slow down, Tillary. Slow down. Who?"

"Mandlestein. Mandlestein," Tillary said. "He's gotten himself involved with those idiotic Guardian Angels. Go see what's going on."

"I can't do that! Where the hell is he?"

"Two cars down from yours."

"On the same train? You sure?"

"Of course I'm sure. Go! I'll monitor and send help if it's needed."

Juan Moncho clicked off, shook Camacho awake and told him they had to go.

"Where? We getting off?" Camacho said.

"Let's go. Follow me."

They went through a couple of nearly empty cars and then into a third one and there was six foot one Bryan Mandlestein, dressed in gold lamé from head to toe, cape and all, bleached blond hair to his shoulders and made up like he was being photographed for the cover of Vogue. Around him six red berets in feathers and buttons, all of them with logoed t-shirts over their winter clothing, were shoving and pushing as they tried to get at Mandlestein. As soon as Mandlestein saw Juan Moncho coming he began clapping his hands. He then jumped up on one of the seats of the train.

"Oh, thank goodness you've come, Robin," he said, sighing. "Please explain to these cretins that they're tastelessly and abominably dressed. Tacky, tacky, tacky," he added, turning to them and pointing his finger at the startled Guardian Angels. "Tell them, okay? I mean you speak their language. Oh, and add that if they're Guardian Angels, then I'm Marlene Dietrich." And then oblivious to their growing anger he went into the singing of some current popular song while gyrating sensuously atop the subway seat. 'Marlene watches from the wall, her mocking smile says it all . . .'"

"Let me at him, José," said one of the Guardian Angels. "I'll kick his faggety ass."

"Word," said a couple more.

"Yo, what's going on brother," said Juan Moncho. "Chill out."

"Hey, mind your own business, shorty," said one of the Guardian Angels. "Or ama bust you upside the head."

"Just take it easy." Juan Moncho said.

Two of the Guardian Angels moved towards Juan Moncho, adopting karate stands, their fingers curled as they crouched.

"My, my," said Mandlestein from his perch. "How grossly butch. Let me turn them into Michael Jackson teeny boppers, Burgos."

Juan Moncho waved Mandlestein off and as soon as the first one made his move, consisting of a high kick, he stepped under and inside, jabbed three times with his left, crossed over with his right and knocked the Guardian Angel out before he hit the floor of the subway car with a thud. The other five Angels rushed Juan Moncho, but as he was getting ready to deliver his next blow, the five turned into young screaming teenage girls made up in pink outfits, their hair chopped in mohawks or dyed the most awful shades of green orange and red, and their clothes looking like they had shopped at the Salvation Army. The subway car doors opened and Mandlestein jumped off the seat.

"Let's go, you beast. You could've hurt that boy. You Latins are so impulsive."

Out the three of them went at Grand Central Station. Camacho was totally sober but nearly in shock. He kept looking from Mandlestein to Juan Moncho, unable to say anything. He was sure the little guy was Johnny Burgos, the lightweight that had gotten killed about ten or eleven years ago.

Mandlestein explained how he'd been sitting up in his cubicle, monitoring the gays in the Village when all of a sudden a friend he knew from fifteen years before when he died was about to commit what amounted to suicide by getting involved with somebody who had been diagnosed as having AIDS.

"Like I couldn't blame him because this boy was divine. I mean, can we talk? Tab Hunter move over, okay? But I couldn't let my friend, Donald, do it and he wouldn't respond to anything I sent down and Tillary told me under no circumstances was I to come down and I told him to buzz off, know what I mean? And now I'm in all sorts of trouble and he's going to report me and I'll probably have to go in front of the All Powerful and all that other garbage. Oh, I'm getting depressed. Look at me. Still dressed in this tacky outfit which is strictly passé. So, what brings you down here?"

Juan Moncho explained about Camacho.

"I'm just gonna stop off at a toy store and get some stuff for his kids. We'll just beam it under their Christmas tree and then get a dress or something for his wife and get him home."

Mandlestein was shocked.

"You have to be kidding. I know what you're thinking. Just cheap stuff and get it over with, right? I know you got it hard with so much responsibility but, puleeze. Okay? Can I speak frankly without you going into your Rocky or Rambo thing, or whatever fantasy it is you think you're playing out?

"Sure, go ahead," Juan Moncho said.

Camacho couldn't take it any longer.

"Say, who are you guys?"

"Quiet, Pancho," Mandlestein said. "Everything's under control."

"My name's not Pancho," Camacho said.

"Okay, then Cisco," Mandlestein said. "Just don't get your panties in a wad, all right?"

"What?" Camacho said, feeling insulted.

"That's okay, Camacho," Juan Moncho said. "Let me handle this," and turning to Mandlestein, told him to go ahead.

Mandlestein explained that part of the reason Puerto Ricans were in such bad shape was because they felt all this guilt about one thing or another and therefore didn't believe they deserved the very best the society had to offer. And that here Juan Moncho had a chance to do it up big and really bring about a miracle and he was settling for some cheap toys and a $19.95 dress for Camacho's wife.

"What did you have in mind?" said Juan Moncho.

"Don't get me wrong, Sheena of the Jungle," Mandlestein said. "I know I'm being a bit selfish because I haven't been shopping in so long but, like how does FAO Schwarz, Bergdorf Goodman, Bloomies and Fred the Furrier sound to you?"

"Are you crazy?" Juan Moncho said.

"Of course, I am, but it's your holy day not mine. I'm already in trouble, so let them put in on my tab. Come on, get out your scanner and get sizes on Lola or Conchita or whatever her name is. What's your wife's name, darling?" he said, turning to Camacho.

"Don't call me that, okay?" said Camacho, going into an extremely awkward boxing stance. "I don't let *patos* talk to me like that."

"Oh, my!" said Mandlestein, backing off as if he were frightened. "Mucho macho! Get our your scanner, Burgos. Although Pancho Villa here doesn't seem to appreciate our effort."

Juan Moncho went into his pocket and retrieved his miniature scanner and punched in Camacho's address. Immediately the screen showed Camacho's living room with the kids sitting around the Christmas tree in their pajamas and Marta Camacho sitting on the sofa crying. Mandlestein snatched the pocket scanner away from Juan Moncho and shoved it at Camacho.

"Take a look, big man," he said.

"Oh, my God," said Camacho. "I'm gonna jump in front of a train."

"No, you're not, sweetie," said Mandlestein. "You're going shopping, whether you like it or not."

"What's he talking about?" Camacho said, turning to Juan Moncho.

"Just do as he says. Don't worry. We'll have you home in less than an hour."

"Oh, goody," said Mandlestein. "Let's get out of here and get a cab. Burgos, make sure they all go to sleep before we start."

Juan Moncho pushed a couple of buttons on his pocket scanner and watched as the kids kissed their mother and went off to bed. Unable to resist the angel induced sleep, Marta Camacho turned off the light and also went to bed.

Within minutes they were inside FAO Schwarz and Camacho was going crazy picking out toys for Alicia, Betty, Rodolfo, Kevin and the baby, Nilsa. He couldn't believe it. He picked out a stuffed elephant the size of a great dane for the baby. Juan Moncho aimed the transporter at the gray form and it disappeared.

"See," Mandlestein said pointing to the scanner.

"Wow," said Camacho, watching as the elephant ended up against the couch where Marta had sat. "You guys are too much! Listen, I'm sorry about what I said about *patos*," he said to Mandlestein.

"That's okay, ducky," Mandlestein said. "Just keep shopping."

From the FAO Schwarz they went to Bloomingdale's and then to Bergdorf Goodman, then to Cartier's where they picked out a watch for Marta and then off to Fred the Furrier where Mandlestein chose a full length sable for her. He wrote down a name and address on a piece of paper and gave it to Camacho.

"Your wife's not half bad," he said, "but she's got to do something about her hair and makeup. Have her go see my friend, Alonzo in the Village. We do miracles, but what he does with women is truly heavenly, okay, sweetie?"

"Sure," said Camacho.

And so it went. When they were finished they stood out in the street with the snow falling. Juan Moncho told Mandlestein that he had to get Camacho home. Mandlestein said he was absolutely exhausted. Since they should both be getting back up, Juan Moncho said, why didn't they use the transporter to get Camacho home. Mandlestein agreed.

"Okay, Camacho," Juan Moncho said. "We gotta go. Merry Christmas and Happy New Year."

"But who are you?" Camacho said.

"If anybody wants to know, just tell them, you met your guardian angel," Juan Moncho said laughing.

Before Camacho could say another word, the angel Juan Moncho pushed three buttons and Camacho found himself in bed next to Marta. He slipped quietly out of bed, tiptoed out of the bedroom, looked in on the children and then peeked into the living room. By the light of the lamppost outside the window he saw dozens of boxes next to the Christmas tree and against the sofa, the outline of the huge elephant.

Edgardo Vega Yunqué was born on the island of Puerto Rico, came to the United States at the age of thirteen and is a resident of New York City. He is the author of *The Comeback*, a novel, 1985; *Mendoza's Dreams*, a novel, 1987; and *Casualty Report*, 1991, a collection of short stories. His fiction has appeared in numerous quarterlies and magazines such as "The Bilingual Review," "The Americas Review," "MBM Magazine," "The Portable Lower East Side," "Bomb," and others. His work can also be found in the following recent anthologies: *Puerto Rican Writers at Home in the U.S.A.*, Open Hand Publishing, Seattle, 1991; *Iguana Dreams*, Harper-Collins, New York, 1992 and *Growing up Latino: Reflections on Life in the United States*, Houghton Mifflin, 1993, *Currents from the Dancing River*, Harcourt Brace, 1994. He has written columns for *New York Newsday* and for *Latino News*. His new novel is *No Matter How Much You Promise to Cook or Pay the Rent You Blew It Cause Bill Bailey Ain't Never Coming Home Again*, and William Morrow will publish *Growing Up Puerto Rican*, an anthology of 20 Puerto Rican fiction writers from the U.S. and Puerto Rico. He is President and Chairman of the Board of the Clemente Soto Vélez Cultural Center, a self-sufficient arts complex in the Lower East Side. Vega Yunqué is the winner of fellowships from the NEA and the NYFA, and is a member of PEN and of the Authors Guild.

7. Nicholasa Mohr, "A Time With a Future (Carmela)"

Nicholasa Mohr's fiction centers on not only the Puerto Rican community but also on the lives of women within this community. A Latina herself, Mohr often addresses the inequality and double standards faced by women within both the Puerto Rican and Anglo societies. In her recent collection of short stories, *Rituals of Survival: A Woman's Portfolio*, she examines the often challenging lives of several New York Puerto Rican females. In "A Time with a Future (Carmela)," Mohr explores the last years of the life of Carmela, who has just lost her husband and now must decide on the future direction of her life. Going against the wishes of her children, she chooses a course of action that surprises her family and friends.

A Time With a Future (Carmela)

"A whole lifetime together, imagine! And now it's over." Edna spoke, holding back tears. "I don't know what I would do if I were Mama, honest."

"Poor Mama," murmured Mary, "she's had such a hard time of it. I'm glad that in these last few years they had each other. Papa was her whole life . . ." Mary stopped and began to sob quietly. Edna put her arms around Mary, who buried her head in her sister's bosom. "Oh Edna, it's so sad to see it all come to an end. The end of something so special."

"Come on, Mary." Edna very gently pushed Mary away from her. "Let's not get like this. Think of Ma. If she sees us crying, it'll be worse for her. We all have to figure this thing out calmly and rationally."

"I know." Mary wiped her eyes and swallowed. "It's . . . the finality of it that's so hard for me to bear, you know? But you're right, we're all Mom's got now, so it's up to us to decide what's best. At her age, it's like you say, she can't be left alone."

"That's more like it, and we can't stay here day after day indefinitely like this. I don't know how long Joe's mother is going to hold out with my kids. How about you? Exactly how long do you think Mark's gonna come home from work to take care of your three and do housework? That's why, when Roberto gets here, I'll discuss what Joe and I have agreed to. Then all three of us have to sit down and decide Mama's future."

Carmela had left her daughters seated in the kitchen, entered the small bedroom of her four-room flat and closed the door, shutting out their voices. She was sick of her daughters' tear-stained faces, their wailing, crying and self-pity. Grown women, with families, acting like children. Carmela shook her head; it was all too much. Her whole body was tired; every bone, every muscle ached. She pulled back the bedspread, kicked off her shoes and lay down.

They had buried Benjamin two days ago, but her daughters had insisted on remaining with her both nights. And that meant Carmela had to make the daybed in the other room, share her own bed with one of her daughters, find more sheets, towels, dishes and all the extra work that was part of caring for others. She had not been able to rest; not as she should, by herself, alone with her private grief and deep sense of relief. There had been too many people at the funeral. Benjamin's friends from the union, neighbors and people she had not seen in years. Carmela felt her eyelids closing with a heaviness from lack of sleep. She had not really slept peacefully in over a week and, before that, for what had seemed like a timeless battle, she had hardly known sleep at all.

Her mind was still filled with him, with Benjamin. When they had laid Benjamin out in the casket, they had pinned a bright scarlet carnation on the lapel of his best suit. The rich red color of the flower contrasted sharply with the dry greyness of his skin and accentuated the dark purple lines of pain that the long illness had etched in his face. Carmela had asked the morticians to replace the red carnation with a white one; this change had made it easier to look at him.

She remembered her Freddie all too vividly. There are things one never forgets, always feels. Like my Freddie, Carmela nodded. His small casket had been laden with flowers. They had placed a bright red rose in his little hands which were cupped together as if in prayer. For him, this had been the right color, matching his full red mouth which was fixed in a serene smile. He appeared to be sleeping and, for one long moment, Carmela had actually believed that Freddie would look up, his dark eyes smiling, and question her. "Where am I, Mami? What am I doing here?" And she would respond, "A bad dream, my baby, Freddie, you and me, we are both having a bad dream."

But it was no dream. Freddie's illness had been unexpected, swift and real. In a matter of days she had lost him. Not like Benjamin; more than a year of waiting patiently for him to die.

At first it had seemed no more than a bad cold. Freddie had a low fever and a sore throat. But he got sicker and his breathing emitted a rasping,

"A Time With a Future: Carmela" by Nicholasa Mohr is reprinted with permission of the publisher of *Rituals of Survival: A Woman's Portfolio* (Houston: Arte Publico Press-University of Houston, 1985)

honking sound, and his small chest caved in, then extended until it seemed about to burst. Carmela was frightened and alone. Benjamin was on the night shift again. While the others slept soundly, Carmela dressed Freddie warmly. She went to a neighbor and asked her to look after the children until she returned from the emergency clinic with Freddie. The bus was not there, and Carmela decided it would be quicker to walk the many long blocks to the emergency clinic. Even through the blankets she could feel Freddie struggling to breathe as she carried him as fast as her feet could take her. At the emergency clinic she explained with great effort in her halting English why she was there, and then waited for her name to be called.

The young doctor spoke gently to her. "You have a very sick baby. He must stay here, in the hospital. Understand . . . mother? Usted comprende? Si, very good." Carmela's head was spinning. She asked "But how? Why? He all right yesterday. He play with his brother and sisters. Por favor, doctor, give to me the medicina, and I take care of my baby in home. Mi casa is much better for him, yes?" The young doctor shook his head. "No! He's too sick to leave hospital." Lifting his hands, he covered his head and face, gesturing to her. "We have to put him in an oxygen tent so he can breathe. He has pneumonia, understand? Muy enfermo niño . . . comprende, madre?" She felt the fear deep inside, shivering as if someone had replaced her blood with ice water. "Por favor, doctor, he never go away from me, he no talk good English too much . . . pero Freddie understands good everything. He no go in school . . . only cuatro, four years." The young doctor nodded reassuringly. "He'll be all right in the hospital, Mrs. Puig, you go home to your casa. Take care of your other children. Then you can come back later and stay with Freddie. The nurse will give you all the information. Don't worry, no apures, we are going to take good care of your baby. Make him well. Go home, get some rest." As they took him away, Freddie turned to her, wide-eyed and scared, fighting for breath.

As soon as Benjamin came home from work, Carmela returned, staying by Freddie's side for the better part of two days. Freddie was not improving, but he had not gotten worse. When he was awake, he smiled at her from under the oxygen tent and she smiled back, telling him all about the things she would get for him after he got well again.

When on the third day she had made her brief visit home to check on the others, Benjamin complained.

"Two days! Two days! I can't stay out another day. Woman, what am I gonna do for money to buy food, pay rent . . . when they dock me? I must get back to work. Freddie's all right now. He's in the best place, in the hospital with the doctors who know better than you what to do." This time Carmela fought back. "But if something should happen to him, I want to be there at his side. Freddie mustn't be alone." Benjamin was unshaken. "I can't be here with the kids, cooking, washing and doing your housework . . . just in case something happens! There's plenty men out there looking for jobs. I'll lose my job . . . woman! If you want to go when I'm not here, call in a neighbor or get a friend. How about Sara, you've done her plenty of favors, eh?" Carmela resisted. "What friends? When do I have time to make friends? Neighbors can't be staying here all day with our kids, and neither can Sara. Besides, she's alone with her own children and worse off than us. There's only you; nobody else can stay here except you, Ben . . . maybe you can ask for part-time work, just a few more days until Freddie is over the crisis . . . maybe . . ." Benjamin shouted, "Stop it!" Full of his own fears, his mind raced with memories of his childhood in a time where death and starvation had dictated his existence. And for two days now, the words to a song he had not heard since he was a small boy would not leave his mind; they played on his lips over and over.

First the tremors,
then the typhoid
follows hunger with every breath
we pray for joy, for better times
but the only relief is the promise of death!

The peasants of his tiny rural village would sing this song during the typhoid epidemic. Benjamin had lost his father, two older brothers and baby sister, leaving only his mother, older sister and younger brother. He was nine when he became head of the household. Sometimes he would get work at the fields or at the sugar refinery, working from sun-up to sundown, bringing home twenty-five, maybe thirty cents a day, depending on the work to be done. Other days he would work chopping wood, running errands and cleaning the hog pens, to be paid in food, usually leftovers, but enough so that they wouldn't starve at home. At thirteen, when his mother died, his sister found work as a domestic and he and his younger brother set out on their own.

"Absolutely not, woman! There's a goddam depression out there. Do you think I'm gonna let us all starve? I ain't selling apples or shoelaces in the street, not when I got a job to go to. And we don't take charity in this family. I go back to work tomorrow and you . . . you can do what the hell you want!" Carmela kept silent. Benjamin had a strong will and his fears justified his reasoning. She understood she could not persuade him.

Carmela had not wanted Freddie to die alone in the hospital, but that's how it had happened. For the next three days, she had only been able to be with him for a few hours, and always with the thought of the others that she left at home, unattended for the most part. That evening when Mr. Cooper, owner of the candy store, sent a message that the hospital had called on the public phone asking her to come right away, Carmela guessed what it was they would tell her.

"Too late. We did everything we possible could." The young doctor was compassionate and visibly upset. "Double pneumonia . . . there was nothing we could give him. All of us did the best we could. We are all very, very sorry, Mrs. Puig, Freddie was a wonderful little boy."

That was in another lifetime, the time of the Great Depression, before the Second World War, before penicillin, antibiotics and miracle drugs. Today it would have been different; children don't have to die from that illness anymore. Medicine, in this lifetime, knows no limits. Look at an old man like Benjamin, eh? Kept alive, full of disease and tortured by pain beyond human endurance. And for what? No future, no hope, only the knowledge that each day he remained alive would be a torment for both of them.

Carmela opened her eyes and yawned, stretching her body. There was no sense in expecting sleep to come, take over and soothe away her weariness. Too much was still happening inside, repeating itself. The past was still the present and the present was not yet real.

When the doctor told her about Benjamin, she had insisted he be told as well. It was too much for her at this time; no longer did she have that kind of strength for others. Besides, Benjamin was a proud man, and it was only right. He had already suspected what the doctors confirmed; he was frightened, but not shocked. Calmly, Benjamin had told her he was resigned to the inevitable, but wanted to ask her for one last favor. And that request stirred and brought to the surface those deep and private feelings of hatred and revenge that can only be felt by one human being for another when they have been as close as Benjamin and Carmela. Then, as he spoke, Carmela felt herself spinning with rage.

"Carmela, no matter how sick I get, don't send me away. Let me die here in my own bed, Carmelita, here with you, buy your side."

A tirade of words she had been nurturing, rehearsing and storing away for that day when she would leave him, walk out, walk out for good, choked Carmela. "Remember Freddie? Remember our son, Benjamin? How he died alone? In a strange place, in a strange bed. Without me by his side. I owed him at least as much as you ask of me. A baby, four years old with no one to comfort him from the fear of death, to guide him gently into the unknown. It all happened thirty-eight years ago, but I remember. And now, today, now . . . you want the right to die here, safe and secure in my arms. I didn't give birth to you! You selfish, hateful man, how well I know you.!"

They had looked at each other silently. He, waiting for her to answer. She, unable to speak, afraid of that explosion of terrible words that would vent her rage. Now it was so easy to hurt him, to make him suffer as she had suffered the death and loss of her child. She couldn't speak, not one word left her lips. Carmela saw him old and tired, bracing himself against death, preparing himself and seeking her help. He spoke again, this time pleading.

"Promise, Carmela, that's all I ask of you. Just this favor and never will I ask you for another thing; I give you my word . . . just don't, don't send me away; no matter what, let me die at home."

Carmela had hidden her resentment and put aside her hatred. Instead, she responded as always, to the unspoken bond that existed between them, that dependency on each other.

And she had promised, "It'll be all right, Benjamin, you can remain at home. No matter how sick you get. Don't worry, I won't let them take you away. You can stay here with me . . . until it's over."

This pact, built on survival, was what held them together; it was what had cemented them to a lifetime of sharing without so much as a day's voluntary separation. That security, that dependency, was the foundation of their marriage; solid and tough, like a boulder of impenetrable granite.

For a full year she had nursed him, giving him medicine, caring for him as he got weaker, almost every minute of the day and night. In time, she had to bathe him, give him the bedpan and finally spoon-feed him. His body, at first, was still strong and straight. They had not slept together for many years and so Carmela had been amazed by his supple body, the muscular limbs and tightness of skin that was unusual for a man as old as Benjamin. But, as he got sicker and lost weight, his body became frail and bent; his skin hung loosely as if lightly tacked onto his bones.

The sleepless nights, when he called out to her for comfort not once, but constantly... the three flights she had to climb, loaded with bundles, began to rip Carmela apart. The burden of his illness gave her not time to rest. Completely exhausted, she decided to speak to him about her promise.

"Benjamin, maybe it's better for you in the hospital. Listen, think about it, please. They can care for you better there, give you stronger medicine, maybe, eh? Look, Benjamin, I'm so tired, because there's nothing more I can do for you. Please, I don't know how long I can hold out... please think about it. I promise, I'll be out to see you every day; every single day I'll be by your side at the hospital, I swear..."

"No, you promised me! And now you talk about sending me out! You said I could stay. Carmela, you've become hardhearted to say this to me. No!" His eyes had filled with tears. Like a child, he clung desperately to her, grabbing her hands, groping at her body. "Please, in the name of God... please don't send me away. Let me die here, with you... you promised!" Carmela had pushed him away, tearing at his fingers, shoving, and struggling, unable to free herself from his fierce grip. "You promised! Now that I'm dying, I don't matter anymore... you can't send me away... you can't ..."

"Selfish man, you deserve to die alone, just like my dead baby! It would be justice to send you away... away from me."

Again the words remained unspoken; instead, she said "All right, stop it! Stop! For God's sake, you can stay. I promise you. But I'm getting some help. I can't do it all alone. All right, I said you can stay!" Only then, after she had reassured him, had Benjamin released her.

Carmela had run away to the other side of the apartment and had put her hands over her ears to shut out his crying. But she still heard his loud sobbing and screaming.

"Carmela, Carmelita, you are a good woman!"

Carmela was able to get some help; a practical nurse came three times a week and later, every day. Benjamin journeyed each day on a long painful road that would lead to death. The kind of merciless journey that comes with cancer. The cancer had started in his lower intestines and finally ran rampant through his body, leaving him helpless, barely able to move. But still he clung to life, determined to put up a battle; fighting to survive was all he knew.

He would call out "Carmela... get me some water. Carmela, I don't want the nurse, tell her to leave. Do something for the pain! Carmela, give me something. Don't leave me, Carmela." And she would hope and pray that before he could utter her name once more, he would stop breathing.

Then, at last, he lapsed into a coma, feebly clinging to life. He would utter sounds and sentences which were, for the most part, unintelligible. Sometimes he screamed out the names of his own parents, brothers and sisters. Events of his childhood, memories of back home filled his mind and escaped from his lips. He spoke mostly in Spanish, laughing, crying and asking questions. No one knew what he wanted and, after two days, no one listened except Carmela. Maybe at this time, Carmela hoped, he would say something about their dead child; but in all his tangled words and gibberish, Freddie's name was never mentioned.

Her children had been at the apartment since their father's latest turn for the worse. That day, they all sat in the kitchen drinking coffee and hot chocolate, waiting for him to die. They shared the vigil, taking turns at Benjamin's bedside. Late that evening, Roberto called his mother and when she returned, they found Benjamin staring blankly, not breathing. A look of peace spread over his face, as if the pain had finally disappeared. Gently, Carmela closed his eyes and mouth, kissed his dry lips and covered his face with the sheet.

Again, thoughts about the funeral, the people, the flowers and Freddie crowded Carmela's thoughts. It was as if her thinking pattern were following a cycle, winding up always with Benjamin's death.

Perhaps she was avoiding this latest part of the whole business? Carmela knew she had to deal with her children, grownups who still insisted on that relationship of mother and child. Now they felt themselves to be in charge. Carmela sighed, almost out of patience. She heard the front door and voices. That would be Roberto, and now her children would begin another discussion about her future.

She had been through their weddings, the birth of their children, marital disputes from time to time; always she had listened and given her support. What they wanted now, and what they might ask of her, created an anxiety that drained Carmela's energy. In a few minutes she would get up and speak to them. Sooner or later they had to talk.

"Mama can come home with me, we'll find the room; Suzie and Gigi can double up . . . " Mary looked at her brother and sister nervously, then continued, "Mark won't mind, honest."

"No," Edna responded. "I think it's better if she comes with me; after all, we have the big house. Nobody will be put out for space."

"I wish I could say it's all right at my house, but the way things are with me and Gloria, well . . ." Roberto hesitated.

"We understand, don't worry," Edna said. "Besides, it's better for Mama to be with her own daughter."

"Financially, I can always help out, you know that," Roberto smiled.

"She's got Papa's pension and some savings; she's all right as far as that goes," Edna said, "but if we need anything more, I'll let you know."

"There's only one thing about her going with you," Mary said. "She's not gonna want to go way out to Long Island. Port Jefferson is too far away from everything for her."

"She'll get used to it. It'll take a little time, that's all. Anyway, you're far away yourself, Mary. Mount Vernon isn't around the corner! And your apartment isn't big enough for another person. Where are you gonna put her?"

"You know what I think? I don't think we are gonna get Mama out of this old apartment, period." Roberto nodded emphatically. "She's too attached to it. Remember the time they took a trip to Puerto Rico, back to Papa's town, to see about retiring there? Ma said she couldn't stand it. She missed the city, her friends, everything. How long have they been living here in this place? Twenty-six years or something like that, right?"

"It'll be better for her to leave here. Personally, I don't know how anybody can live here, in this city, if they can get out . . ." Edna shook her head. "The noise, the pollution, the crime! Oh, I know I wouldn't want my kids here. When we were kids, maybe it was different . . . it just seems worse today . . ."

"Mama said it's not too bad since they put up all the new middle-income buildings. She says it's better than ever with new shops and all kinds of interesting people around. Ma says she can go right to Broadway and buy anything she wants at any time of the day or . . ."

"Stop being so naive . . ." Edna interrupted. "Mary, how long can Mama stay by herself? She's sixty-six. In a few years, when she can't cope, then what?" It'll be a lot worse to get her out of here. I'm not going to be commuting back and forth. And I

know you, Mary . . . you too, Roberto, especially the way your marriage is going, who knows where you'll be, eh?" No, we have to make a decision between us and stick to it. Now, listen to what Joe and I have planned . . ." Edna paused, making sure her brother and sister were listening. "Mama has a fairly good income from Papa's pension, so she won't be a financial burden to anyone. She's in good health, except for some arthritis not and then, but nobody ever hears her complain. And, she has some savings . . . all right, then. With a little more than half her savings we can convert the playroom area on the lower level of my house into living quarters for Mama. Like a kind of efficiency apartment, with her own kitchenette and half-bath. She won't need much more because she will have the rest of the house as well. This is necessary because we all know how independent Mama is. After that initial investment, I won't charge her rent or anything. She can live there as long as she wants . . . I mean, for the rest of her days."

Roberto opened his mouth to speak, but thought better of it. Instead, he shrugged and smiled, looking at Mary. She smiled back. After a long silence, Mary said, "It sounds pretty good . . . what do you think, Roberto?" "Well, so far it's the best plan, and also the only plan. There's only one thing, like I said, Ma's gotta go for it." "She will," Edna said, "but it's up to us to convince her. The two of you better back me on this. Understand? We have to be united in this thing? Well?" Mary and Roberto nodded in agreement. "Good," Edna continued, "now, what to do with this place? Mama's got all kinds of pots and pans . . . look at all of this furniture and junk. I suppose she'll want to take some of this with her . . . let's see . . ."

Carmela sat up, put on her shoes and placed the bedspread neatly back on her bed. She heard the voices of her children. Well, she might as well get it over with. Carmela opened a bureau drawer, removed a small grey metal box and opened it. She searched among her valuable papers; the will she and Benjamin had made, the life insurance policy she had taken out on herself many years ago and still faithfully paid every month, some very old photographs, letters from her children as youngsters and from her grandchildren. Finally, she found the large manila envelope with all the material she was looking for. She closed the box and put it back. Then she walked into the kitchen where her children were waiting.

"Ma, how you feeling?" Roberto kissed his mother lightly on the forehead.

"How about something to eat, Ma?" Edna asked. "Some tea? Or a little hot broth?"

"No," Carmela sat, holding the envelope in her hands. "I'm fine; I'm not hungry."

"Mama, you should eat more, you're getting too thin . . . it's not good for you. You should eat regularly, it could affect your . . ."

"Ma . . ." interrupted Edna, ignoring Mary. "We have to have a serious talk."

"I wasn't finished," snapped Mary.

"Mama's not hungry!" Edna looked directly at Mary. "All right?"

"Listen . . ." Roberto spoke. "Why don't I go out and get us all something to eat. Chinese or Cuban . . . so nobody has to cook."

"Sit down, Roberto." Edna then continued in a quiet, calm voice, "We have all the food we need here . . ." Turning to Carmela, she went on, "Mama, now that Papa isn't here anymore . . . we want you to know that you have us and you don't have to be alone. You are our responsibility now, just as if you had Papa. We all know this . . . don't we?" She turned to Mary and Roberto.

"Yes."

"Oh yes, Mama."

"We've all discussed this a great deal, just between ourselves. And, we've decided on a plan that we know you'll like. Of course, we want to talk it over with you first, so that we have your approval. But, I'm certain that when you hear what it is, you'll be pleased."

"Oh yes, Mama, wait until you hear what Edna . . . what we . . . oh, go ahead, Edna, tell her . . ." Mary smiled.

"Joe and I agreed and thought this out carefully. You . . . are coming to live with us, Mama. With me, Joe and the kids. We are the ones with a big house. Mary's in an apartment and Roberto doesn't exactly know where he's gonna settle; not the way things are right now. I know how proud you are and how independent, so you'll want to contribute something. Here's what we think . . . you know my house is a split level and there's room for expansion, right?"

Carmela felt an urge to open the envelope at that moment and tell them, so that Edna could stop talking nonsense,. But instead, she listened, trying to hide her impatience.

". . . so that your savings, or part anyway, can pay for your private apartment. Of course, as I said, you don't need such a big area, because you can share the house with the rest of us. Outside, you can take a section of the lot, Mama, if you want to have a vegetable garden or flowers. The kids would love

it, and of course Joe and I won't take a cent, you can live the rest of your days rent free. You know Joe's pleased, he wants you to feel welcomed in our home." Edna was almost out of breath. Well, there, I've said my piece . . . now what do you think, Mama?"

All three waited for Carmela to respond. She held out the envelope.

"I've got something to show all of you." Carefully she removed its contents and spread several sheets of paper out on the kitchen table. "I suppose I should have said something before this, but with your father's illness and everything else . . ." Carmela gestured that they come closer. "Here we are . . . take a look. It's a co-op. The building's only been up about three years. Everything is brand new. My apartment is on the sixteenth floor, on the northwest corner, just like I wanted, with lots of windows and it's got a terrace! Imagine, a terrace . . . I'm gonna feel rich . . . that's what. Look . . . kids, here are the floor plans, see? I got one bedroom, a living room-dining room, a brand-new kitchen. Oh, and here's an incinerator for garbage. They've got one on every floor and a community room with all kinds of activities. I heard from some of the people who live there, that there are some well-known experts, lecturers, coming in to speak about all kinds of subjects. The best part is that it's right here, around the corner, on Amsterdam Avenue. On the premises we have a drugstore, stationery and delicatessen. You know, I put my name down for this with a deposit right after Papa got sick. He hadn't wanted us to move, but once I knew how things would be, I went ahead. They called me just before Benjamin died, when he was almost in a coma, and asked if I could move in around the first of the month. I took a chance . . . I knew he couldn't last much longer, and said yes. That's in two weeks!" Carmela was busy tracing the floor plans with her fingers showing them the closets and cabinet space. "Here? See, I've paid the purchase, my savings covered the amount. You are all welcome to come and sit on the terrace . . . wait until you see how beautiful it is . . ."

"Mama . . ." Edna's voice was sharp, "what about what I just said? I finished explaining to you . . . a very important plan concerning your future. What about it?"

"I'm moving the first of the month, Edna," Carmela continued to look at floor plans. "But, I thank you and your husband for thinking of me."

"Is that it, Mama?"

"Yes, Edna."

"You already signed the lease, paid the money and everything?"

"Yes, all I have to do is move in, Edna."

"Well . . . I'm glad to see you figured it all out, Mama." Edna looked at Mary and Roberto; they avoided her eyes. "There's just one thing, eh? Who is gonna look after you when you can't . . . ?" You are sixty-six, ma! Sixty-six!"

"Not you, Edna." Carmela looked at her children. "Or you, Mary, or you, Roberto."

"Mama, I don't think you are being practical. Now I'm too far away to be here if anything happens! If you get sick . . . and so is Mary. And as far as Roberto is concerned . . ."

"I'll manage."

"Manage? Please, Mama. Mary, Roberto, what do you have to say? Don't you think Mama should have asked us first about this? Mama, you should have spoken to us! After all, we are your children."

"I didn't ask any of you to come here when Papa was so sick, did I? I never called or bothered you. I took care of all of you once, and I took care of him. . . . now, I want the privilege of taking care of myself!" There was a long silence and Carmela continued. "Thank you Edna, Mary, Roberto; you are all good children. But I can take care of myself; I've done it all my life."

"If that's the way you see it, Mama, I'm with you." Roberto said. "Right, Mary?"

"Okay . . . I guess . . ." Mary smiled weakly at Edna.

"All right, Mama." Edna stood up. "Go ahead . . . but remember, I tried my best to work something out for you. When something happens, you wont have anybody near you."

"I appreciate your good intentions, Edna, but it's all settled."

"When are you moving in, Mama?" asked Mary.

"I hope on the first, but since the landlord here knows me so well after twenty-six years, and we always paid our rent, I might be able to stay a few days extra, if things are not ready at the new place. I've already arranged everything with the movers and with the super of the new building and . . ."

They spoke for a while and Carmela talked excitedly about her new apartment.

"I feel better now that you all know . . . in fact," a feeling of drowsiness overcame her, "I think I might take a nap."

"Mama," Edna said, "we are all gonna have to leave soon, you know, get back to our families. But if you need us, please call."

"Good," Carmela smiled, "we should all get back to our own business of living, eh? The dead are at peace, after all. You were all a great help. Your husbands and children need you, and you too, Roberto . . . Gloria and the kids would like to see you, I'm sure."

"Go on, Mama, take your nap. Edna and I will cook something light, and then I think I'll call Mark to pick me up."

Carmela put everything back into her envelope and left. She closed her door and lay down, a sweet twilight state embraced her; it seemed to promise a deep sleep.

"Papa isn't even buried more than two days and she's acting like he's been dead forever." Edna was on the verge of tears. "She looks so happy . . . I don't understand it. You would think . . . Oh, I don't know anymore!"

"I'm sure she feels bad," Mary said, "it's just that she's also happy about her new apartment."

"She feels bad, all right. Mama doesn't want to show it, so that we don't feel worse than we already do," Roberto said.

"Well then, why is it that when Papa died she hardly cried. A few tears and moist eyes, but you can't call that crying!"

"Well, what do you want from her?" Roberto snapped.

"I don't know! She should be sorry . . . yes, that's what; I want her to be sorry!"

"What do you mean, sorry?!" Roberto whispered angrily.

"He was her husband of a lifetime, and my father, I . . ."

"Shh . . ." Mary snapped, "stop it!"

"How do you know what she feels inside? Leave her alone! It's always what you want? What about what she wants?"

"Go on, defend her. You've always been her favorite; mama's boy!"

"Quit that shit!" Roberto went towards Edna.

"For God's sake," Mary whimpered, "we're acting like kids . . . what's happening?"

"That's right, whimper like a baby, Mary." Edna began to cry, "that's all you know how to do. Everybody else has to make your decisions . . ."

"This is ridiculous," Roberto said, "I'm leaving."

"Go on . . . walk out, that's what you always do, you've done it to your own family now."

"Screw you . . . bitch!" Roberto called out, then slammed the front door.

"Come on, Edna, please stop it. What's the use of fighting? Mama's made up her mind. Let's make supper and forget about all of this. Roberto will come back after he cools off. You better call Joe; I think it's time we went home."

The two sisters began to open the refrigerator and pantry to prepare the evening meal. Mary turned to Edna, who was still sobbing quietly.

"What's the matter now?"

"I . . . wish she would be sorry . . ."

Carmela stood on the small terrace of her new apartment. She looked down at the city laid out before her. In between and over some of the buildings she could see the Hudson River and part of the George Washington Bridge. The river was dotted with sailboats and small craft that slipped in and out of sight. Overhead she had a view of a wide blue sky, changing clouds competing with the bright sun. Flocks of birds were returning home now that winter was over. Carmela took a deep breath. There was a warmth in the air; spring was almost here. In a couple of weeks she could bring out her new folding chair, lounger and snack table. Soon she would bring out her plants. New buds would begin to sprout, growing strong and healthy with the abundant sunlight and fresh air.

Carmela missed no one in particular. From time to time her children and grandchildren visited. She was pleased to seem them for a short while and then was even happier when they left. In a few days it would be a whole year since Benjamin's death. It seemed like yesterday sometimes, and sometimes it was like it never happened.

She rarely thought about Benjamin. Memories of her days as a young girl became frequent, clear and at times quite vivid. Before Carmela had married at sixteen, she had dreamed of traveling to all the many places she had seen in her geography book. After school she would often go with her brothers to the docks of San Juan just to watch the freighters and big ships.

"When I grow up I'm going to work and travel on those ships," "Carmelita, don't be silly, you can't. Girls can't join the navy or the merchant marine."

How she had wished she had been born a boy, to be able to travel anywhere, to be part of that world. Carmela loved the water; ocean, sea, river, all gave her a feeling of freedom.

She looked out from her terrace at the river, and a sense of peace filled her whole being. Carmela recognized it was the same exhilarating happiness she had experienced as a young girl, when each day would be a day for her to reckon with, all her own, a time with a future.

8. EARL SHORRIS, "SOMEONE FROM CUBA"

"Six weeks after arriving in the U.S.," a recent newspaper story reported about two Cuban immigrants, "Lestor Torres and his cousin Pavel Cruz have enrolled in English classes, obtained Florida driver's licenses and discovered a suburban singles bar called Cafe Iguana." What indeed has made many Cuban-Americans (and many recent arrivals at that) some of the most politically and economically successful Latinos in the U. S. today? Earl Shorris in his third essay on a major Latino group ("Fulano de Cuba," "Someone from Cuba") tackles this difficult question.

Shorris begins by stressing that Cuba itself has always been rather of a crossroad of cultures in the Caribbean; peoples from other continents would first land on that island and then proceed to other parts of the New World. Thus, for internationally-minded Cubans, learning English is a critical step to progress once in the U.S. Shorris next defines the word "exile" and how many Cubans view life in the U. S. as an experience which will return to them the status once enjoyed in pre-Castro Cuba, perhaps a desire to succeed found in the concept of *atrevimiento*. Finally, Shorris speculates on the future of the new generation of Cuban Americans born in the U.S. for whom the memory of Castro and Cuba is not even a souvenir of childhood.

FULANO DE CUBA

Fulano is a very old Spanish word for someone of uncertain identity, a so-and-so, that less than memorable person the English call a bloke or a chap, the one known in American English as a guy or you-know (as in whatsisname). Fulano, zutano, mengano play the role of Tom, Dick, and Harry or the butcher, the baker, the candlestick maker. Fulano isn't real, no one bears that name; fulano, doesn't play first base or marry your niece; he pays no taxes, eats no food, and leaves no mess behind; he's nobody.[1] If by some error of madness, alcohol, or utter failure of the imagination, a child were named Fulano, his life would be a trial for he would be no one and everyman, rich and poor, short and tall, Colombian, Cuban, Dominican, Mexican, Puerto Rican, Spanish, and so on. In the case of fulano the wound is minor, one person obliterated. "Latino" is another matter, a deed, a name into which millions disappear.

Since the nationalists that make up the ethnic group known as Latinos are not randomly distributed across the United States, but tend to cluster in certain areas, most Anglos think of all Latinos as being like the people who live nearby. In the northeast, for example, Latinos are thought to be Puerto Rican. The identification of Puerto Ricans with New York City is so strong that they are sometimes referred to as Neoricans or Nuyoricans. In Miami, Latinos (who prefer to be called Hispanics there) are thought to be Cuban, although the Nicaraguan refugees may broaden the definition by the end of the 1990s. Californians and Texans think of Latinos as Mejicanos or Mexican-Americans or chicanos. Chicagoans have a problem, for that city has neither a Mejicano nor Puertorriqueño nor Cubano majority; it is a city with a large Latino population.

Salvadorans live in Los Angeles, San Francisco, and Hempstead, N.Y. Cubans and Puerto Ricans have moved into New Jersey in roughly equal numbers. Even in New York City, once the capital of Puerto Rican immigrants, perhaps half a million Dominicans have moved in, along with a huge Colombian colony, and a growing number of Central Americans and Mexicans. There are also sizable communities of Spaniards and Sephardim (or Spanish Jews) in the city. In every city, even Miami (which is dominated by Cuban exiles) and Los Angeles (which would rank as one of the largest cities in Mexico, if one simply counted the number of Mexican citizens living there), other nationalities have made their presence felt.

To many Latinos drawing the distinctions among the nationalities constitutes a kind of game, like a quiz program. Everyone has a theory about everyone else. Some are amusing, all are accurate, and every nuance is important. A few people are better situated than others to draw the distinctions. Raymond del Portillo, who headed up San Francisco's initial effort at bilingual education, is the son of a Cuban father and a Mexican mother. On the Cuban side his great-grandfather wrote the Cuban national anthem. On the Mexican side his grandfather crossed the Sierra Madres three times while fighting with the Villistas during the Mexican Revolution of 1910. His wife, Carlota, is Puerto Rican, raised in Puerto Rico and New York.

From his unique viewpoint del Portillo offers these observations about the cultural extremes of the three nationalities. "Cubans," he said, "are aggressive, assertive, and sometimes appallingly arrogant. There is a steadfastness and loyalty among Mexican-Americans, but their docility is sometimes disappointing. And the feistiness of the Puerto Rican is understandable. They're tough, very tough, either because of life on the island or prejudice in New York; they're tough, but not bitter."

Leobardo Estrada, a demographer at UCLA whose work takes him to every Latino community in the country, says that a visitor must prove himself in different fashion for each group. For the Cubans, the litmus test is language: One must not

---

1. In some parts of Latin America, "fulano" has taken an opposite meaning, as in "Es un fulano," He's a somebody.

From LATINOS: A Biography of the People by Earl Shorris. Copyright © 1992 by Earl Shorris. Reprinted by permission of W.W. Norton & Company, Inc.

only speak Spanish, one must speak the language well, with a vocabulary of synonyms and the ability to use arcane verb forms. Puerto Ricans judge a person by his or her familiarity with the island; one must know not only the cities, but the towns and villages as well. To establish oneself with Mexican-Americans, it is necessary only to be a professor, so great is the reverence for education in the Mejicano and Mexican-American culture.

A young woman in New York offers a somewhat different view. To Rose Vega, who left an executive position in New York City government to attend law school, Puerto Ricans and Dominicans, the dominant groups in New York, are quite different. "Puerto Ricans just want to party all the time," she said. "Dominicans are smooth talkers; they're full of lavish compliments." Vega, whose parents are Puerto Rican and Spanish, finds Spaniards, like her father, stern and very proud, particularly when it comes to language: The Spaniards frown upon both Puerto Rican vocabulary and pronunciation.

The difference between stereotypes and cultural distinctions is sometimes very subtle. Instead of relying on my own judgment, I asked people from the various nationalities to describe their own cultures. Guarione M. Diaz,[2] executive director of the Cuban American National Council, said in response to the challenge to convey in a word the essence of the Cuban character, "Atrevimiento," which means bold or daring. Others, lacking the precision of Diaz, said "aggressive" or "hard-working," but the tone was always the same.

A few people tried to draw distinctions between the early Cuban refugees and the Marielitos, who came out much later and were said to have been undesirables, criminals and lunatics that Fidel Castro wanted to get rid of. But it became clear after a while that the real distinction between the two wave of emigrants was mainly in the level of their education and the color of their skin; many of the Marielitos were black, while almost all of the first wave of emigrants were white.[3]

About 10 percent of the Marielitos were actually criminals, but all of them were painted into convict's stripes. Still, six or seven years after arriving

here, they were climbing the Cuban economic ladder, following the same pattern of daring and evincing the same confidence in their ability to solve problems. There is a story in Miami about *atrevimiento* and the plumbing in many of the houses. It is said to be unlike the plumbing anywhere else in the world. The reason is that Cubans who came over in the sixties took whatever work they could get. When there was work for plumbers, they said they could do plumbing, and they did, but an autodidact is not necessarily a successful plumber. Most of the work they produced is apparently so strange and convoluted that when it breaks no real plumber can figure out how to repair it.

The most poignant description of exile life is contained in the story of the Cuban dog, a wretched little thing, with a short, ragged tail, thin haunches, and sorry, splayed paws. As it was walking down a Miami street it came across a group of large American dogs, with big tails and shiny coats. "Look at that bedraggled beast," the American dogs said. They laughed at the little Cuban and insulted him for being so small and powerless. The Cuban dog endured the insults for a few moments, then he said, "Go ahead, laugh. You see me as I am now, but in Cuba I was a German shepherd."

It is not a humble tale. No Mexican would tell such a story. The Cuban dog knew who he was, and he knew the transitory nature of power. It is really a story about the failure of American dogs to recognize one of their own, perhaps even a member of a superior culture. Unlike other Latinos, the Cuban has nothing of the supplicant in his culture; he has been wronged, and he means to set the world aright. The nature of the immigrant is to flee the past; the exile seeks only the return of his former glory; he wants only the opportunity to act upon his nostalgia.

---

3. The difference in class origin between the first and last (Mariel) waves was profound.

In the first wave, 1959-1962, 31 percent were professional, technical, and managerial (compared with 9.2 percent of the entire Cuban population); 33 percent clerical or in sales (compared with 13.7 percent of the entire population); 8 percent were semi-skilled or unskilled, 7 percent were service workers, and 4 percent were agricultural workers. Only 4 percent had less than a fourth grade education (compared with 52 percent of the entire population), and 36 percent had completed high school or had some college (compared to 4 percent for the entire population).

By 1967, only 18 percent of the Cuban immigrants were professional, technical, and managerial, and when the Marielitos arrived thirteen years later, the number had fallen to 8.5 percent. The Mariel group included large numbers of machine operators, transportation operators, and people who simply classified themselves as laborers.

---

2. I have followed each person's choice in the use of accents in proper names. Diaz is spelled without the accent on his business card. Guarione is an Indian name which has several variant spellings.

The wit of the Cubans, which is often self-deprecating, the classic survivor's sigh in the form of a joke, helps to overcome the aggressiveness in business, social, and cultural life that is almost universally ascribed to them. Although Cuba has historically had a taste for philosophy, the exile has favored practical life. Eating and paying the rent became paramount for people who left their homes with nothing but the powers of mind for capital.

The middle class is resourceful, but anxious; there is no theory of property that denies the comfort of capital. The nature of the bourgeoisie is to understand economic reverses as a fall from grace. Hell is doing without, and the lowest circle of Hell is watching one's children do without. In exile, the hungers of the Cuban middle class took precedence.

Andrea Camps, the elegant doyenne of Latino society in Houston, remembers coming to the United States. Her husband, a physician, was in Central America. She and her children lived alone in Miami on welfare payments of $100 a month. "Rent was $67.50," she said. "We had to live on the rest. I suffered from hunger, because the food was for the children. I drank water to fill myself up." She laughed. "It was not so bad, really, I lost a lot of weight, and because there was no money for cigarettes, I gave up smoking." The little laugh, the gallantry, are not fraudulent: she typifies the exile at her most successful; she keeps her sorrows to herself.

No one seeing her now could imagine Andrea Camps poor, moving in 1963 to Detroit for several years because she could not bear the discrimination against Cubans in Houston. She sits at a conference table in the little mansion that houses the Hispanic Cultural Institute of Houston, a woman of perfect fingernails and solemn coif, clothed by Saks, tough-minded and tall, elitist, still sensual, a woman. Yet something about her style doesn't work as she would like it to; her hair is red, her skin is olive, an unsuccessful mix, too far from nature's intent, yet not far enough. Her husband delivers sixty babies a month, she has a perfect grasp of style; she can leap over all but one hurdle on the way to the U.S. upper middle class—she cannot extirpate the sun from her skin.

But she will try. It is the Cuban way. As Andrea Camps, who brought a Ph.D. with her from Cuba, said, "We Cubans are aggressive, progressive. We make the opportunity; it is not given to us."

She and her husband and children came back to Houston in 1977. Detroit was a success for them. She taught at Wayne State University. Her husband did well in his practice, their children attended the exclusive and expensive Cranbrook Academy. But there is still prejudice, she feels. "They resent us, the Cubans, here, because we are successful. A lady said to me, 'I can't believe you are Cuban. You don't even speak like a Cuban. You are not very loud.' They also call us the Jews of the Caribbean, but they say it in a pejorative way. I think that they think we are too concerned with money, but maybe we had to learn. The Cubans are very generous with money. For a Cuban, the problem is not to have money, but to be able to make money."

In Houston, as in Los Angeles, the Cubans rose quickly to become an elite among Latinos. Most of the Latino doctors are Cuban. The Hispanic Cultural Organization is run by Cubans, and when they have an annual ball, complete with king and queen and their court, it is the Cubans who invite one of the more social Anglo families to reign over the ball, for the Cubans wish to move out into Anglo society in East Texas. They do not understand themselves as Latinos, but as citizens of the world. Cuba was a crossroads, a place where justice winked, a palimpsest of racism, the only place in the hemisphere in which sophistication and evil make an Old World arrangement.

But Cuba was then, now the Cubans are also fulanos, the inheritors of new responsibilities, especially when they live outside Miami. Señora Camps sees their role in Houston as bolstering the entire Latino community. "The Mexicans who come here . . . have given the Anglos their version of Hispanics. They are people who go to bad schools, who get a feeling of pessimism. We are trying to present them with role models; we are trying to prove to them that their pessimism is wrong."

She remembers Cuba fondly, but return is not an option for her. "We Cubans cannot go back," she said. "we have to go forward." Then she sighed, and the tensions that give pace to her life disappeared for a moment. She looked away, and when she turned back toward me, I saw for a moment the children, the hard years, the toll it takes of a woman when she refuses to fail. "To leave Cuba," she said, "is a spiritual liberation, because we have lost our fear of the future."

To be a Cuban in Miami is to live in a special country, somewhere between the United States and history. Miami and Cuba have been tied together culturally and economically since Cuba dominated the hemisphere in the sixteenth century. Eighth Street, now known as Calle Ocho, began changing from a predominantly Jewish neighborhood to the Cuban section in the 1950s. That was when my wife's uncle opened a restaurant there. It was a tiny place, but comfortable; business was conducted entirely in Spanish. They did not seek English-speaking customers. The advantage of Miami, the pleasure and the opportunity of Miami, was that they didn't have to speak English.

The entire city changed after the refugees began coming out in the early sixties. Although they were poor at first—every Cuban, especially those who became rich, has a tale to tell about the struggle of those first few years—they were given asylum, the right to work, and financial assistance from the federal government. More than anything, the right to work legally gave them the chance to use their skills. The professional class took some time to get licensed to practice and the businessmen had to work day and night at difficult jobs to get the capital to go into business, but they managed.

They followed the Cuban system of doing business known as *socios* or *socioismo*,[4] an exaggerated form of the old boy network. In the system of socios one does not approve a loan or accept a contract based upon objective criteria, as U.S. businessmen are supposed to do; knowing the person, being a friend or even an acquaintance, is more important than a Dun & Bradstreet rating. The system worked, helped along by the high level of education and the willingness to take on any challenge, the daring Guarione Diaz talks about, and what he calls a lack of reverence for persons or position. The Cuban exiles, primarily middle- and upper middle-class, soon became middle- and upper middle-class again.

Never before had there been a group of exiles quite like them, not even the White Russians who carried out more royalist baggage than worldly capabilities, not even the German Jews who came to the U.S. in the nineteenth century; no group of newcomers in the United States had ever moved so quickly from penury to prosperity; Fidel Castro had given the middle-class engine of the Cuban economic system to his worst enemy.

Exiles are not emigrants, however. They come to the new country laden with bitterness. Although time and comfort bank the fires of what might have been, action turns into a rage of words, and danger

dies slowly into nostalgia. Ambition is the exception, the only barrier to a happy old age. And even ambition tires of action in old men; it turns to dominoes or politics. It isn't easy to find a bomb thrower in Miami anymore. The members of the Brigada 2506, those brave and foolish men who landed at the Bay of Pigs, have opened a museum.

The Greeks understood exile as a form of capital punishment: not travel, relocation, or emigration, but death. Nothing else radicalizes a person quite so thoroughly, nothing makes one quite so daring, as to be already dead. Thus, the politics of Miami in the first quarter of a century of exile were those of the risen dead. What many interpreted as a sinister quality in the exiles was merely the freedom from morality of those who are already in purgatory. These angelic exiles threw bombs, landed at the Bay of Pigs, worked for the CIA, ranted on the radio.

But exiles grow old, even when they consider themselves the risen angels of righteousness. The hands of the once dead warriors tremble; they are better at business or dominoes. The celebration of anniversaries drains their radicalism now. Real death will soon replace the symbolism of exile. Their backs ache; they know more doctors than arms merchants. The Cuban American National Foundation, once a junta of fanatics, jockeys for influence with political contributions and the promise of votes and appeals to the guilt of the host country that sent them naked onto the beaches of the Bay of Pigs.

The right wing, which was motivated by bitterness and nationalism in the beginning, is driven now by the wildest ambition. Jorge Más, a charming businessman, who unquestionably loves both Cuba and the United States, expects to be the first democratic, or at least the first non-communist, leader of Cuba after the Castro regime finally falls. He denies that, of course, but not with much vehemence.

As an anti-Castro fanatic, Más was not a dangerous man. He was a leader of the Cuban right, which supplied lunatics to the CIA and the Nixon Administration. As some people pointed out, in soft voice, it was not healthy for the image of the Cuban community to be in the business of leasing loonies to government and quasi-government agencies. But Más and his Cuban American National Foundation have recently learned that it is better to be in charge of the asylum. And in the United States, they learned, that can be done with cash contributions and a few votes.[5] He and other officials of the foundation told me that they don't throw bombs anymore, and I believe them.

---

4. Castro coined the word to condemn the establishment professionals and businessmen of prerevolutionary Cuba.

It is very difficult to disbelieve anything that Jorge Más says. He is a round faced man with a receding hairline, hospitable and informal, but crisp, quick, scheduled. When my wife and I visited with him, he served Cuban coffee for the digestion and straightforward responses for the tape recorder. He had been warned by his staff at the foundation that my politics were liberal-left,[6] and I warned him again before we spoke. He seemed to like the idea, to be pleased at the thought of combat.

Only once during a long conversation did he stray from the reasoned clarity that is so surprising in a man who leads what is often described as the radical right fringe of Cuban-American politics. And even then his response to a question about bombs was only a jesuitical kind of madness: He said that the people who had bombed the Cuban leftists in Miami were agents of Castro intent upon discrediting the actions of the anti-Castro right.

The thought disturbed him. It led him into paths of mind that were bizarre. He spoke of people who sent clothing or money or food to relatives in Cuba. They were all agents of the Castro government, he said. It was a trick, this sending of money to relatives, these cash payments for burials and such. Castro needed the hard currency. For an instant he saw agents everywhere. Then the telephone rang.

He had a cryptic conversation in Spanish. "I can't give you any details now," he said, "but we are buying one of the oldest and largest businesses of its kind in Florida."

He had been rescued by business. He was charming again, although still intense, the man who was shown in the photograph with President Ronald Reagan, the man who had access to the office of the Secretary of State of the United States of America, one of the few who saw Secretary James Baker without appearing on the public calendar. He smiled and drank his tiny coffee. The informality returned. We spoke of family, of Cuban things, not politics. He recalled his early years in exile.

It was difficult, listening to the ordinariness of the man, to remember that the Mercedes Benz parked outside beside the Porsche had not always belonged to Jorge Más; it had been the personal armored car of Anastasio Somoza of Nicaragua. There was no craziness apparent in the man; he did not look at us with a fanatic's glare. He looked like the person who had been photographed in Angola, dressed in a bush jacket, inspecting the situation as if he were a head of state, not merely the enemy of Fidel Castro who had sent troops there.

He spoke of freedom, of his appreciation of dissent. He said he had contributed $10,000 of his own money, "the legal limit," to the campaign of the liberal, Senator Howard Metzenbaum. In his voice there were hesitations, a quality of fulmination that came more from his frustration with English than from his temper. He had been generous in the contest between us, giving away the advantage; we spoke in my language, not his.

In Joan Didion's book on Miami, Jorge Más is a part of the sinister paranoia of the radical right. And I think she was only partly correct, but ill-served by her own humorlessness. The Cubans who came in the first wave of exile are more Spanish than Caribbean, and it must be remembered that there are two Spains: the Spain of the Inquisition and that of Miguel Cervantes, the inventor of Don Quixote, a Spain of certainty and irony, of paranoia and hope, of death and laughter. There was a time in Miami when the foundation ran an inquisition; whoever did not oppose Fidel Castro wholeheartedly was suspect, to be ostracized, tortured in a social sense, destroyed in business, in a political auto-da-fé. And Jorge Más Canosa was the Grand Inquisitor.

He was also the knight from the plain of La Mancha. When a commissioner of the city of Miami insulted him, Más challenged the commissioner to

---

5. The extent to which political action committee money and personal donations from Cuban exiles, as well as votes, have penetrated two morally corrupt administrations—those of Ronald Reagan and George Bush—was revealed in the summer of 1990 when the U.S. government, under intense pressure from the Bush Administration, released the terrorist pediatrician, Orlando Bosch from prison. An editorial in the *New York Times* of July 20, 1990, concluded:

"In the name of fighting terrorism, the United States sent the Air Force to bomb Libya and the Army to invade Panama. Yet now the Bush Administration coddles one of the hemisphere's most notorious terrorists. And for what reason? The only one evident is currying favor in South Florida."

In the classic pattern of exile thinking, Cuban moderates in Miami saw a more complex plan behind the freeing of Bosch. They believed the government had given Bosch to the right in exchange for a promise to react mildly to the opening of dialogue with the Castro government. As usual in Latin American politics, the moderates were wrong.

6. The use of the term left in speaking of Latin America and the United States presents serious problems, because the left in the United States is more like the center in Latin America. The continuing rightward drift of the U.S. Supreme Court as well as the executive branch makes drawing the distinction even more difficult. It is not my impression that the anti-Castro Cuban-exile rightists are necessarily economic rightists. Marilyn Kalusin and Rene Silva of the CANF deal with Democrats as well as Republicans. Silva described the complexity of Cuban views with a joke: "When there are two Jews, you have three opinions, when there are two Cubans, you have three organizations."

a duel! "Yes, I did," he said. "It's what I was referring to you about the emotions and the passions. Yes, I did."

"Can you tell me about that?" I asked.

"This is nothing new. This is something as old as mankind. We were living in a society here where people used to offend each other every day and call names on each other. And I had never gone into that situation. This man used a very unfortunate situation which had nothing to do with politics to offend what I think was my honor.[7] And I said, 'Look, I don't want to debate with you publicly. I don't want to exchange names, that's up to you. If you feel that I have offended you or I feel that you have offended me, I will challenge you in a duel. Let's clean your name, your thinking that I have hurt you, and we'll clean mine. Let's see who comes out the winner, period, that's it.'

"He didn't accept. I will do it. I don't have any problem with that. I have a lot of respect for many presidents and vice-presidents of this country who did it before, statesmen around the world; there's nothing new to it. It's all out of fashion, yes, but you know, all fashions always find a way to come back. Nowadays there's pants with cuffs and polyester coats, there's nothing new. I didn't invent that.

"We were going to do it in Central America. It's forbidden here in this country. I'm a law-abiding citizen.

"He turned it down immediately, and he quit right there and it was over. Can you find a better way to do something better to the community? Otherwise, we would have been throwing mud back and forth for weeks and weeks and weeks forever. This way, it's only two hours.

"It's just to show you, I'm not a conventional guy."

Like the other son of Spain who wished to return to the time of good knights and great deeds, Jorge Más sees grandeur where reality is something less. He did, in truth, challenge the offending commissioner to a duel. But the commissioner did not decline. He accepted.

"Choose your weapons," said Más in the grand tradition of the duel.

"Water pistols," the commissioner answered, with the ferocity of a real windmill, "at twenty paces."

---

7. The cause of the argument was a real-estate deal between the commissioner and Más. When the deal went sour, Más accused the commissioner of being a communist.

The tragic side of the Spanish character also exists in the Cuban exile community of Miami. There is in Little Havana a portrait photographer, Ketty Gort, a woman whose utterly deliberate smile frames the tragedy of civil war and exile. "I am divorced," she said. "I had, how could you say it, a political divorce." She is a grandmother now, a woman of business, but when she spoke of her marriage, her voice became that of the little bride, the young mother. "We were in the beginning political exiles from Batista. That's how we came to this country.

"We were living in New York then. We had our two kids, but we went back in 1960. I thought it was fine. I went to Cuba, and I stayed about a year. For me it was a contrast, because I was already used to the way over here, and I started seeing things that I didn't like, but I never said anything to him until I came here to the States to see my folks. While I was here, that's when he called me, and he said, 'You better come back right away, because if you don't come back everything is finished. I feel socialista, Marxista, Leninista.'"

She is a little woman who wears big eyeglasses; she is sturdy and as realistic as small business or a two-line telephone. But for a moment she was possessed by tears. She seemed to stagger. "He was in favor of the revolution, and he'd like to stay in Cuba. What am I supposed to do?

"It was very difficult, because I married with my first fiancé, my first love in life. I was very much in love with him. It was very hard; it was a decision you have to make between really being a wife and a woman or saving your kids.

"I don't like people who start complaining that Castro took this, this sugar cane plantation or took a house, took this. For me, he didn't take any money, any material thing, but he did something very bad for me: He destroyed my marriage; he took away the father of my two sons."

Her granddaughter, who was born in 1980, is more practical that Ketty Gort. The girl refuses to say the name of Fidel Castro, as if it were a dirty word; she indicates with coy pointing that he belongs in Hell. The girl has learned the lesson of reaction early. But the woman who lost her husband to Marxism is a Democrat, which she says is not a popular position in Little Havana. If she has a hero in the community, it is not a rightist, but Jorge Valls, the socialist who spent twenty years and forty days in Cuban prisons and emerged with his leftist politics and Catholicism intact. They have never met, although they are both in Cuban Miami and they are both among the few who understand that a revolution is also a civil war. For her, exile and tragedy provided the strength to raise her sons; for him, "Exile is worse than a sentence of death, much worse. Exile is like trying to breathe and not finding enough air. But exile is also one of the greatest experiences."

Like everyone who has studied the exile community, Lisandro Pérez, a sociologist at Florida International University, focuses on the first wave. Data on the Marielitos, Castro's castaways, is still fragmentary. Moreover, they don't please the earlier exiles, whose reputation and statistics they have sullied.

"Here selectivity of migration draws disproportionately from middle and upper-middle strata," Pérez said, speaking of the first wave. "High aspirations for social mobility—Cubans also had high expectations." He notes that Cuban women work to help the family, calling them "instrumental, not career oriented."

"Cubans are not fatalistic," he said. "Cubans are a take-charge sort of people." He relates much of this aspect of Cuban character to the role of the Catholic Church in pre-Castro Cuba. "In the 1950s churches were popular because one priest would give the homily while the other proceeded with the ceremony in Latin. So the service was over in fifteen minutes and people could go on with their business.

"The challenge to the Church in 1960-61 took place before Vatican II. The Church opposed the government, but had no effect. The Church was weak as a political institution. However, the Church has been important here in the refugee movement, very important in the beginning."

Those with the other view of the Catholic Church's power in Cuba argue that Castro has recently attempted some rapprochement with the Church because he understands how the Church affected the work ethic in prerevolutionary Cuba. The very fatalism that Pérez says does not exist in the Cuban culture is the element Castro seeks to bring back, for the Cuban communists have apparently decided that only a fatalistic person can work hard for little earthly reward. And the fuel of fatalism is the afterlife.

Pérez said Cuba was "a secular rather than an insular society, a collection of ports," a crossroads of culture and commerce. And he is, of course, correct about the effect of Cuba's geographic and economic position upon the educated class of Cubans, many of whom came to the United States.

For those who remained behind, largely the less affluent, Castro's sociologists have made what amounts to an interesting self-criticism: The Cuban economy depended upon the promise of an afterlife to maintain high levels of productivity despite the disparity in wages and living standards. However, during the glorious years of success and foreign aid Castro and the middle- and upper middle-class intelligentsia who helped him overthrow Batista forgot that one needs a reason to suffer in life on the edge of absolute misery; people must make excuses to their children for giving them less than they need.

It was a form of what Lisandro Pérez and others term arrogance, but what I think is closer to self-deception, following the Greek view that *apate* (deception) is a result of human blindness and *logos*. Although it is sometimes difficult to remember, given all the turmoil around his Marxist-Leninist ideas, Fidel Castro is a Cuban, and it is his perfectly Cuban combination of daring and self-deception that has led to his successes and his failures. I have no doubt that on his deathbed, when the inward debate of soul takes precedence, Fidel Castro will call for a priest.

In other areas, language for one, Lisandro Pérez has a penetratingly amusing view of the Cuban exile in America. The English-only movement, in his view, is not for the Cubans. "To learn English is consistent with the notion of social mobility." He gives as an example the Belen Jesuit School, now in Miami, recalling that Fidel Castro attended the Belen School in Cuba. The institution has been moved whole to Miami, but "they teach in English: They have only one hour of Spanish every day. It is a Cuban institution in English."

He believes that "all ethnic communities have an expiration date. Cultures do change." At the same time he refers to the enclave theory of Alejandro Portes: "You can live here," he says, "without speaking English; the Spanish community is institutionally complete."

The differences between Cubans and other Latinos, which are greater than the differences among all other groups, are apparent to Pérez. "There is an absence of minority-group orientation. Cubans have a very high self-concept—at times there is a certain arrogance—that's very different from the self-concept of Mexican-Americans and Puerto Ricans." He offers an anecdote to make his theory concrete: At a meeting a Mexican complained of being unable to get a bank loan because he was Mexican. Surprised, a Cuban businessman said that when he started his business he couldn't get bank loans because he was poor, not because he was Cuban. The Cuban said, "Now, I own twenty stores and everybody wants to lend me money, and I'm still Cuban."

Lisandro Pérez is a big man, ursine, bearded; he overflows his tiny office. A small sharp nose comes out of his soft, round face, a surprise—insight leaping out of caution. Perhaps that is not so good for him; he must be careful. Florida International University is not a place that appreciates daring; its president, Modesto Maidique, has cowered publicly before the demands of the political right. Lisandro Pérez has nothing to say about the Cuban American National Foundation. I cannot blame him for his caution. He has a wife and children, and although he does not say it, he cannot help but be aware of the inability of the Cuban exile community to grasp the concept of freedom in the United States. It is a community of old people, and the institutional completeness of which he speaks has kept the Cubans from experiencing much of the best of America.

Pérez said, "I'm not sure that Cubans feel a brotherhood with other Latin Americans. The Cuban connection was more with Spain and the U.S." Unfortunately, much of that connection was with the worst of the United States; the mafia, the government that supported Batista, the plantation owners who were glad to exploit Cuban labor, the racists who came to have sex with the mulatas populating the hundred of whorehouses that existed in Havana on the eve of the revolution. Even the most sophisticated exiles have not learned to appreciate fully the United States' concept of political protection for the minority, the loyal opposition.

Younger Cubans are quite different. They have virtually no interest in island politics. For them Miami has become what Cuba was to their parents. Diana Campoamor lives in San Francisco with her teenage son, who thinks of Miami as home. That's where his grandparents live, where he spent his first few years, where his roots are. Christina Gelabert went to Boston College, worked in communications in New York and Europe, married, had two children, and then brought her non-Cuban family back to Miami with her. Although I have known her for many years and still think of her as a little girl with dimples, she has grown into a strikingly beautiful woman, tall, slim, and still with the Gelabert dimples. Her life in Miami has nothing to do with

politics. She earns her living in Miami, as she did in New York, as a writer. Christina was born in Cuba and raised partly in Spain, but she is fond of saying, "I don't write with an accent." And she doesn't. Nor does she live with an accent, except perhaps for her closeness to her family, all of whom (both parents and her brother and sister) are architects.

Diana Campoamor is politically liberal; she worked for the Mexican American Legal Defense and Education Fund in California. Christina Gelabert, who is a few years younger, is apolitical. Both are divorced, which is, according to social scientists at the Cuban American Council, typical; they claim that Cuban women have the highest divorce rate of any identifiable group in the United States.

The second great distinction in the Cuban community, even greater than age, is class. Despite the popular misconception, all Cubans are not rich, even though they are more affluent as a group than other Latinos. Those who came from a working-class background in Cuba do not have the same "high self-concept" as the richer and better educated first wave. They say that most people think of Cubans as loud, always having to let everyone know they're around. And the burden of the Marielitos has fallen very heavily on them.

The work ethic has not deserted these Cubans, but they work at different kinds of jobs. They drive trucks or wait on tables or do the routine tasks of factories. And they do not live in elegant beachfront homes; they live in apartments in New Jersey or bungalows in Hialeah. Their expectations are lower, but they are not without dreams. They want to move out of Little Havana, where the crime rate is high and the good stores have mostly closed and gone to the suburbs. Little Havana belongs to the old people now, and Nicaraguans and Salvadorans are moving in. The effort to rejuvenate the neighborhood may not succeed. It is the new areas that fill the dreams of the working-class Cubans, and they are determined to find some way to get there. Generally, it will mean that every member of the family works; both parents, perhaps even a grandparent, and all the children who have finished school. In such families of strivers, it is not out of the ordinary for most of the working family members to have more than one job; thus a family of two parents, two grown children, and two high-school age children might have eight or ten jobs between them.

Older Cubans say they will return to Cuba as soon as Castro dies or is deposed. The younger generation is interested only in going back to visit. How many older Cubans really would go back is impossible to gauge. Meanwhile, the pain of the exile does not recede. Arturo Rodríguez, a painter who lives in Little Havana, continues his series of dreams of exile, producing works in which he always sees himself with a missing or disjointed limb.

Rolando Fernández, a young psychiatrist in Miami, treats many old people. Perhaps he does so because he has the cherubic smile and good humor of the grandson every old man or woman dreams of. Perhaps it is simply that the community is old and the supply of patients is determined by demographics. Every day, Dr. Fernández, the patron of avant-garde painters and writers, cousin of Roberto Fernández, one of the exile's most imaginative novelists, goes to his office to minister to the old angels of exile, the dead who are dying again, quietly now, forever now.

He tells of one of his patients, an old woman who had not seen her daughter, who remained behind in Cuba, for more than twenty years. Under an agreement that permits brief visits to the United States by relatives from Cuba, her daughter came to Miami. The old woman, who had been depressed, was happy during the visit of her daughter, but when the daughter had to return to Cuba, the old woman fell into a deep depression and was hospitalized.

Dr. Fernández does professionally what has become the familial vocation of many of the children of the exile—he comforts the dying. There are so few children and so many old people that the burden weighs heavily in the community of memories.

Massive changes will be coming to the exile community soon. Relations between the United States and Cuba will eventually improve, with or without the fall of Castro. But even more certainly the time of the old exiles is coming to an end. The new generation is not much interested by ancient wars. They are Miami people, and they are not like the old Cubans; they want to be free to make their own way in the world, yet they know that cannot happen until the exile is resolved in politics and time.

9. MARGARITA MONDRUS ENGLE, "NIÑA" AND "SINGING TO CUBA"

Margarita Mondrus Engle's world is really the intermeshing of two cultures, that of the United States and Cuba; this duality reflects the fact that her mother was Cuban and her father American (her parents met when her father arrived in Cuba to paint scenes from the city of Trinidad). Engle's professional pursuits are also double, for she writes both as a professional journalist and as an author of fiction. Her short stories have been published in *Nuestro*, *The Americas Review*, *Revista Interamericana*, and other publications.

Perhaps her best writing, both fiction and non-fiction, deals with her native Cuba, where she has returned several times to reflect on her roots. In the short story "Niña," Engle describes the reactions of a young girl as she returns to Cuba shortly after the Communist revolution to visit her *abuela*. While on the island, she meets another girl named "Niña," who teaches the narrator a new set of values that differ from those of the protagonist's home, Los Angeles. In "Singing to Cuba" (from Engle's first novel, *Singing to Cuba*, 1993), the narrator as a grown woman returns in the role of a tourist to Havana. There, she confronts the trappings of Castro's totalitarian regime with her cousin, Miguelito. Undeterred, the two wander about Old Havana, examining the past of decaying marble mansions and speculating what the future might hold for them and for Cuba.

NIÑA

My mother was afraid it might be our last chance to visit her family in Cuba. The revolution was almost two years old, and already there was talk of an impending crisis.

At the airport in Miami she gave us three instructions.

"Never tell anyone you are tomboys."

"Why?"

"They wouldn't understand. Also, don't tell the other children about your allowance. You have more money in the bank than their fathers make in a year."

"So?"

"So, they would feel bad."

"Oh."

"And most important, don't bring animals into your grandmother's house."

"But Mom . . ."

"No animals. They don't like having animals in the house. Do you understand?"

At the airport in Havana we released the caterpillars we had hidden in our luggage.

"Just in case there are no butterflies here," my sister and I reassured each other.

We had no idea what to expect, but the island did not disappoint us. Abuelita's house was on the outer fringe of Havana, and there were animals everywhere. We put lizards in beds, and tarantulas and scorpions in the living room. The fisherman who lived across the street gave us a ripe swordfish snout to play with. When it really started to stink, my mother threw it on the roof, where it rotted quickly in the sun.

The fisherman's daughter asked me if I had money for ice cream. "Yes," I said with pride. "I have eighty dollars in the bank, which I saved all by myself."

"Dollars? Really?" I could see she didn't believe a word of it. I squirmed inside, remembering my mother's admonition.

"Well, I have something better," the girl offered. "Crabs. When my father gets home, you can have one to cook for your dinner."

She was right, of course. The crabs were better than my money. Her father came home with a truckload of them, bright orange crabs as big as cats. We put ours on a leash and led it up and down the street until it died.

My sister liked dogs better than crabs. She begged my mother for a can of dog food for my great-grandmother's mangy hound. We had to go all the way downtown, to Woolworth's, just to find dog food in cans. It cost more than a month's supply of real food, corn meal, black beans, and rice.

Just to make sure there were no sins left uncommitted, I went across the street and told the fisherman's daughter I was a tomboy.

"Oh, no," she said, horrified. "You're not a tomboy, don't worry. You will be fine." She fluffed her petticoats and curled a lock of hair with her fingers.

My collection of revolutionary bullets was growing. They were everywhere—in Abuelita's front yard and in the weeds where we searched for tarantulas, which we caught with wads of gum attached to strings. There were bullets in the open fields beyond the city, and in the passion vines which clung to the walls of houses.

On one of my solitary expeditions I wandered far beyond those walls, beyond the open fields, and into a mud-floored hut with a thatched roof and many inhabitants. The family greeted me as if I had some right to invade their home. The children came outside to introduce me to their mule, their chickens and the sensitive Mimosa plant which closed its leaves at the touch of a child's fingers.

One of the children was called Niña, meaning "girl." I assumed her parents had simply run out of names by the time they got around to her. In Niña's case, her name was no more unusual than her appearance. She was hardly there, just bones and eyes, and a few pale wisps of hair bleached by malnutrition.

"Doesn't she get enough to eat?" I asked my mother when I reached home.

"They say she has a hole in her stomach."

"Niña" by Margarita Mondrous Engle is reprinted with permission from the publisher of *Short Fiction by Hispanic Writers of the United States* (Houston: Arte Publico Press-University of Houston, 1993).

One day I was standing in the sun of the front porch, watching a black storm cloud sweep across the sky, bringing toward me its thunder and lightning, which fell only in one small corner of the sky. A motionless circle of vultures hung from the cloud, listless, with black wings barely trembling in the wind.

"Come in," my mother warned. "Don't forget your uncle was killed by lightning, right in his own kitchen."

I ignored her. If it could happen in the kitchen, then why bother to go inside? I was just as safe outside.

Niña crept up to the porch, smiling her death's head smile, like the skull and crossbones on a bottle of medicine.

"Here," she said, offering me half of the *anon* fruit she was eating. I took it. Together we ate and stared and smiled at each other, not knowing what to say. We both knew my half of the seedy, juicy fruit was going into my body, making flesh and fat, while hers was going right out the gaping invisible hole in her stomach.

Something like a shiver passed through my shoulders.

"Someone stepped on your grave," Niña giggled.

"What do you mean?"

"They say when you shiver like that it's because someone stepped on the spot where your grave will be."

I stared at Niña's huge eyes, wondering who could have been cruel enough to inform her that she would ever have a grave.

When we trooped down the street to the bingo games at my great-grandmother's house, Niña tagged along. An endless array of uncles and cousins filed in and out, a few boasting revolutionary beards and uniforms, but most outfitted in their farmers' Sunday best, their hands brown and calloused.

Niña was quiet. She poured burnt-milk candy through the hole in her stomach, and watched. The size of her eyes made her watching feel like staring, but no one seemed to notice. Children like Niña surprised no one.

On the anniversary of the revolution, the streets filled with truckloads of bearded men on their way to the mountains to celebrate. A man with a loudspeaker walked along our street announcing the treachery of the Yanquis. I was listening inside my grandmother's house. Suddenly his voice changed.

"Let me clarify," he was saying, "that it is not the common people of the United States who we oppose, but the government which has . . ." I stopped listening. Niña was at the open door, smiling her bony smile.

"I told him," she said very quietly, "that you are from *Estados Unidos*. I didn't want him to hurt your feelings."

At the beach, my sister and I went swimming inside shark fences. We imagined the gliding fins beyond the fence. Afterwards, our mother extracted the spines of bristly sea urchins from the soles of our feet.

We visited huge caverns gleaming with stalactites. How wonderfully the Cuban Indians must have lived, I thought, with no home but a cave, nothing to eat but fruit and shellfish, nothing to do but swim and sing. "We were born a thousand years too late," I told my sister.

With a square old-fashioned camera, I took pictures of pigs, dogs, turkeys, horses and mules. Not once did it occur to me to put a friend or relative into one of my photos. I was from Los Angeles. There were more than enough people in my world, and far too few creatures. When my uncle cut sugarcane, it was the stiff, sweet cane itself which caught my eye, and the gnats clinging to his eyes. His strong arms and wizened face were just part of the landscape. When my cousins picked *mamonsillo* fruit, it was the tree I looked at, and not the boys showing off by climbing it. I thrived on the wet smell of green land after a rain, and the treasures I found crawling in red mud or dangling from the leaves of weeds and vines. I trapped lizards, netted butterflies, and once, with the help of my sister, I snared a vulture with an elaborate hand-rigged snare. Our relatives were horrified. What could one do with a vulture? It was just the way I felt about everything which mattered to them. If the goal of the revolution was to uproot happy people from their thatched havens, and deposit them in concrete high-rise apartment buildings, who needed it? Thatched huts, after all, were natural, wild, primitive. They were as good as camping. When my mother explained that the people living in the *bohíos* were tired of it. I grew sulky. Only an adult would be foolish enough to believe that any normal human being could prefer comfort to wildness, roses to weeds, radios to the chants of night-singing frogs.

I knew the hole in Niña's stomach was growing. She was disappearing, vanishing before my eyes. Her parents seemed resigned to her departure. People spoke of her as if she had never really been there. Niña was not solid. She didn't really exist.

On the day of her death, it occurred to me to ask my mother, "Why didn't they just take her to a doctor?"

"They had no money."

I went out to the front porch, abandoning the tarantula I had been about to feed. As I gazed across the open fields toward Niña's *bohío*, the reality of her death permeated the humid summer air. In my mind, I sifted through a stack of foals and ducks, caterpillars and vultures. Somewhere in that stack, I realized, there should have been an image of Niña.

SINGING TO CUBA

When I dressed like a foreigner and stayed inside the tourist zone, official guides watched my movements closely. Hotel maids, waitresses, and taxi drivers made incessant inquires about my solitary activities. Yet I found that if I dressed like a Cuban and spoke like a Cuban, remaining stoically silent most of the time, speaking to strangers only when necessary, and addressing them as comrade when I did, then I would be watched even more carefully, by the ubiquitous men in *guayaberas* who stood on every street corner, flanked every ration line, and rode every *guagua*, monitoring the sporadic whispered conversations.

I decided I was best off dressing like a tourist when alone and like a Cuban when accompanied by relatives. Although officially I was prohibited from visiting relatives, and officially my cousins were denied the right to speak to foreigners, I found that every cousin I visited expressed a strong desire to behave like ordinary families in ordinary places, going out in public together, walking and talking together as if the absurd array of small deranged laws did not exist.

Miguelito, more than any of the others, loved to walk up and down the streets of Old Havana with me, pointing out historical sites and discussing our lives just as if we were not taking any risk by being seen together. When he wanted to go out, Aurora made him carry my wedding picture in his pocket, with the letter *Abuelita* Amparo had written when she sent it, to prove we were really cousins and not just a heretofore quiet dissident, finally bursting, speaking openly to a foreigner.

Miguelito sometimes sang as we walked. He sang about a marble house which crumbled while its residents were asleep. Both ceiling and floor caved in, and a woman, still reclining on her bed, told the neighbors that at first she thought it was just a dream but when she woke up, her leg was broken, and she could see the sky. Aurora had assured me that all of Miguelito's songs were true, taken from the seemingly impossible things which, in Cuba, she laughed, happened every day.

He sang about a poet who lived alone in a house by the sea. A storm carried away one half of his house, taking with it his typewriter and his entire library, leaving him to dwell in the other half, still writing about the sunset and the sea, while waves came swirling about his feet, coming in through the gap where once there had been a wall.

Sometimes, before going out, Miguelito would hang a big antique silver crucifix around his neck. It was the kind of jewelry Cubans were not supposed to have kept after the revolution. Soon after the Maximum Leader took control of the island, its inhabitants had been ordered to turn in all their guns, money, jewelry, and other valuables, so that everyone could start over with nothing. Nearly everyone gave up their firearms, but even the most dedicated communist bureaucrats buried their valuables rather than turn them over. Now, with the economy collapsing, the government was luring the heirlooms and jewelry out of hiding by allowing Cubans to sell hoarded valuables in exchange for shopping privileges in otherwise prohibited dollar stores.

When Miguelito wore his big silver crucifix, he looked like a foreigner, like a lean moustached cowboy from nineteenth-century Texas or Mexico. He left the top button of his shirt open to make sure the crucifix showed and he walked with pride, relieved to be taking a step so bold and defiant. He told me that as a Cuban, wearing a crucifix in public could brand him as a second-class citizen, faithful in a land still officially atheistic. Within his own neighborhood, he was taking a risk. In the tourist zone, he felt anonymous and spoke freely of the elation he felt when disregarding the usual elaborate code of conduct.

When Miguelito, with his crucifix, and I, with my foreign clothes and camera bag, walked through Old Havana together, we both felt safe. When we rode the beet-and-mustard-striped *guagua*, we knew we were, like all Cubans, vulnerable. Few tourists braved the crowds and heat of the Cuban *guagua*. Most confined themselves to Tourist-Taxis and air-conditioned tour buses. In the *guagua* Miguelito and I stood out as the only people daring to converse. My cousin was so tired of silence that even on a crowed *guagua* he would lean his head down toward the window and say without lowering his voice, "This is all I have ever known. In my entire life, this is all I have ever seen." People would look away, pretending they hadn't heard.

Excerpt from SINGING TO CUBA by Margarita Mondrous Engle is reprinted with permission from the publisher (Houston: Arte Publico Press—University of Houston, 1993).

With a sweep of his hand he would indicate everything beyond the window, decaying marble houses, winged statues, hordes of young men on bicycles, the sea wall, the harbor, El Morro Castle. When the *guagua* passed La Cabaña Fortress, I was relieved to see my cousin remain quiet. No matter how much he wanted to point out the dungeons, such overt defiance would be foolish.

I looked out at the tourists snapping photographs of each other standing next to the cannons. I couldn't help thinking of all the names I read each month, when my human rights bulletins arrived, of men arrested for joining a movement of artists seeking freedom of expression, and human rights monitors arrested by State Security, held without charge.

On the *guagua*, surrounded by silent Cubans, Miguelito went on asking about the U.S., my family, my friends, my life. He asked about my schooling, my wedding, about jobs, vacations, grocery shopping. He asked about childbirth and books, movies and music. He asked about rhythm-and-blues singers, and about the irrigated orchards near my arid northern home, and about the coyotes which roamed the orchards hunting jackrabbits, roadrunners and ground squirrels. We rode many different *guaguas* along many different routes, past Revolution Square with its tanks and armed guards, past a colonial cemetery with its magnificent variety of carved angels, past an enormous white monument to José Martí, and the towering Soviet Embassy, a skyscraper which pierces the Cuban sky with its listening apparatus for spying on U.S. communications systems. Miguelito named the landmarks as we passed them. I didn't want my cousin to keep taking chances, so I asked if we could get out and walk.

The streets of Havana were filling with tourists as Cuba prepared to host the Pan American Games. Tourists from Europe and Latin America were flooding the hotel zone and the secret police could hardly keep up with their massive efforts to monitor the movements of Cubans to ensure that they didn't violate the rule against speaking to foreigners. The Neighborhood Committees were being trained as riot squads. In every crowd of Cubans, police informers were planted to disrupt any incipient protest through Acts of Repudiation, by mobilizing groups of citizens to surround and beat anyone who openly voiced discontent.

Descriptions of Acts of Repudiation came in the monthly human rights bulletins. Committee members surround the house of a dissident or they surround him on the streets. They chant slogans and create the appearance of a spontaneous pro-government demonstration. The Act of Repudiation can go on for hours or it might end abruptly with the arrest of its target. Sometimes the dissident's house is ransacked. Family members and visitors may be held captive inside the house. Acts of Repudiation are effective because they instill in the dissident a fear of isolation, creating the illusion that only he and his family are unhappy with a system loved by multitudes. The Act of Repudiation is designed to stimulate a wave of self-doubt and to terrify bystanders who swear they will never speak out and place their families in such a precarious position.

Miguelito and I had just emerged from a *guagua*. The afternoon sky had suddenly clouded over and a light rain was beginning to fall. As we walked, we found ourselves surrounded by blue-uniformed civil police. Miguelito kept right on talking and gradually the blue uniforms drifted away. Soldiers replaced them. Again we were surrounded. Still, my cousin kept talking. The cluster of soldiers walked beside us, behind us, and in front. I counted fourteen of them.

Looking beyond them, at the crumbling walls, I noticed a small red cross and a child's handprint, the only graffiti I had seen since arriving in Havana. I felt like someone discovering pictographs in a prehistoric cave. They reminded me of a story by Reinaldo Arenas called "Singing from the Well," about a child who starts scribbling on tree trunks, sending his stern family into a flurry of accusations when they decide he is crazy.

I thought of Anacaona, the ten sisters who emerges as Cuba's first all-female singing group after three years of hiding inside their Havana house during the anarchy of Machado's overthrow in the early 1930s.

How many artists must now be waiting behind closed doors, practicing secretly, waiting for the day when they could come out of their houses singing and dancing!

I withdrew the camera from my bag and began fussing with the lens as I walked. Then I started snapping photographs of the soldiers. One of them waved his semiautomatic weapon at me in a threatening gesture that meant to stop. I smiled and turned the camera toward the broken walls of the houses around me. I pointed the lens toward the roofless apex and disintegrating columns of a once-elegant building that looked like the ruined remains of some ancient Greek temple.

Beside me, Miguelito was smiling, looking as fearless and confident as any newly arrived foreigner still unaware of the vast network of vigilant guides, secret police, and informers. The soldiers glanced at each of us, then at each other. They shrugged, grinning, and moved away, pursuing some young Cuban women who had begun to flirt with them. Soon they were walking far ahead of us, surrounding the girls, who were laughing and conversing with them in loud fast voices, still sounding as I remembered from 1960, raucous and musical, like wild parrots joined by small song birds as they all fed from the same fruit tree.

10. JULIA ALVAREZ, "SNOW"

In addition to Mexican-Americans, Puerto Ricans, and Cuban Americans, there are many other American communities that have been traditionally brought under that umbrella term Latino. Many U.S. Latinos trace their roots to Central America and South America. Due to several bloody civil wars and oppressive regimes in this area during the 1980s (such as Nicaragua, El Salvador, Argentina, Chile), many Latinos from these regions are rather recent arrivals. Joining these groups are a significant number of individuals from the Caribbean area, above all from the Dominican Republic.

Julia Alvarez was born in the Dominican Republic and came to the United States when she was ten years old. She since has written poetry (such as *Homecoming*, 1986) and also prose fiction. The reading here is from her acclaimed novel *How the Garcia Girls Lost Their Accents* (1991). The narrator in "Snow" recounts her first months in New York City and how bomb shelters and snowflakes at first disoriented her world view.

Snow

Our first year in New York we rented a small apartment with a Catholic school nearby, taught by the Sisters of Charity, hefty women in long black gowns and bonnets that made them look peculiar, like dolls in mourning. I liked them a lot, especially my grandmotherly fourth-grade teacher, Sister Zoe. I had a lovely names, she said, and she had me teach the whole class how to pronounce it. *Yo-land-da.* As the only immigrant in my class, I was put in a special seat in the first row by the window, apart from the other children so that Sister Zoe could tutor me without disturbing them. Slowly, she enunciated the new words I was to repeat: *laundromat, cornflakes, subway, snow.*

Soon I picked up enough English to understand holocaust was in the air. Sister Zoe explained to a wide-eyed classroom what was happening in Cuba. Russian missiles were being assembled, trained supposedly on New York City. President Kennedy, looking worried too, was on the television at home, explaining we might have to go to war against the Communists. At school, we had air-raid drills: an ominous bell would go off and we'd file into the hall, fall to the floor, cover our heads with our coats, and imagine our hair falling out, the bones in our arms going soft. At home, Mami and my sisters and I said a rosary for world peace. I heard new vocabulary: *nuclear bomb, radioactive fallout, bomb shelter.* Sister Zoe explained how it would happen. She drew a picture of a mushroom on the blackboards and dotted a flurry of chalk marks for the dusty fallout that would kill us all.

The months grew cold, November, December. It as dark when I got up in the morning, frosty when I followed my breath to school. One morning as I sat at my desk daydreaming out the window, I saw dots in the air like the ones Sister Zoe had drawn—random at first, then lots and lots. I shrieked, "Bomb! Bomb!" Sister Zoe jerked around, her full black skirt ballooning as she hurried to my side. A few girls began to cry.

But then Sister Zoe's shocked look faded. "Why, Yolanda dear, that's snow!" She laughed. "Snow."

"Snow," I repeated. I looked out the window warily. All my life I had heard about the white crystals that fell out of American skies in the winter. From my desk I watched the fine powder dust the sidewalk and parked cars below. Each flake was different, Sister Zoe had said, like a person, irreplaceable and beautiful.

From HOW THE GARCIA GIRLS LOST THEIR ACCENTS. Copyright © by Julie Alvarez, 1991. Published by Plume, a division of Penguin USA, New York, and originally published by Algonquin Books of Chapel Hill. Reprinted by permission of Susan Bergholz Literary Services, New York. All rights reserved.

11. JUDITH ORTIZ COFER, "THE LATIN DELI: AN ARS POETICA"

Despite differences in customs, foods, and even political perspectives, Latinos in the United States are bound together as a community through collective roots in Europe, Africa, and the New World as well as by their experiences in America itself. One writer who has addressed the essential unity of Latinos is the Puerto Rican poet Judith Ortiz Cofer. After spending most of her childhood in New Jersey, Cofer began to write poetry and prose fiction (*The Line of the Sun*, *Silent Dancing*). In "The Latin Deli: An Ars Poetica" (from *The Latin Deli*, 1993), the poet reminds us not only of the specific characteristics of various Latino groups in America but also of the ties that bind this people together. Cofer employs a local Latin Deli to demonstrate that the qualities of uniformness and uniqueness are not mutually exclusive, and that the memories of past the and hopes for the future can be intertwined on a daily basis.

THE LATIN DELI: AN ARS POETICA

Presiding over a formica counter,
plastic Mother and Child magnetized
to the top of an ancient register,
the heady mix of smells from the open bins
of dried codfish, the green plantains
hanging in stalks like votive offerings,
she is the Patroness of Exiles,
a woman of no-age who was never pretty,
who spends her days selling canned memories
while listening to the Puerto Ricans complain
that it would be cheaper to fly to San Juan
than to buy a pound of Bustelo coffee here,
and to Cubans perfecting their speech
of a "glorious return" to Havana—where no one
has been allowed to die and nothing to change until then;
to Mexicans who pass through, talking lyrically
of *dólares* to be made in El Norte—
                                    all wanting the comfort
of spoken Spanish, to gaze upon the family portrait
of her plain wide face, her ample bosom
resting on her plump arms, her look of maternal interest
as they speak to her and each other
of their dreams and their disillusions—
how she smiles understanding,
when they walk down the narrow aisles of her store
reading the labels of packages aloud, as if
they were the names of lost lovers; *Suspiros*,
Merengues, the stale candy of everyone's childhood.
                                    She spends her days
slicing *jamón y queso* and wrapping it in wax paper
tied with string: plain ham and cheese
that would cost less at the A&P, but it would not satisfy
the hunger of the fragile old man lost in the folds
of his winter coat, who brings her lists of items
that he reads to her like poetry, or the others,
whose needs she must divine, conjuring up products
from places that now exist only in their hearts—
closed ports she must trade with.

"The Latin Deli: An Ars Poetica" by Judith Ortiz Cofer is reprinted with permission from the publisher of *The Americas Review,* Vol. 19, No. 1 (Houston: Arte Publico Press—University of Houston, 1991).